S0-AZR-806

SHADOWMAN

BIRTH
RITES

JUSTIN JORDAN | PATRICK ZIRCHER | BRIAN REBER

CONTENTS

Writers: Justin Jordan and Patrick Zircher
Artist: Patrick Zircher
Colorist: Brian Reber
Letterer: Rob Steen
Cover Artist: Patrick Zircher
Assistant Editor: Josh Johns
Executive Editor: Warren Simons

Shadowman #1 Variant Cover by Dave Johnson
Shadowman #2 Variant Cover by Dave Johnson
Shadowman #3 Variant Cover by Dave Johnson
Shadowman #4 Variant Cover by Dave Johnson

Collection Cover Art: Patrick Zircher

VALIANT

Peter Cuneo
Chairman

Dinesh Shamdasani
CEO and Chief Creative Officer

Gavin Cuneo
CFO and Head of Strategic Development

Fred Pierce
Publisher

Warren Simons
VP Executive Editor

Walter Black
VP Operations

Hunter Gorinson
Marketing and Communications Manager

Atom! Freeman
Sales Manager

Travis Escarfullery
Production and Design Manager

Rian Hughes/Device
Trade Dress and Book Design

Jody LeHeup
Associate Editor

Josh Johns
Assistant Editor

Peter Stern
Operations Coordinator

Ivan Cohen
Collection Editor

Steve Blackwell
Collection Designer

Russell Brown
President, Consumer Products,
Promotions & Ad Sales

Shadowman®: Birth Rites.
Published by Valiant Entertainment, LLC. Office of Publication:
424 West 33rd Street, New York, NY 10001. Compilation copyright
©2013 Valiant Entertainment, Inc. All rights reserved. Contains
materials originally published in single magazine form as
Shadowman® #1-4. Copyright ©2012 Valiant Entertainment, Inc.
All rights reserved. All characters, their distinctive likenesses
and related indicia featured in this publication are trademarks
of Valiant Entertainment, Inc. The stories, characters, and
incidents featured in this publication are entirely fictional. Valiant
Entertainment does not read or accept unsolicited submissions of
ideas, stories, or artwork. Printed in the U.S.A. Second Printing.
ISBN: 9781939346001.

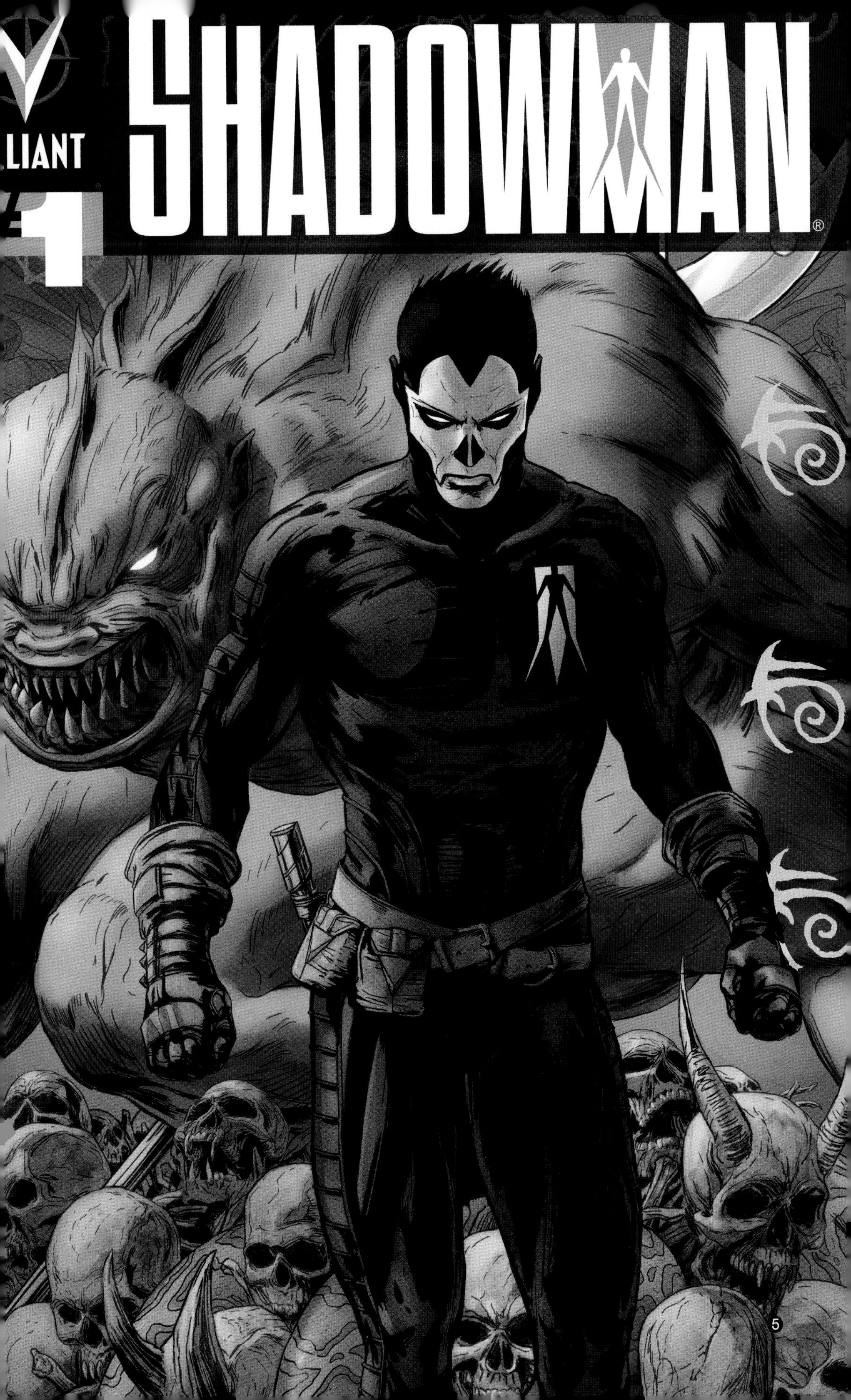

VALIANT
#1
SHADOWMAN

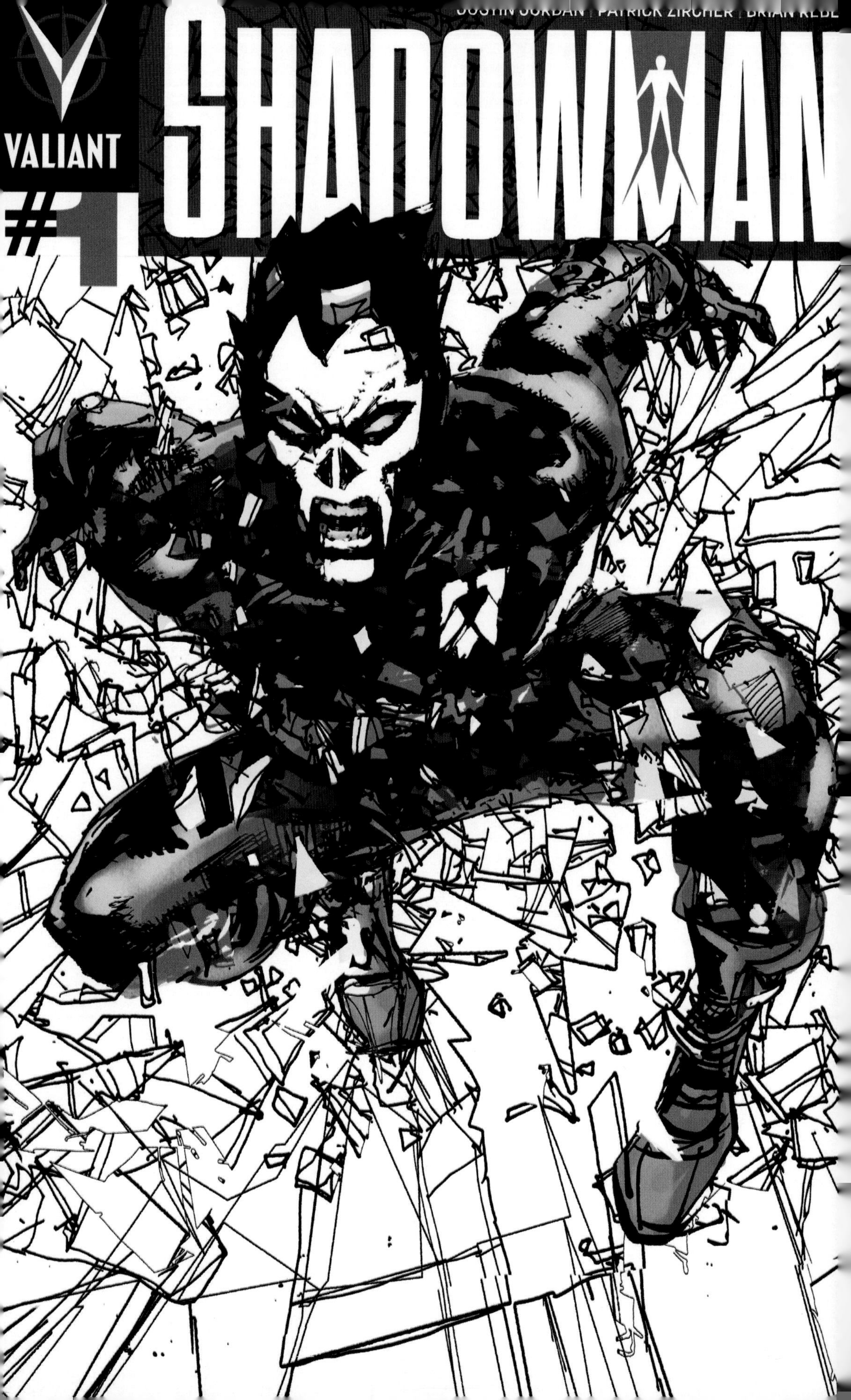
VALIANT
#1
SHADOWMAN

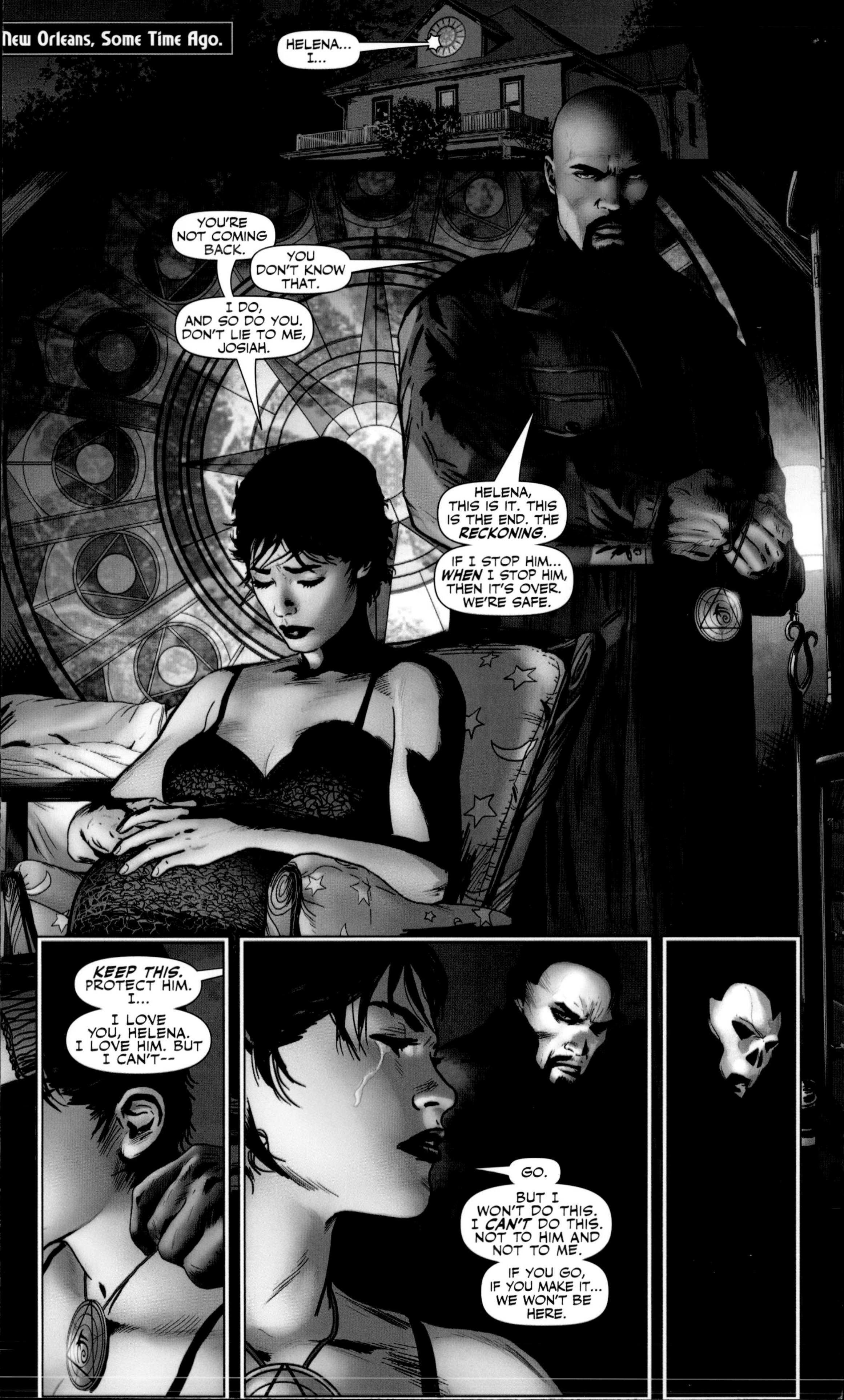
New Orleans, Some Time Ago.
HELENA... I...
YOU'RE NOT COMING BACK.
YOU DON'T KNOW THAT.
I DO, AND SO DO YOU. DON'T LIE TO ME, JOSIAH.
HELENA, THIS IS IT. THIS IS THE END. THE RECKONING.
IF I STOP HIM... WHEN I STOP HIM, THEN IT'S OVER. WE'RE SAFE.
KEEP THIS. PROTECT HIM. I...
I LOVE YOU, HELENA. I LOVE HIM. BUT I CAN'T--
GO.
BUT I WON'T DO THIS. I CAN'T DO THIS. NOT TO HIM AND NOT TO ME.
IF YOU GO, IF YOU MAKE IT... WE WON'T BE HERE.

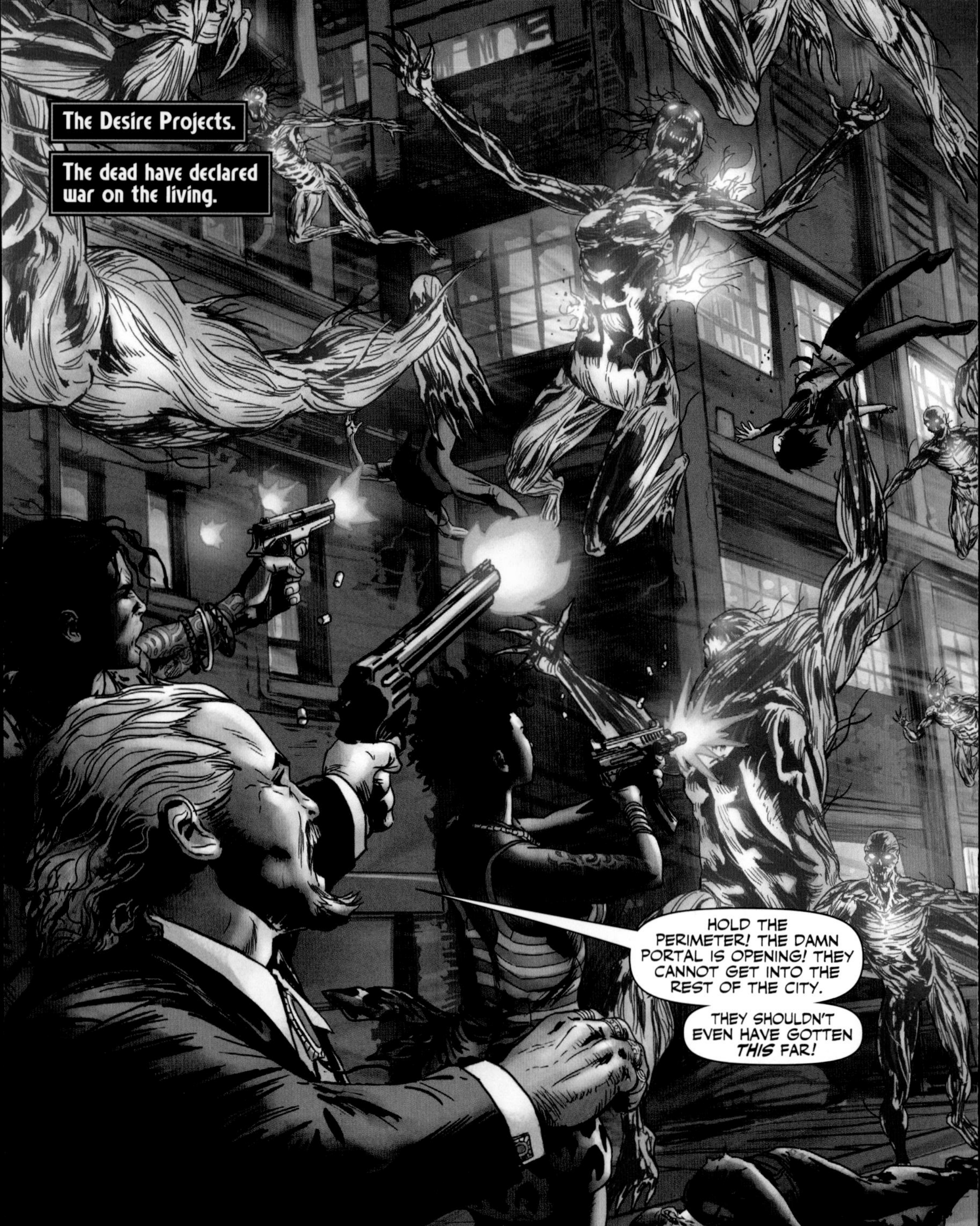

The Desire Projects.
The dead have declared war on the living.
HOLD THE PERIMETER! THE DAMN PORTAL IS OPENING! THEY CANNOT GET INTO THE REST OF THE CITY.
THEY SHOULDN'T EVEN HAVE GOTTEN *THIS* FAR!

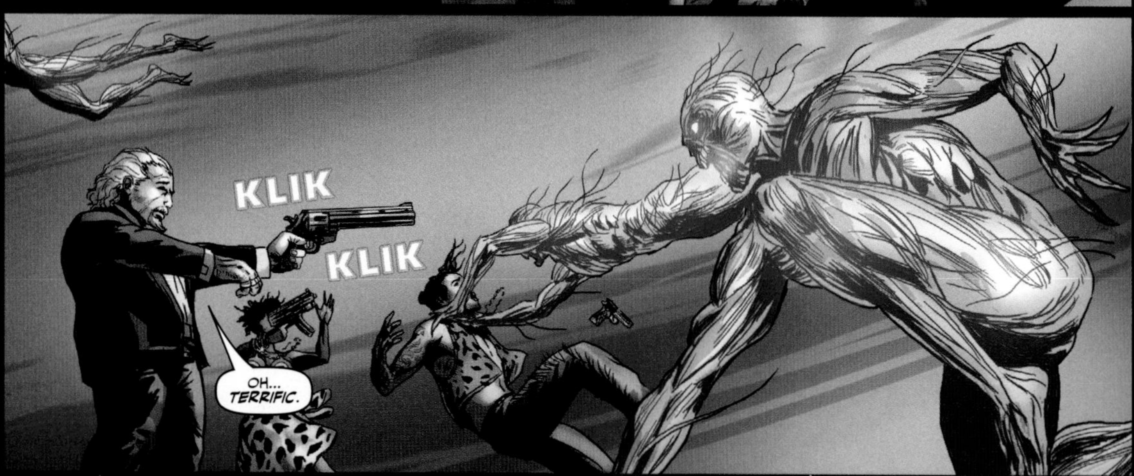

KLIK
KLIK
OH... *TERRIFIC.*

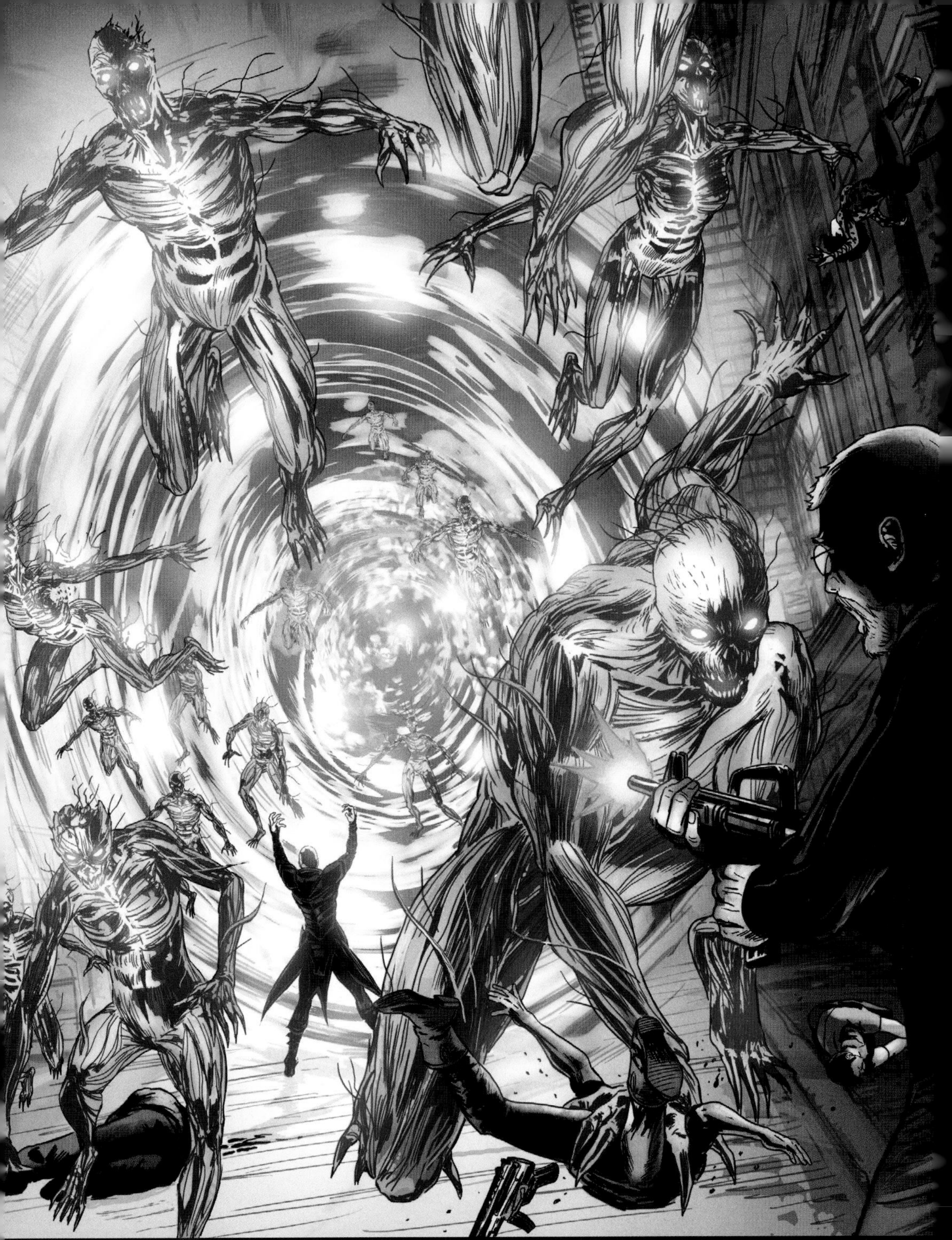

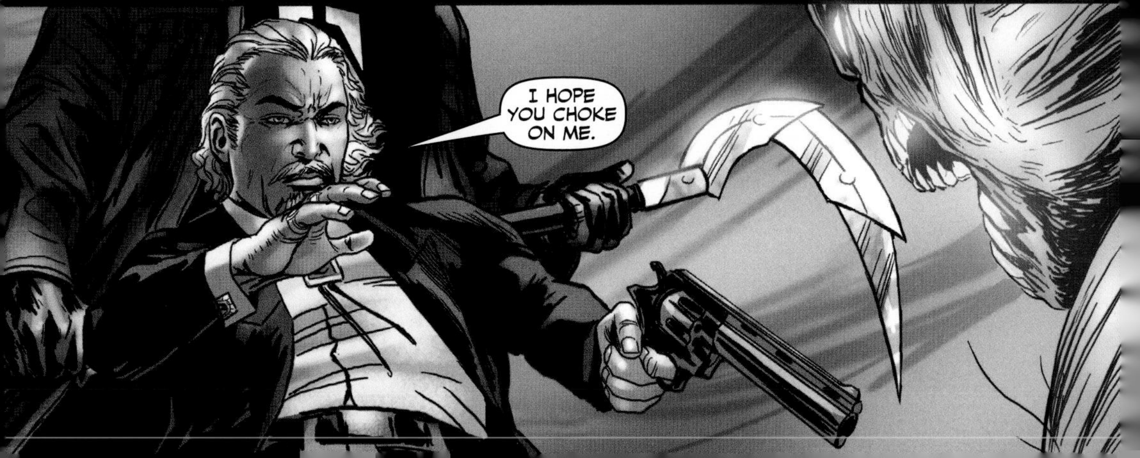
I HOPE YOU CHOKE ON ME.

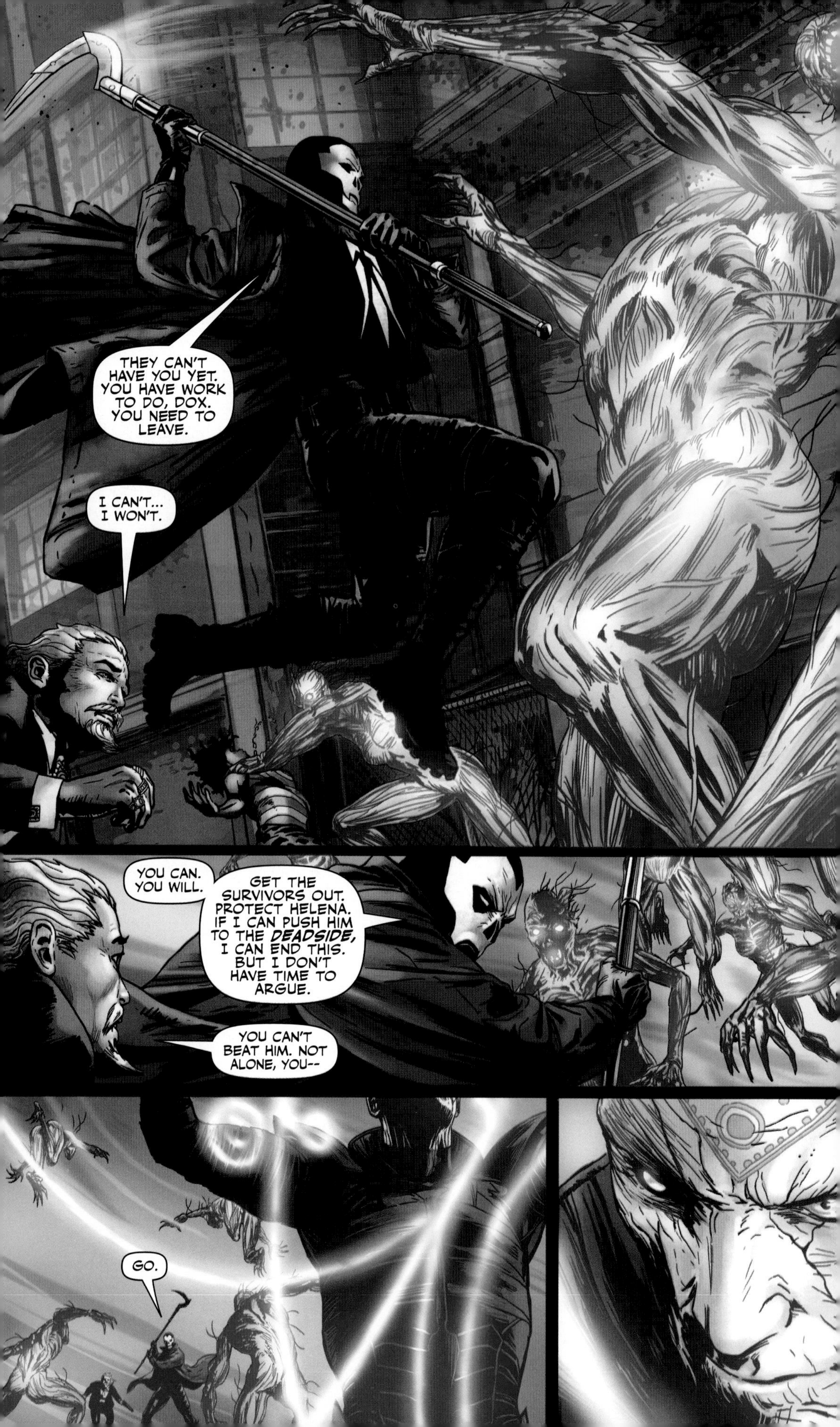
THEY CAN'T HAVE YOU YET. YOU HAVE WORK TO DO, DOX. YOU NEED TO LEAVE.
I CAN'T... I WON'T.
YOU CAN. YOU WILL.
GET THE SURVIVORS OUT. PROTECT HELENA. IF I CAN PUSH HIM TO THE ***DEADSIDE,*** I CAN END THIS. BUT I DON'T HAVE TIME TO ARGUE.
YOU CAN'T BEAT HIM. NOT ALONE, YOU--
GO.

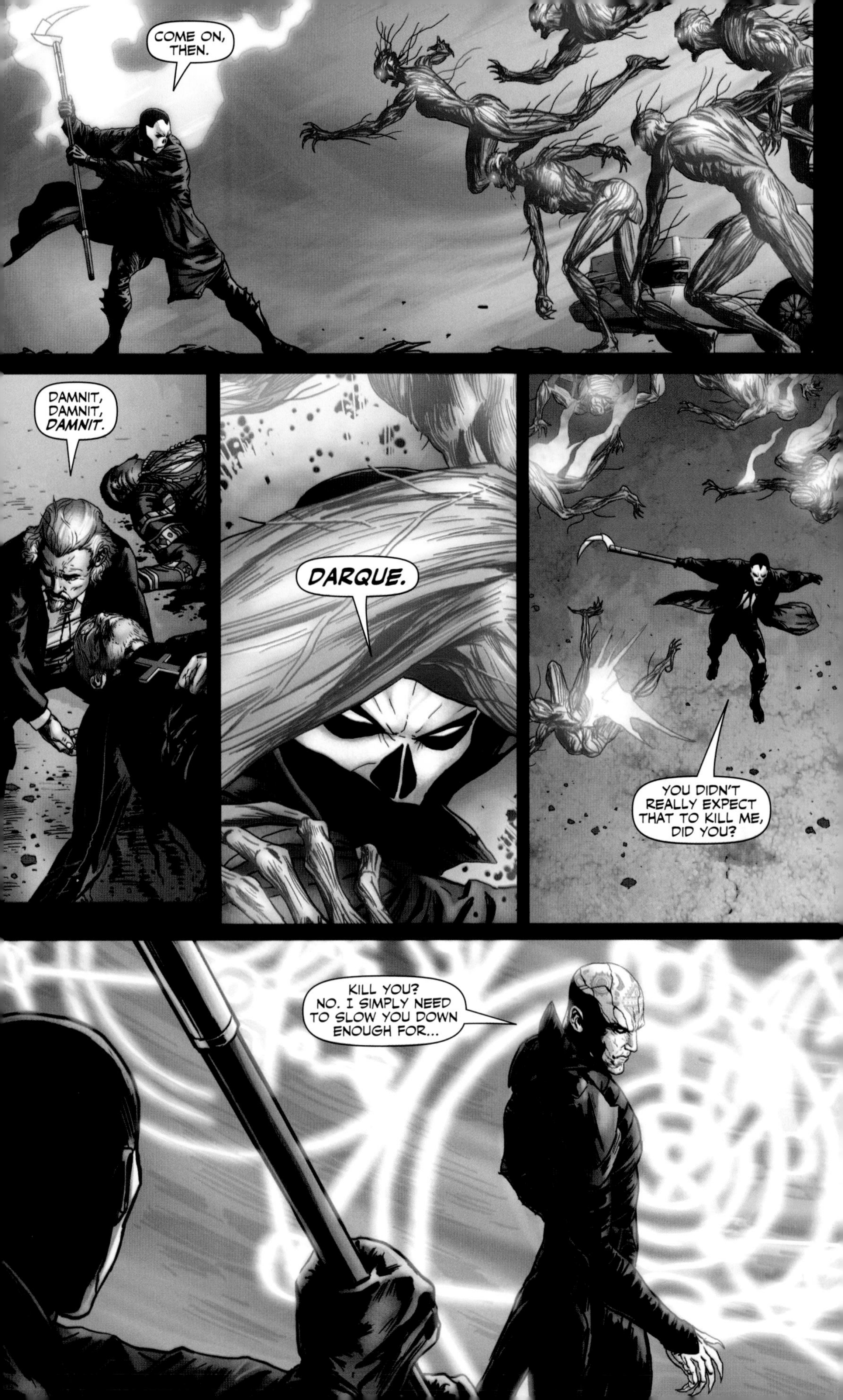
COME ON, THEN.
DAMNIT, DAMNIT, DAMNIT.
DARQUE.
YOU DIDN'T REALLY EXPECT THAT TO KILL ME, DID YOU?
KILL YOU? NO. I SIMPLY NEED TO SLOW YOU DOWN ENOUGH FOR...

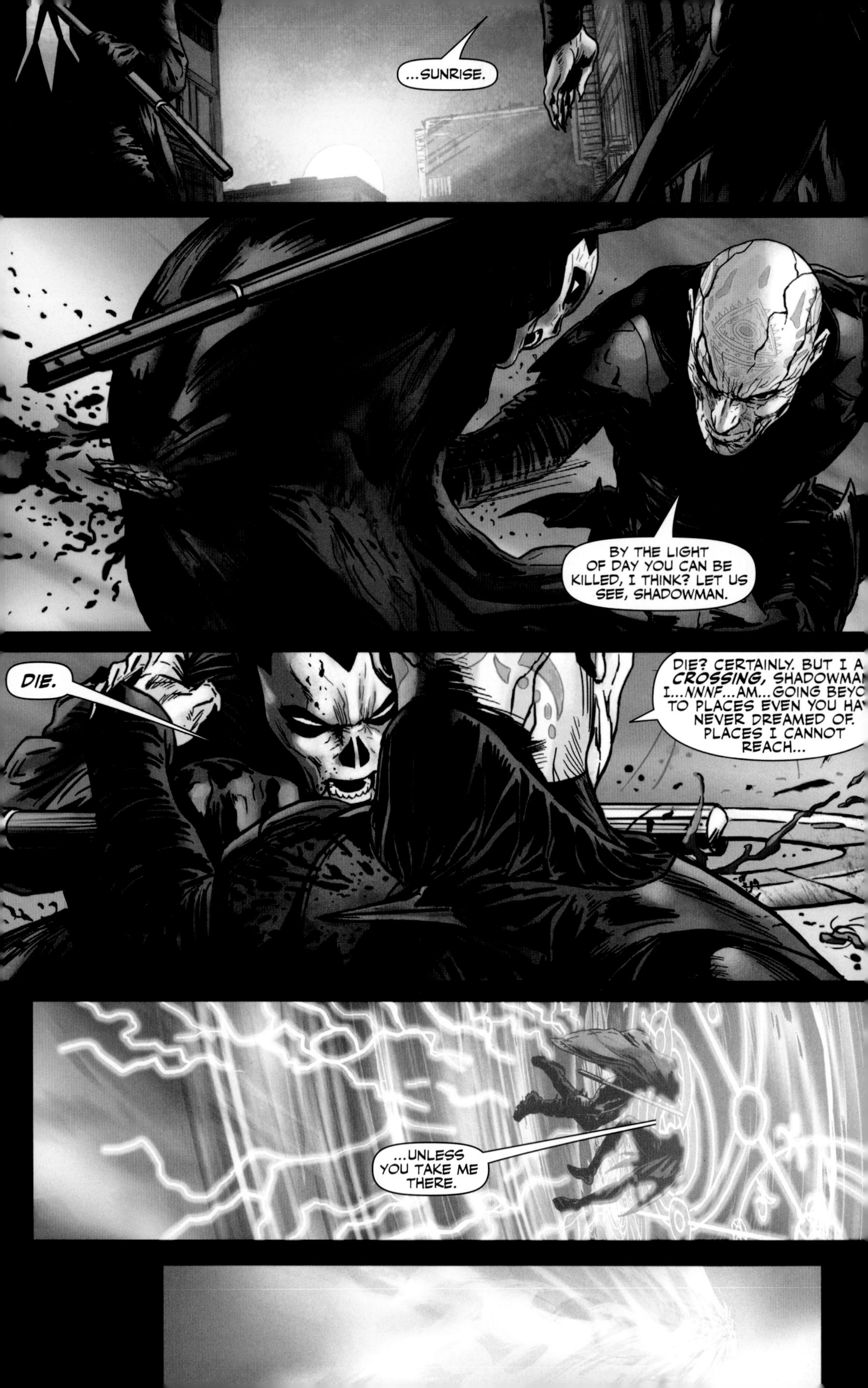
...SUNRISE.
BY THE LIGHT OF DAY YOU CAN BE KILLED, I THINK? LET US SEE, SHADOWMAN.
DIE.
DIE? CERTAINLY. BUT I A CROSSING, SHADOWMA I...NNNF...AM...GOING BEYO TO PLACES EVEN YOU HA NEVER DREAMED OF. PLACES I CANNOT REACH...
...UNLESS YOU TAKE ME THERE.

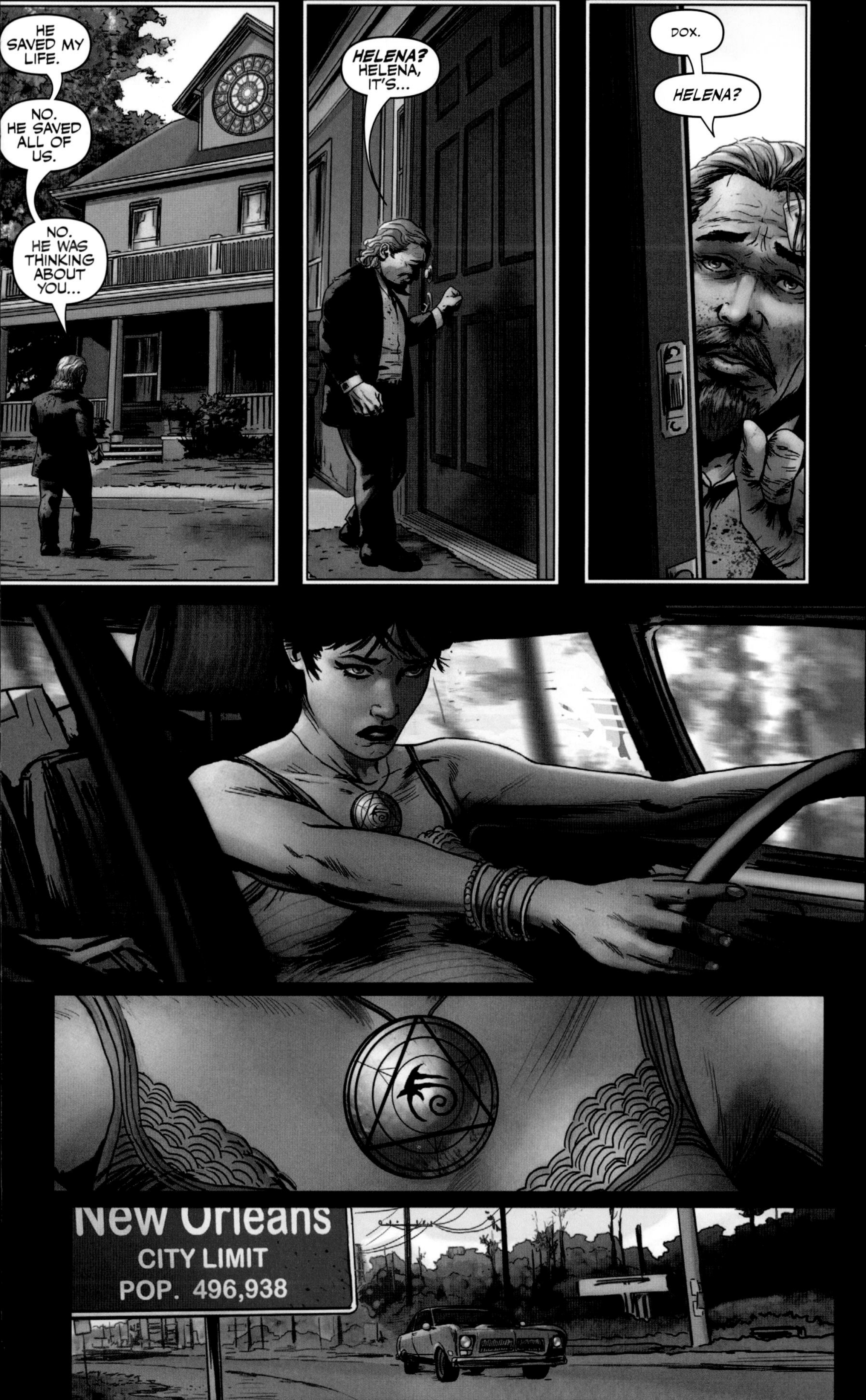
HE SAVED MY LIFE.
NO. HE SAVED ALL OF US.
NO. HE WAS THINKING ABOUT YOU...
HELENA? HELENA, IT'S...
DOX.
HELENA?
New Orleans
CITY LIMIT
POP. 496,938

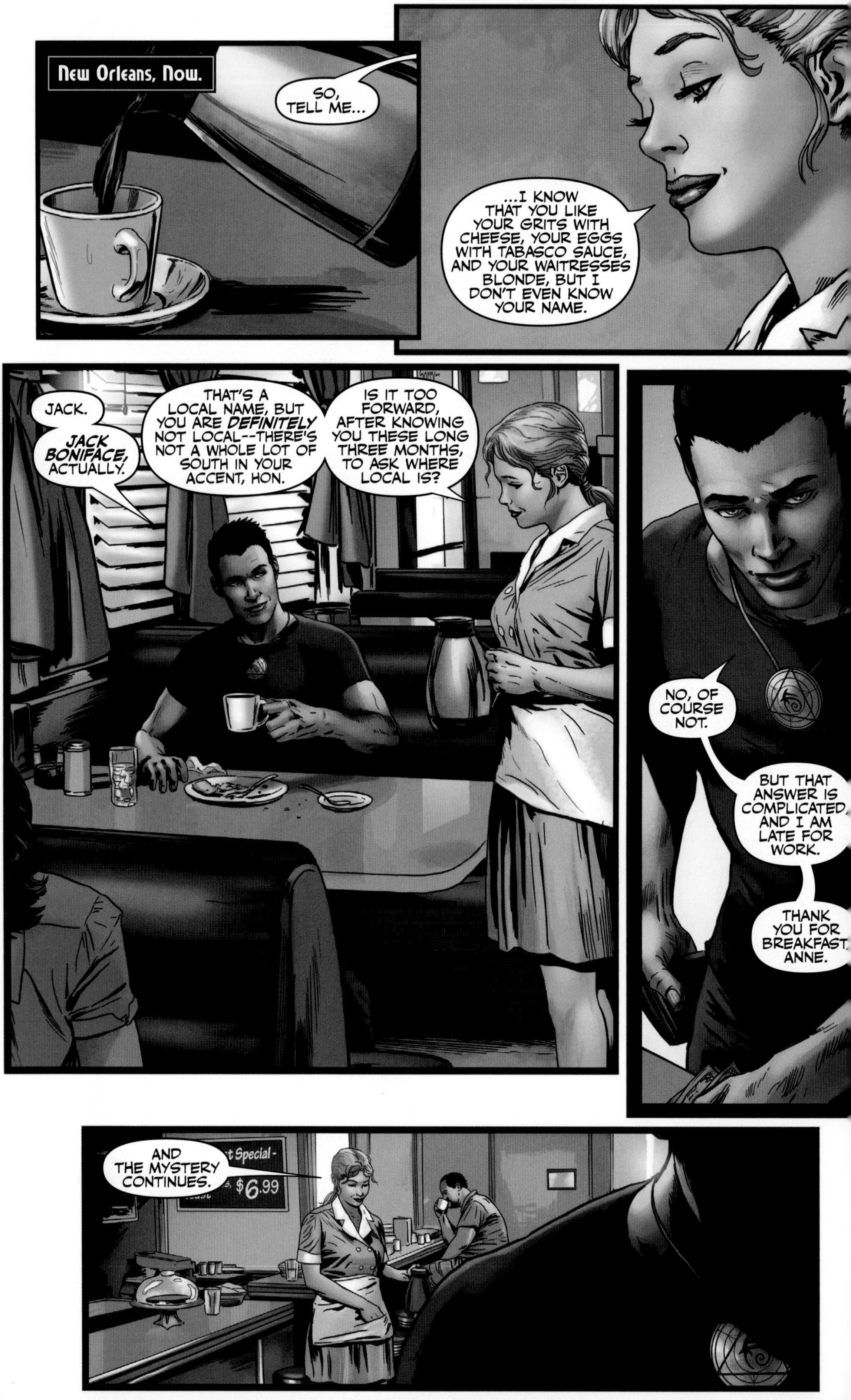
New Orleans, Now.
SO, TELL ME...
...I KNOW THAT YOU LIKE YOUR GRITS WITH CHEESE, YOUR EGGS WITH TABASCO SAUCE, AND YOUR WAITRESSES BLONDE, BUT I DON'T EVEN KNOW YOUR NAME.
JACK.
JACK BONIFACE, ACTUALLY.
THAT'S A LOCAL NAME, BUT YOU ARE DEFINITELY NOT LOCAL--THERE'S NOT A WHOLE LOT OF SOUTH IN YOUR ACCENT, HON.
IS IT TOO FORWARD, AFTER KNOWING YOU THESE LONG THREE MONTHS, TO ASK WHERE LOCAL IS?
NO, OF COURSE NOT.
BUT THAT ANSWER IS COMPLICATED, AND I AM LATE FOR WORK.
THANK YOU FOR BREAKFAST, ANNE.
AND THE MYSTERY CONTINUES.
$6.99

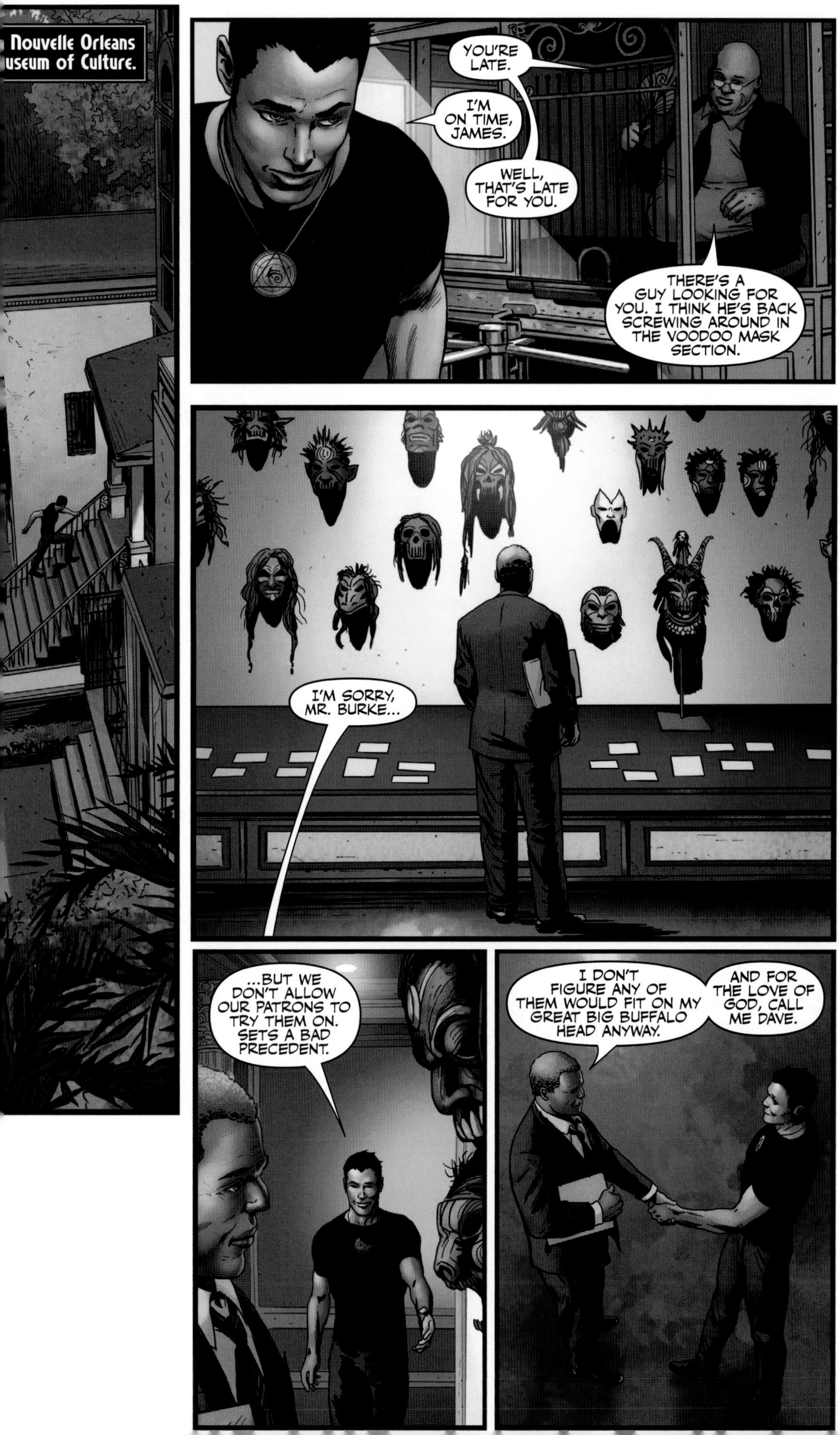
Nouvelle Orleans
useum of Culture.
YOU'RE LATE.
I'M ON TIME, JAMES.
WELL, THAT'S LATE FOR YOU.
THERE'S A GUY LOOKING FOR YOU. I THINK HE'S BACK SCREWING AROUND IN THE VOODOO MASK SECTION.
I'M SORRY, MR. BURKE...
...BUT WE DON'T ALLOW OUR PATRONS TO TRY THEM ON. SETS A BAD PRECEDENT.
I DON'T FIGURE ANY OF THEM WOULD FIT ON MY GREAT BIG BUFFALO HEAD ANYWAY.
AND FOR THE LOVE OF GOD, CALL ME DAVE.

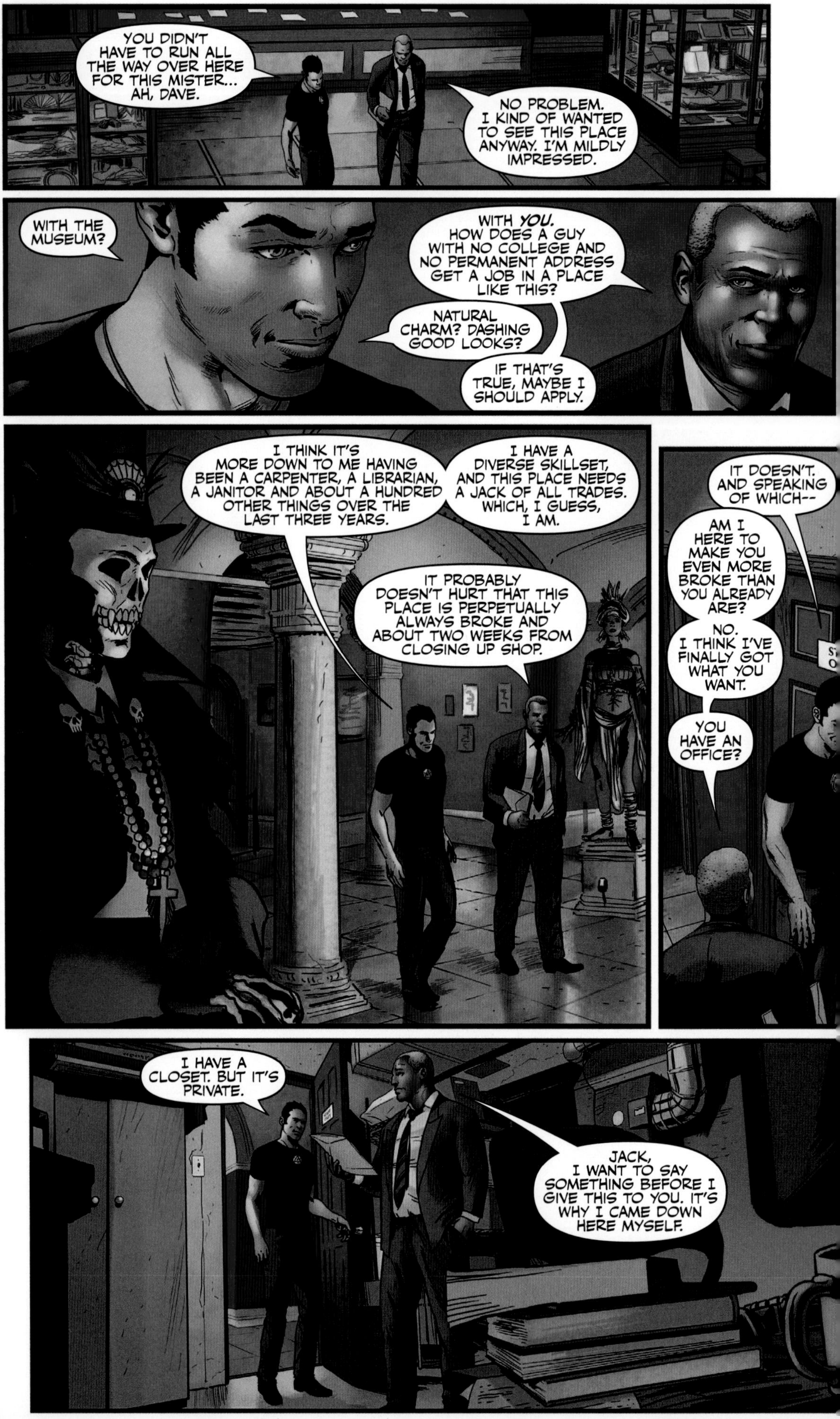

YOU DIDN'T HAVE TO RUN ALL THE WAY OVER HERE FOR THIS MISTER... AH, DAVE.
NO PROBLEM. I KIND OF WANTED TO SEE THIS PLACE ANYWAY. I'M MILDLY IMPRESSED.
WITH THE MUSEUM?
WITH *YOU.* HOW DOES A GUY WITH NO COLLEGE AND NO PERMANENT ADDRESS GET A JOB IN A PLACE LIKE THIS?
NATURAL CHARM? DASHING GOOD LOOKS?
IF THAT'S TRUE, MAYBE I SHOULD APPLY.
I THINK IT'S MORE DOWN TO ME HAVING BEEN A CARPENTER, A LIBRARIAN, A JANITOR AND ABOUT A HUNDRED OTHER THINGS OVER THE LAST THREE YEARS.
I HAVE A DIVERSE SKILLSET, AND THIS PLACE NEEDS A JACK OF ALL TRADES. WHICH, I GUESS, I AM.
IT PROBABLY DOESN'T HURT THAT THIS PLACE IS PERPETUALLY ALWAYS BROKE AND ABOUT TWO WEEKS FROM CLOSING UP SHOP.
IT DOESN'T. AND SPEAKING OF WHICH--
AM I HERE TO MAKE YOU EVEN MORE BROKE THAN YOU ALREADY ARE?
NO. I THINK I'VE FINALLY GOT WHAT YOU WANT.
YOU HAVE AN OFFICE?
I HAVE A CLOSET. BUT IT'S PRIVATE.
JACK, I WANT TO SAY SOMETHING BEFORE I GIVE THIS TO YOU. IT'S WHY I CAME DOWN HERE MYSELF.

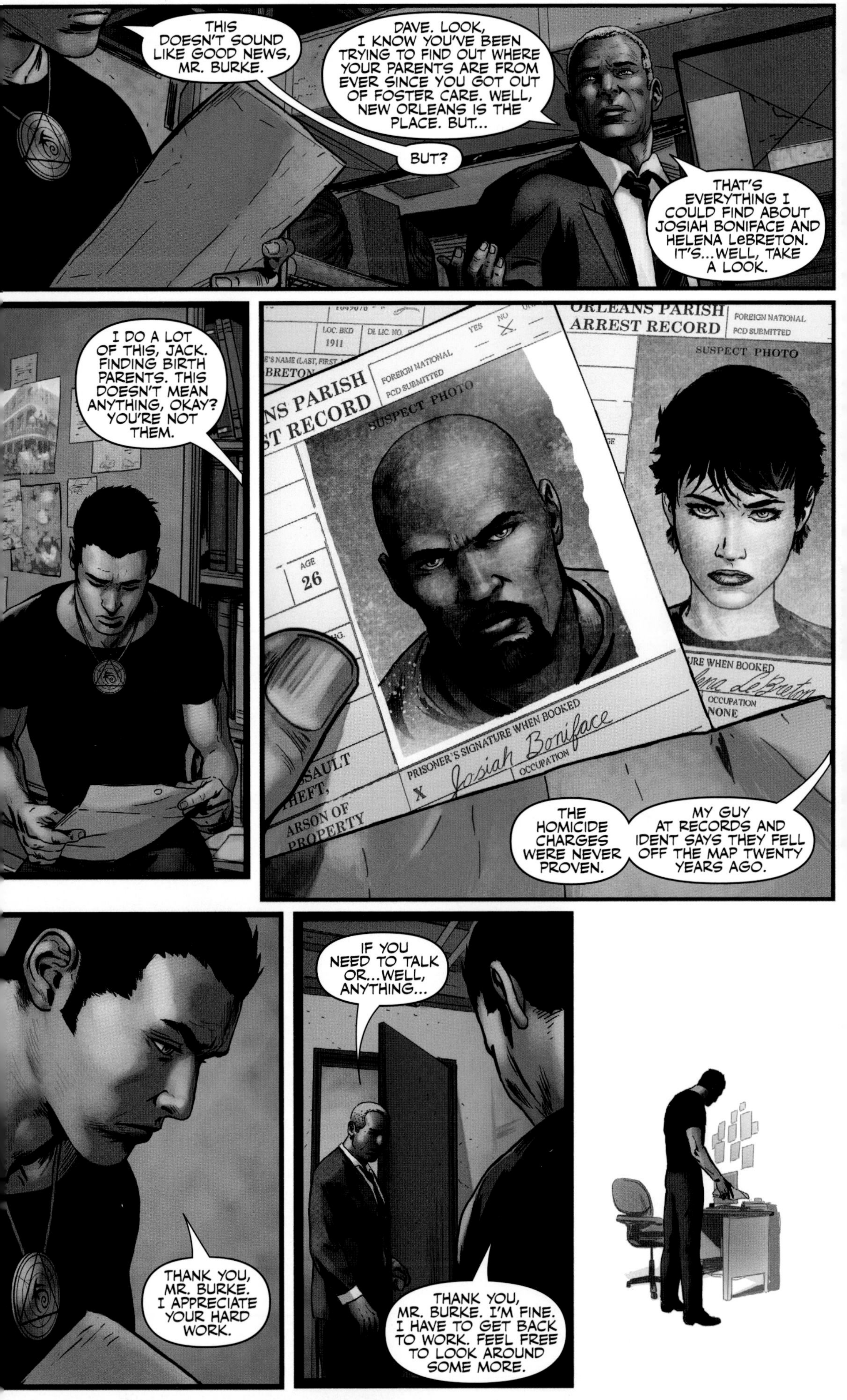

THIS DOESN'T SOUND LIKE GOOD NEWS, MR. BURKE.
DAVE. LOOK, I KNOW YOU'VE BEEN TRYING TO FIND OUT WHERE YOUR PARENTS ARE FROM EVER SINCE YOU GOT OUT OF FOSTER CARE. WELL, NEW ORLEANS IS THE PLACE. BUT...
BUT?
THAT'S EVERYTHING I COULD FIND ABOUT JOSIAH BONIFACE AND HELENA LeBRETON. IT'S...WELL, TAKE A LOOK.
I DO A LOT OF THIS, JACK. FINDING BIRTH PARENTS. THIS DOESN'T MEAN ANYTHING, OKAY? YOU'RE NOT THEM.
ORLEANS PARISH
ARREST RECORD
FOREIGN NATIONAL
PCD SUBMITTED
SUSPECT PHOTO
LOC. BKD
1911
AGE
26
PRISONER'S SIGNATURE WHEN BOOKED
Josiah Boniface
OCCUPATION
NONE
ASSAULT
THEFT,
ARSON OF PROPERTY
THE HOMICIDE CHARGES WERE NEVER PROVEN.
MY GUY AT RECORDS AND IDENT SAYS THEY FELL OFF THE MAP TWENTY YEARS AGO.
THANK YOU, MR. BURKE. I APPRECIATE YOUR HARD WORK.
IF YOU NEED TO TALK OR...WELL, ANYTHING...
THANK YOU, MR. BURKE. I'M FINE. I HAVE TO GET BACK TO WORK. FEEL FREE TO LOOK AROUND SOME MORE.

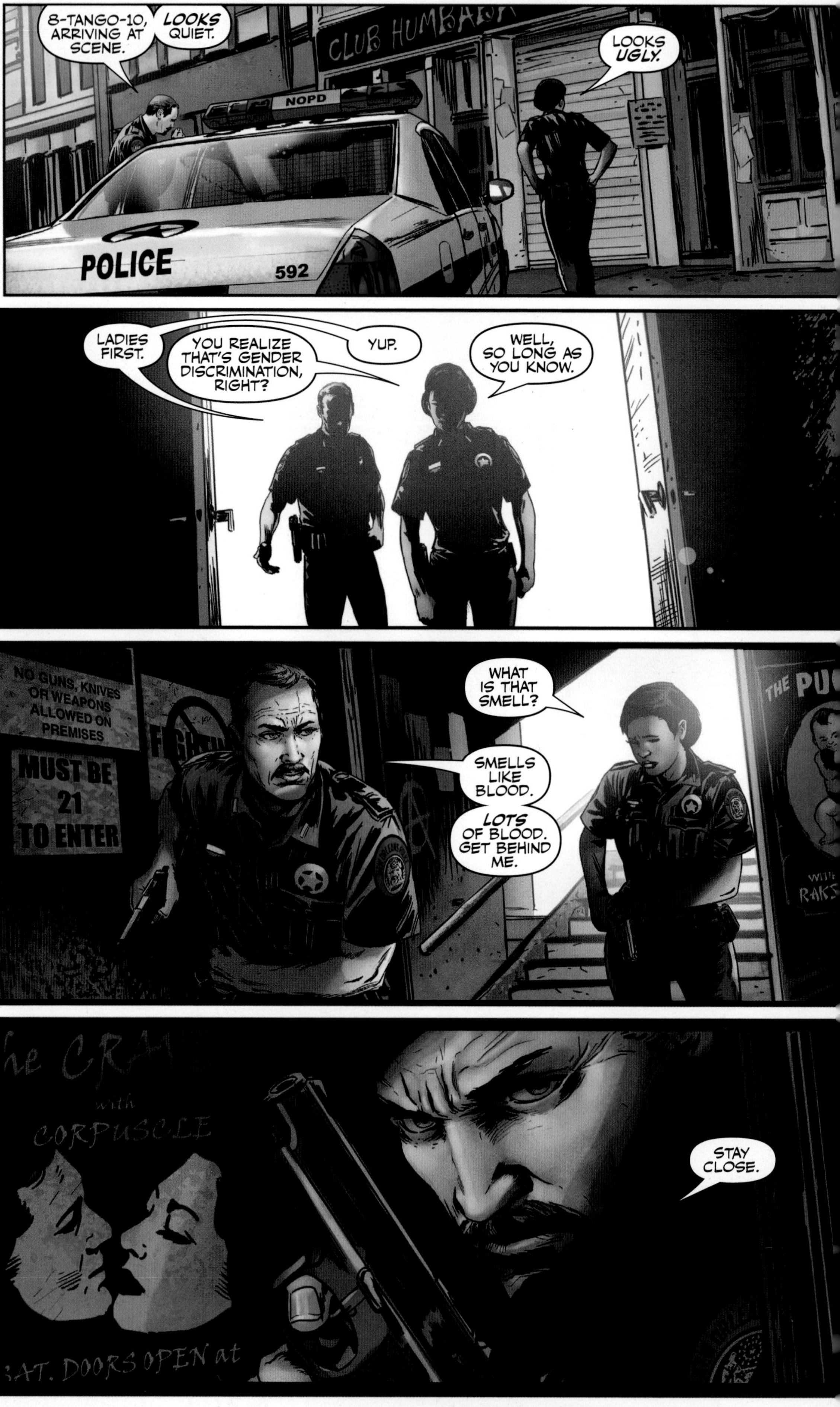

8-TANGO-10, ARRIVING AT SCENE.
LOOKS QUIET.
LOOKS UGLY.
NOPD
POLICE
592
LADIES FIRST.
YUP.
YOU REALIZE THAT'S GENDER DISCRIMINATION, RIGHT?
WELL, SO LONG AS YOU KNOW.
NO GUNS, KNIVES OR WEAPONS ALLOWED ON PREMISES
MUST BE 21 TO ENTER
WHAT IS THAT SMELL?
SMELLS LIKE BLOOD.
LOTS OF BLOOD. GET BEHIND ME.
with
CORPUSCLE
STAY CLOSE.

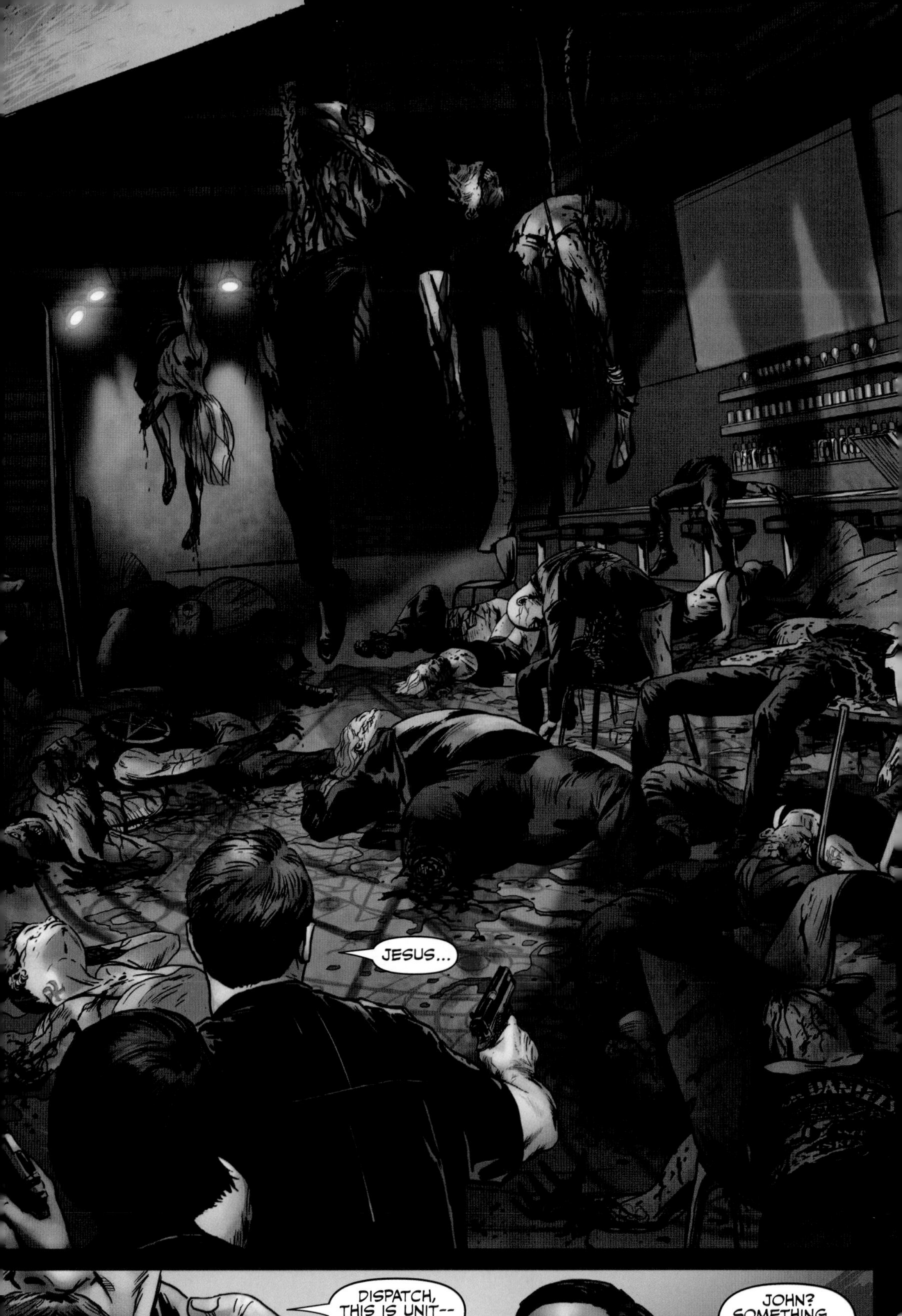
JESUS...

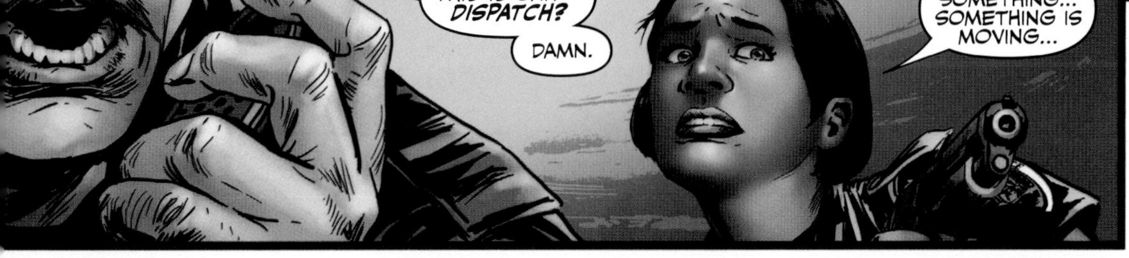
DISPATCH, THIS IS UNIT-- *DISPATCH?*
DAMN.
JOHN? SOMETHING... SOMETHING IS MOVING...

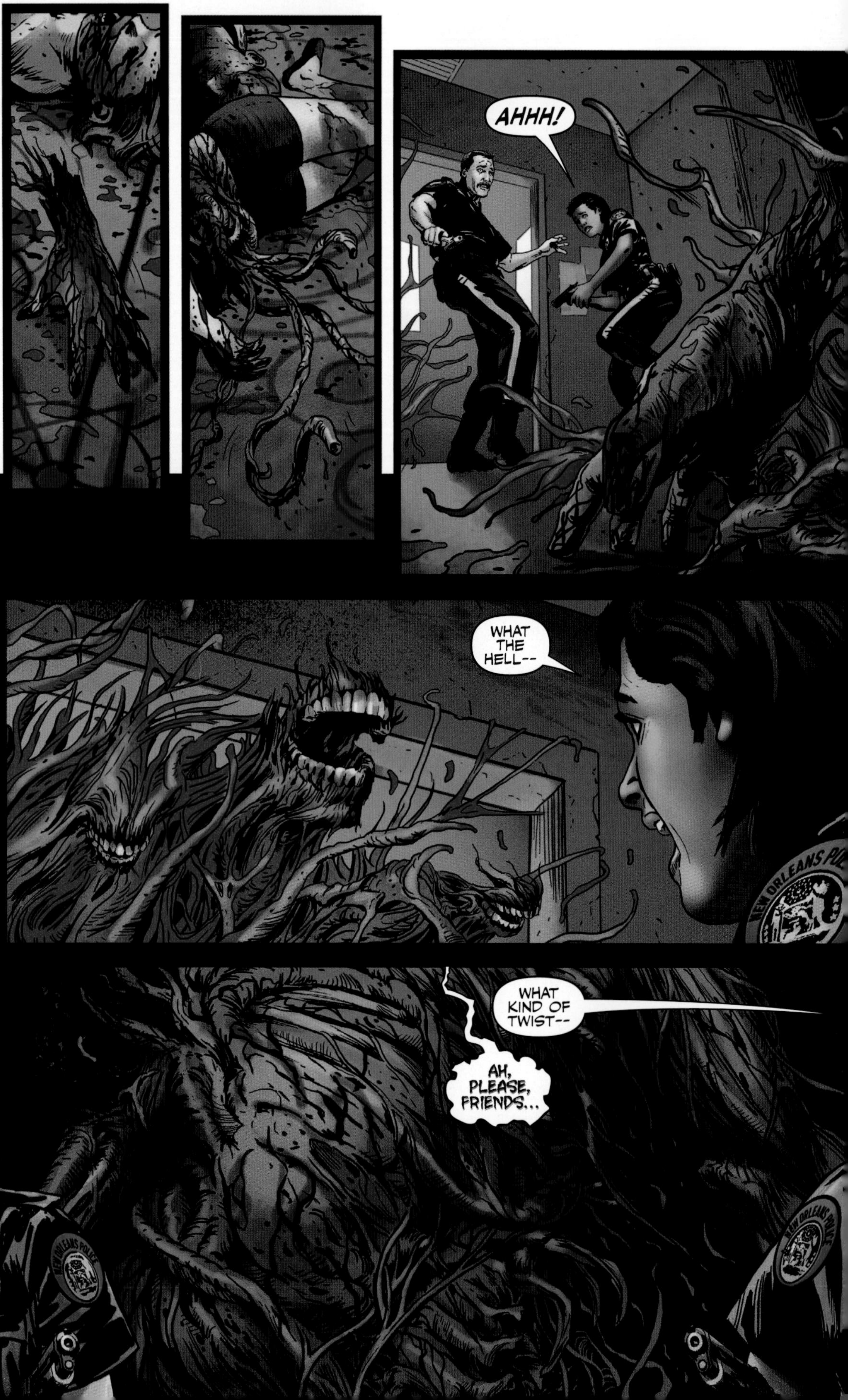
AHHH!
WHAT THE HELL--
WHAT KIND OF TWIST--
AH, PLEASE, FRIENDS...

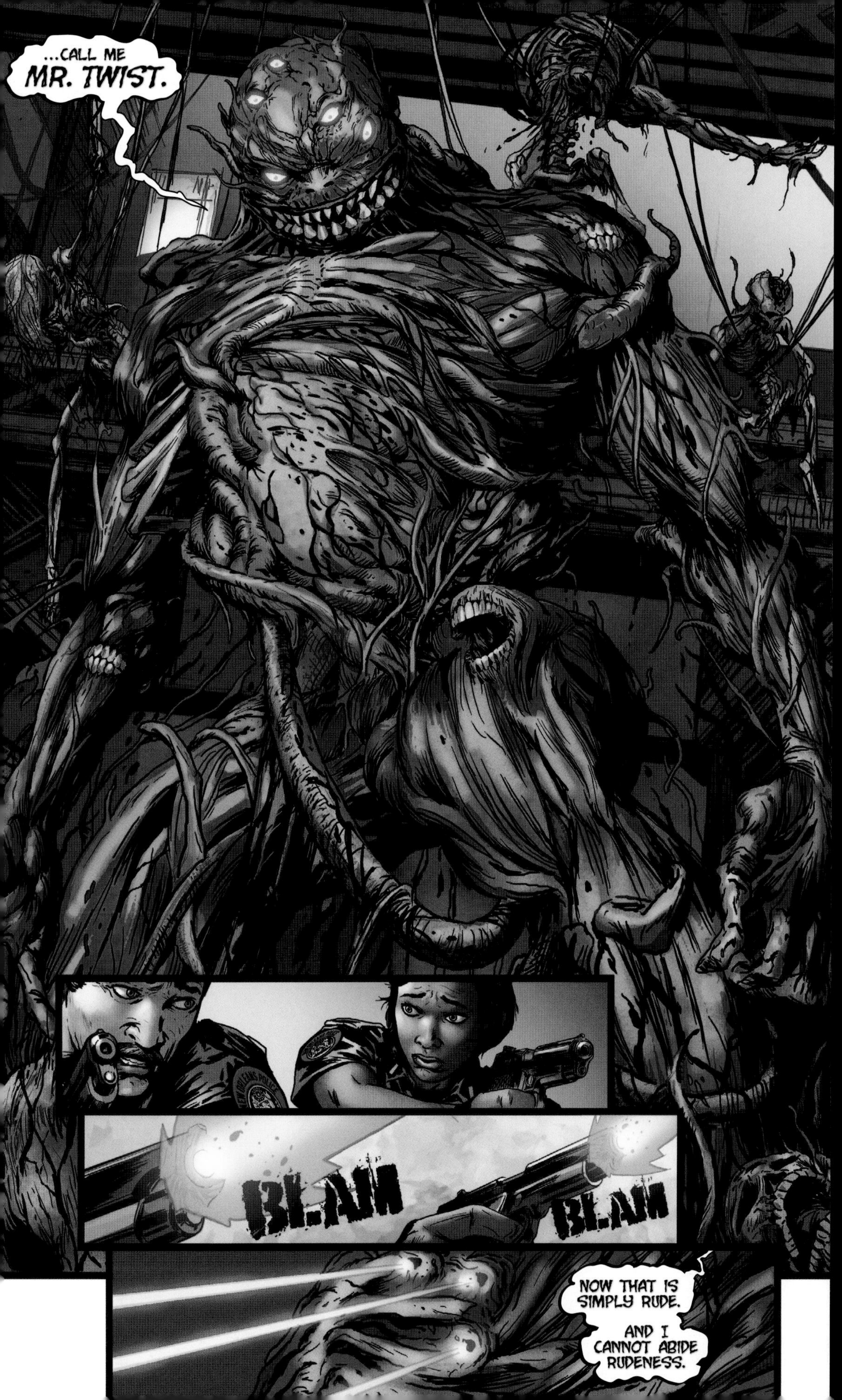
...CALL ME MR. TWIST.
BLAM
BLAM
NOW THAT IS SIMPLY RUDE.
AND I CANNOT ABIDE RUDENESS.

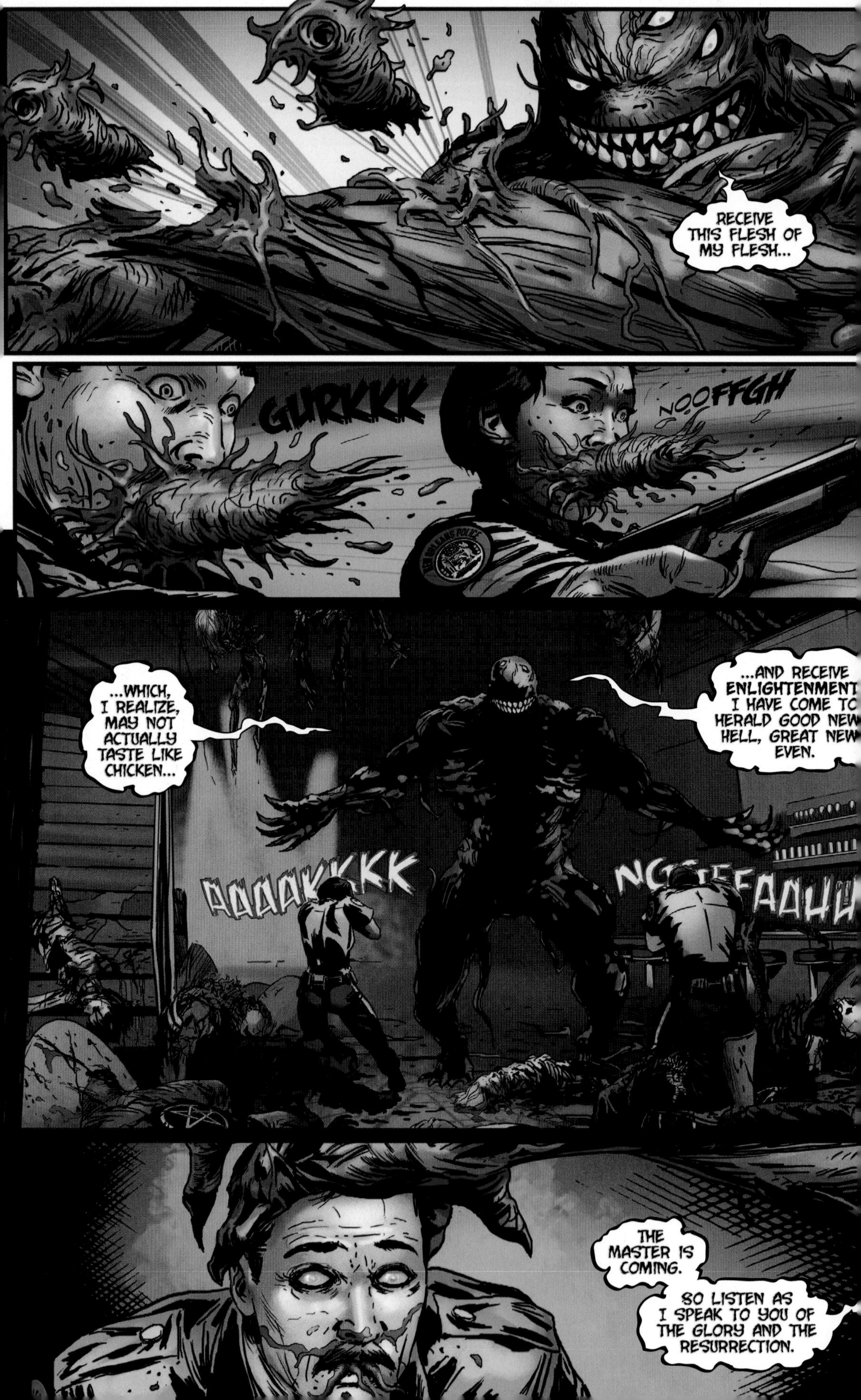
RECEIVE THIS FLESH OF MY FLESH...
GURKKK
NOOFFGH
...WHICH, I REALIZE, MAY NOT ACTUALLY TASTE LIKE CHICKEN...
...AND RECEIVE ENLIGHTENMENT I HAVE COME TO HERALD GOOD NEW HELL, GREAT NEW EVEN.
AAAAKKKK
THE MASTER IS COMING.
SO LISTEN AS I SPEAK TO YOU OF THE GLORY AND THE RESURRECTION.

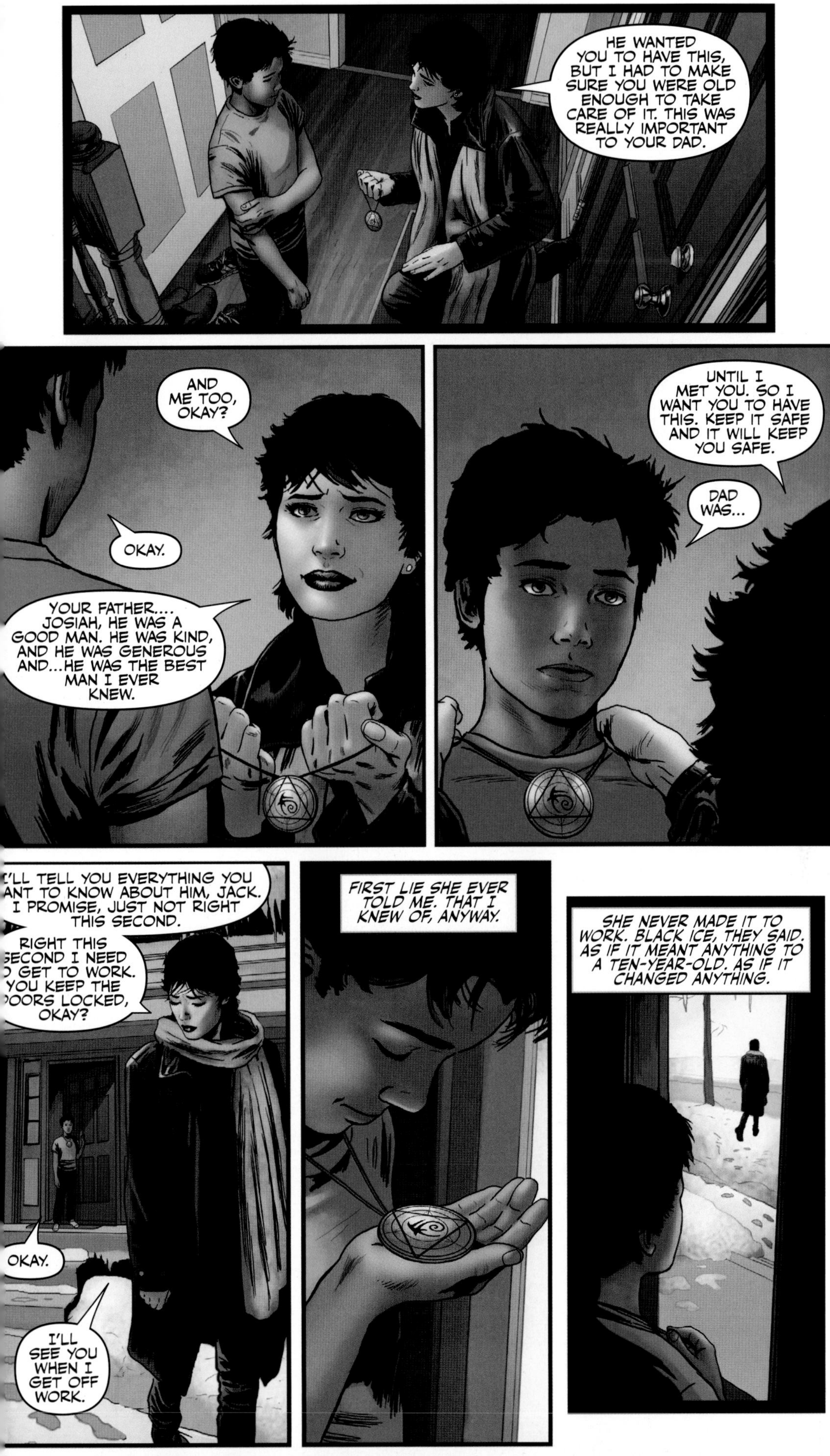
HE WANTED YOU TO HAVE THIS, BUT I HAD TO MAKE SURE YOU WERE OLD ENOUGH TO TAKE CARE OF IT. THIS WAS REALLY IMPORTANT TO YOUR DAD.
AND ME TOO, OKAY?
OKAY.
YOUR FATHER.... JOSIAH, HE WAS A GOOD MAN. HE WAS KIND, AND HE WAS GENEROUS AND...HE WAS THE BEST MAN I EVER KNEW.
UNTIL I MET YOU. SO I WANT YOU TO HAVE THIS. KEEP IT SAFE AND IT WILL KEEP YOU SAFE.
DAD WAS...
I'LL TELL YOU EVERYTHING YOU WANT TO KNOW ABOUT HIM, JACK. I PROMISE, JUST NOT RIGHT THIS SECOND.
RIGHT THIS SECOND I NEED TO GET TO WORK. YOU KEEP THE DOORS LOCKED, OKAY?
OKAY.
I'LL SEE YOU WHEN I GET OFF WORK.
FIRST LIE SHE EVER TOLD ME. THAT I KNEW OF, ANYWAY.
SHE NEVER MADE IT TO WORK. BLACK ICE, THEY SAID. AS IF IT MEANT ANYTHING TO A TEN-YEAR-OLD. AS IF IT CHANGED ANYTHING.

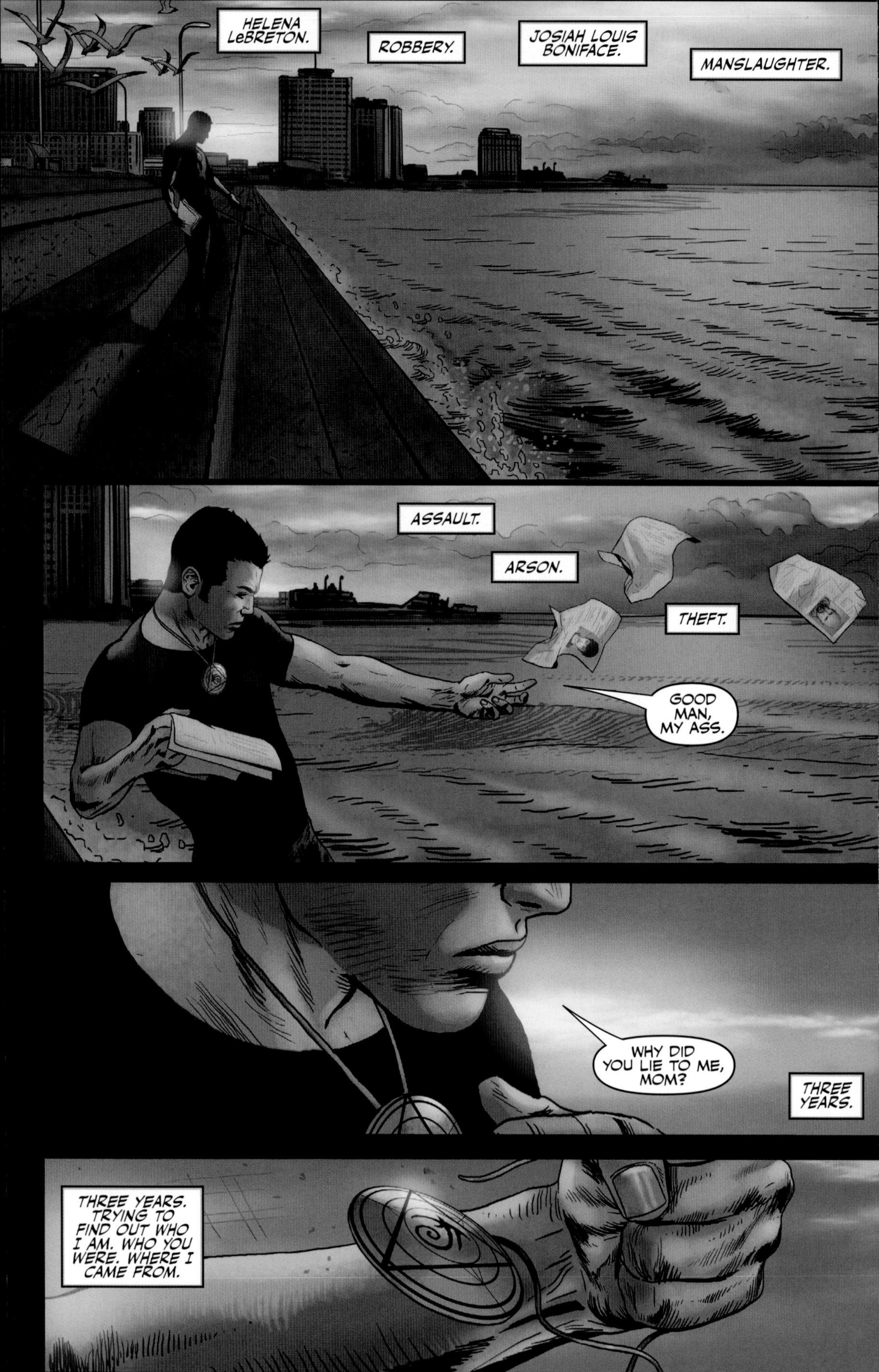
HELENA LeBRETON.
ROBBERY.
JOSIAH LOUIS BONIFACE.
MANSLAUGHTER.
ASSAULT.
ARSON.
THEFT.
GOOD MAN, MY ASS.
WHY DID YOU LIE TO ME, MOM?
THREE YEARS.
THREE YEARS. TRYING TO FIND OUT WHO I AM. WHO YOU WERE. WHERE I CAME FROM.

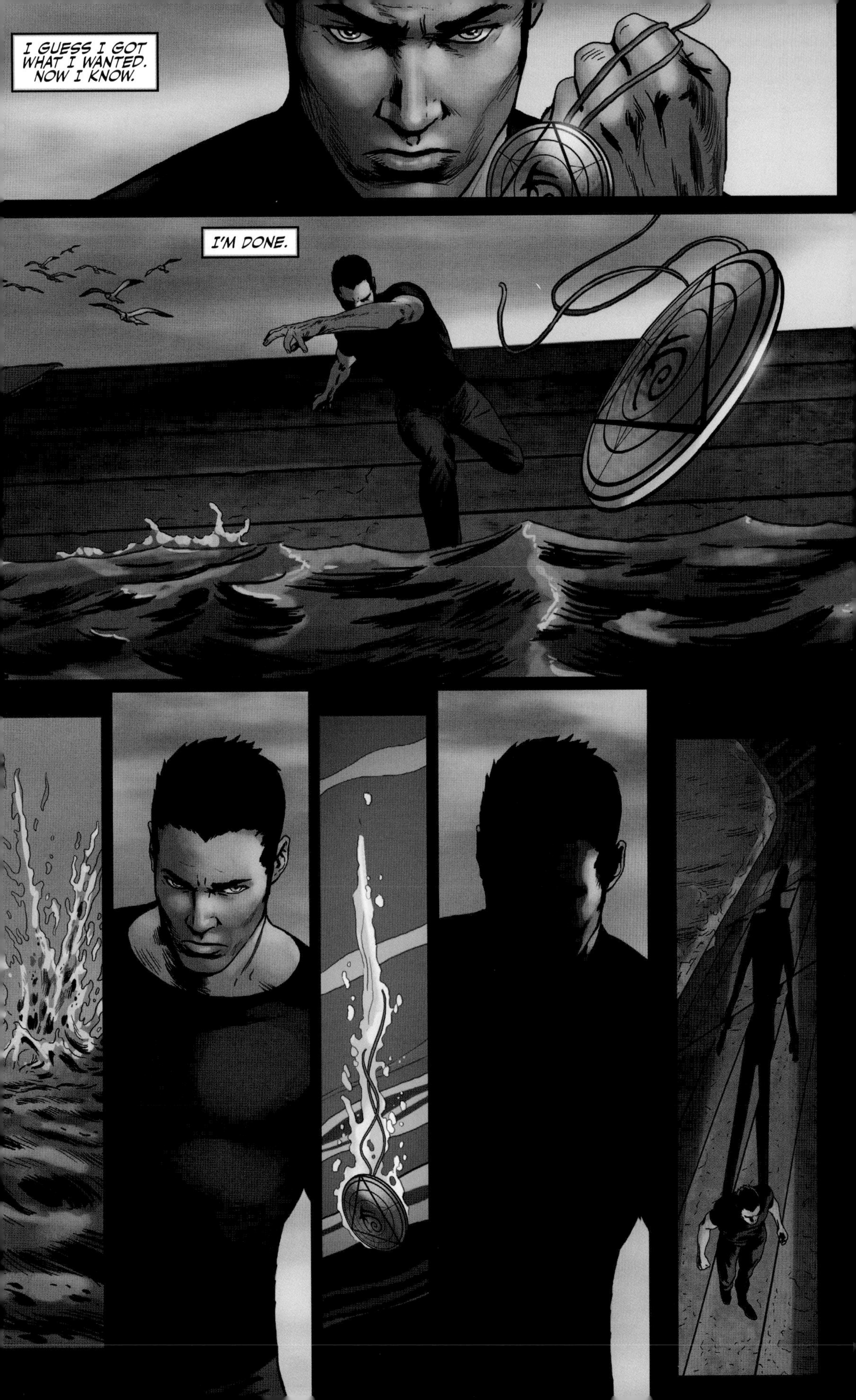
I GUESS I GOT WHAT I WANTED. NOW I KNOW.
I'M DONE.

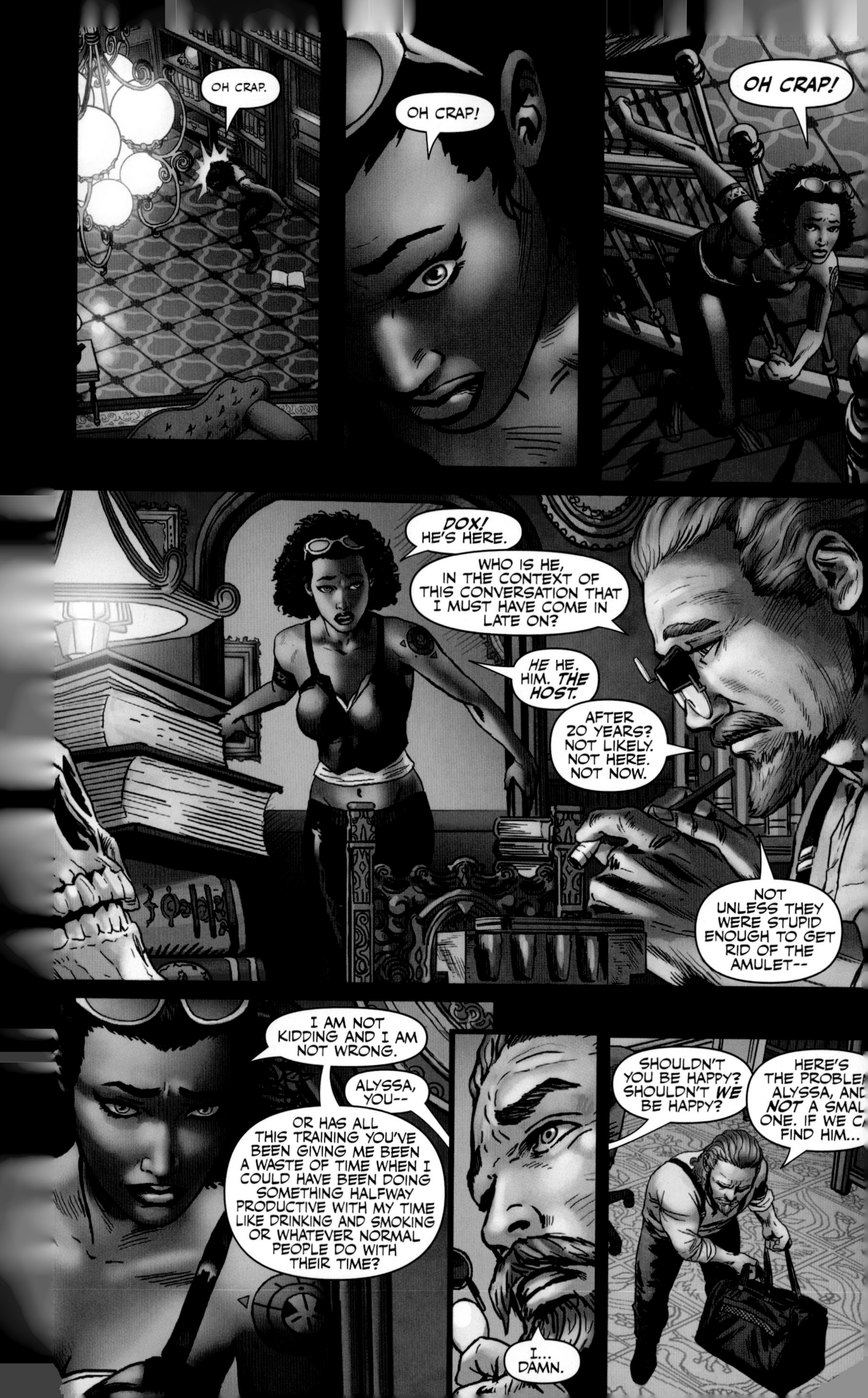

OH CRAP.
OH CRAP!
OH CRAP!
DOX! HE'S HERE.
WHO IS HE, IN THE CONTEXT OF THIS CONVERSATION THAT I MUST HAVE COME IN LATE ON?
HE HE. HIM. THE HOST.
AFTER 20 YEARS? NOT LIKELY. NOT HERE. NOT NOW.
NOT UNLESS THEY WERE STUPID ENOUGH TO GET RID OF THE AMULET--
I AM NOT KIDDING AND I AM NOT WRONG.
ALYSSA, YOU--
OR HAS ALL THIS TRAINING YOU'VE BEEN GIVING ME BEEN A WASTE OF TIME WHEN I COULD HAVE BEEN DOING SOMETHING HALFWAY PRODUCTIVE WITH MY TIME LIKE DRINKING AND SMOKING OR WHATEVER NORMAL PEOPLE DO WITH THEIR TIME?
I... DAMN.
SHOULDN'T YOU BE HAPPY? SHOULDN'T WE BE HAPPY?

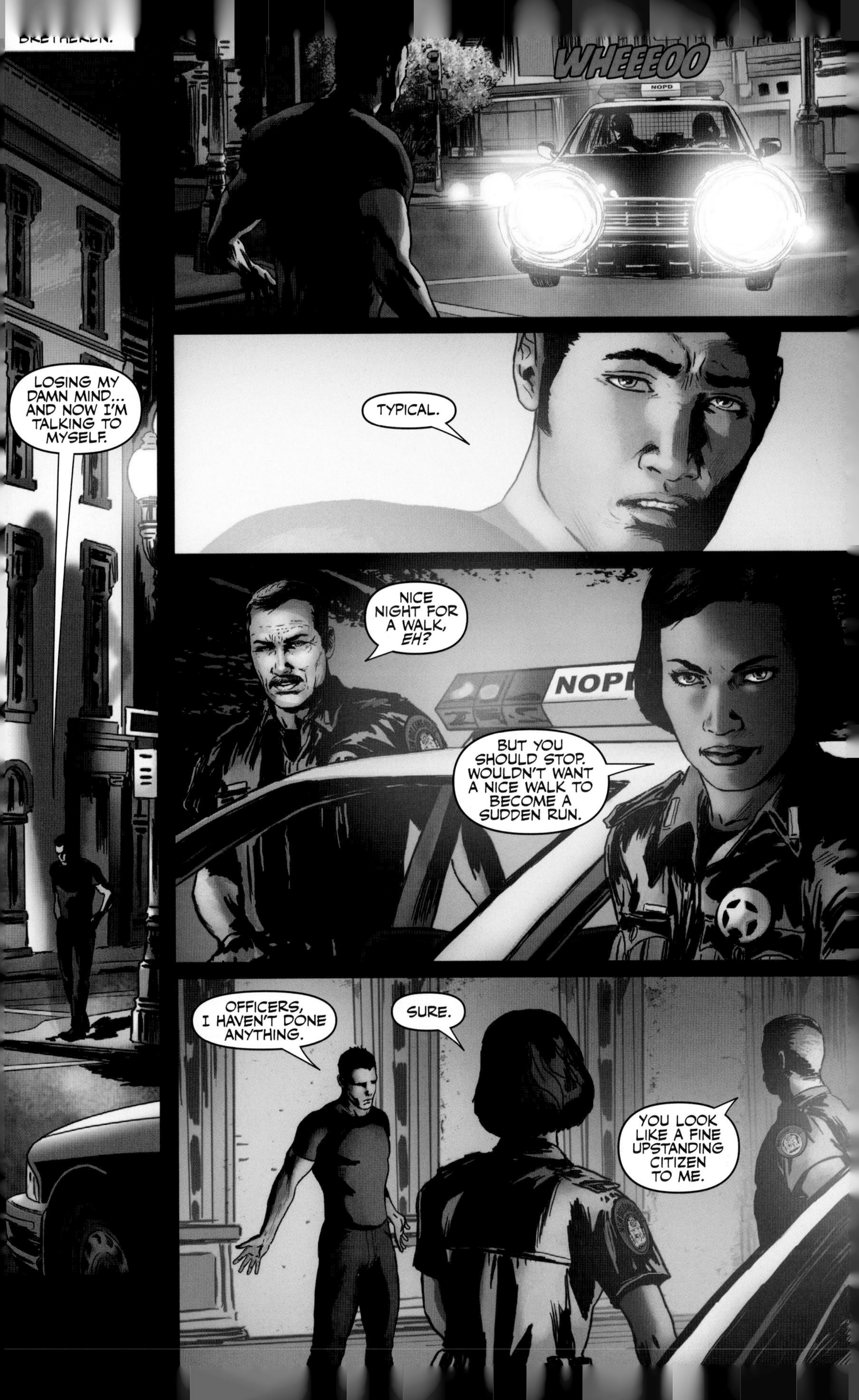

LOSING MY DAMN MIND... AND NOW I'M TALKING TO MYSELF.
WHEEEOO
NOPD
TYPICAL.
NICE NIGHT FOR A WALK, *EH?*
NOPD
BUT YOU SHOULD STOP. WOULDN'T WANT A NICE WALK TO BECOME A SUDDEN RUN.
OFFICERS, I HAVEN'T DONE ANYTHING.
SURE.
YOU LOOK LIKE A FINE UPSTANDING CITIZEN TO ME.

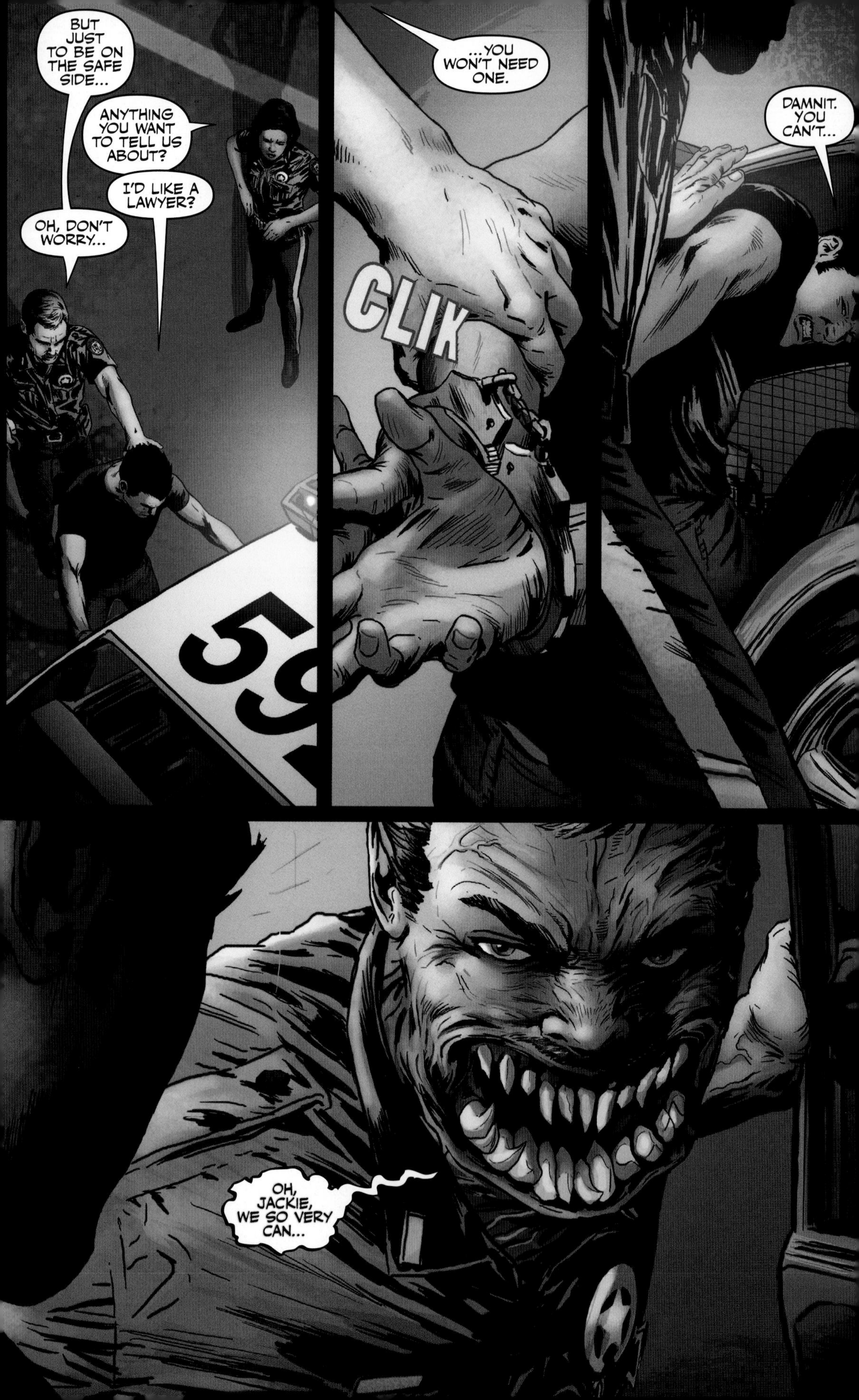
BUT JUST TO BE ON THE SAFE SIDE...
ANYTHING YOU WANT TO TELL US ABOUT?
I'D LIKE A LAWYER?
OH, DON'T WORRY...
...YOU WON'T NEED ONE.
CLIK
DAMNIT. YOU CAN'T...
OH, JACKIE, WE SO VERY CAN...

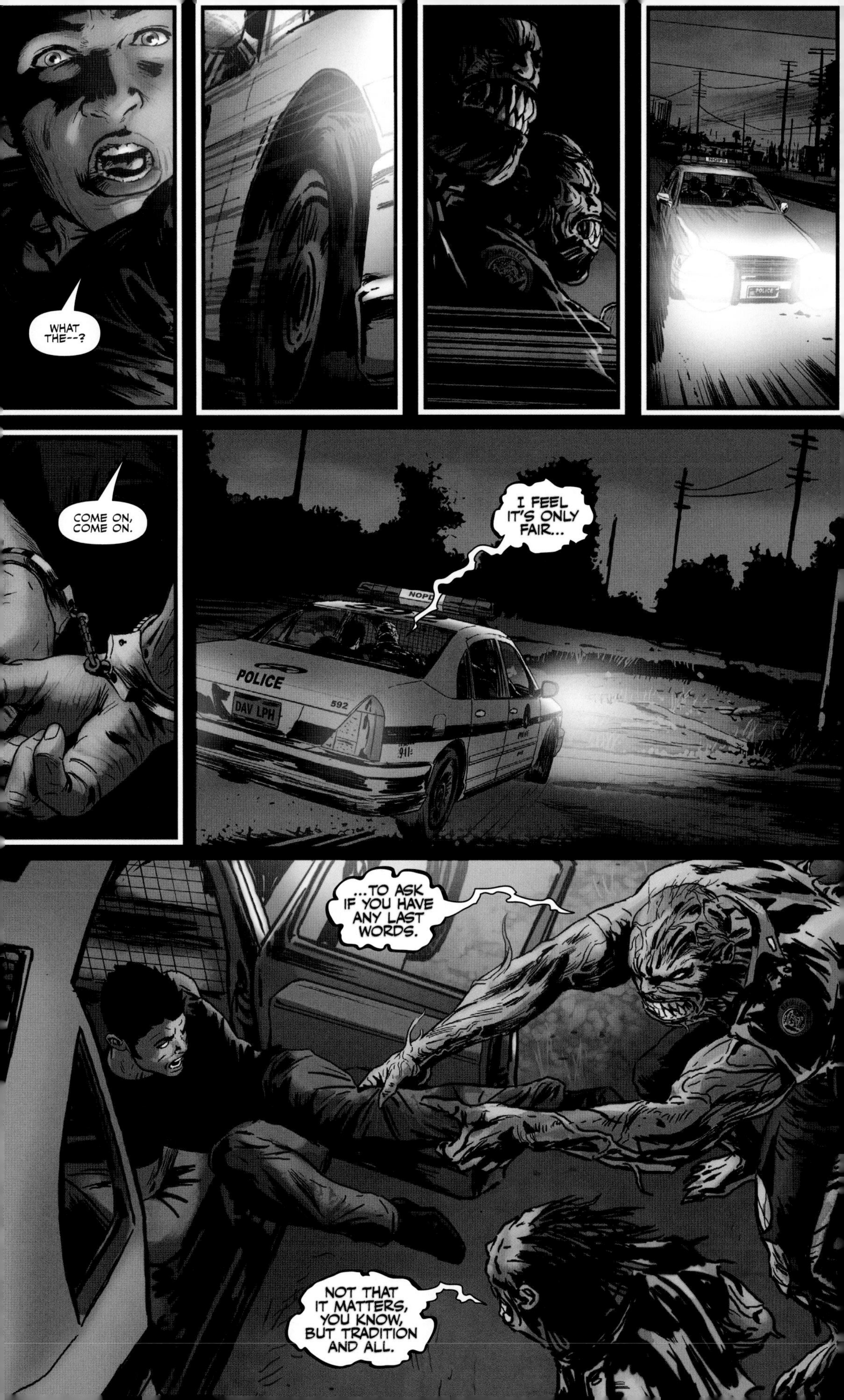
WHAT THE--?
NOPD
POLICE
COME ON, COME ON.
I FEEL IT'S ONLY FAIR...
NOPD
POLICE
DAV LPH
592
911
...TO ASK IF YOU HAVE ANY LAST WORDS.
NOT THAT IT MATTERS, YOU KNOW, BUT TRADITION AND ALL.

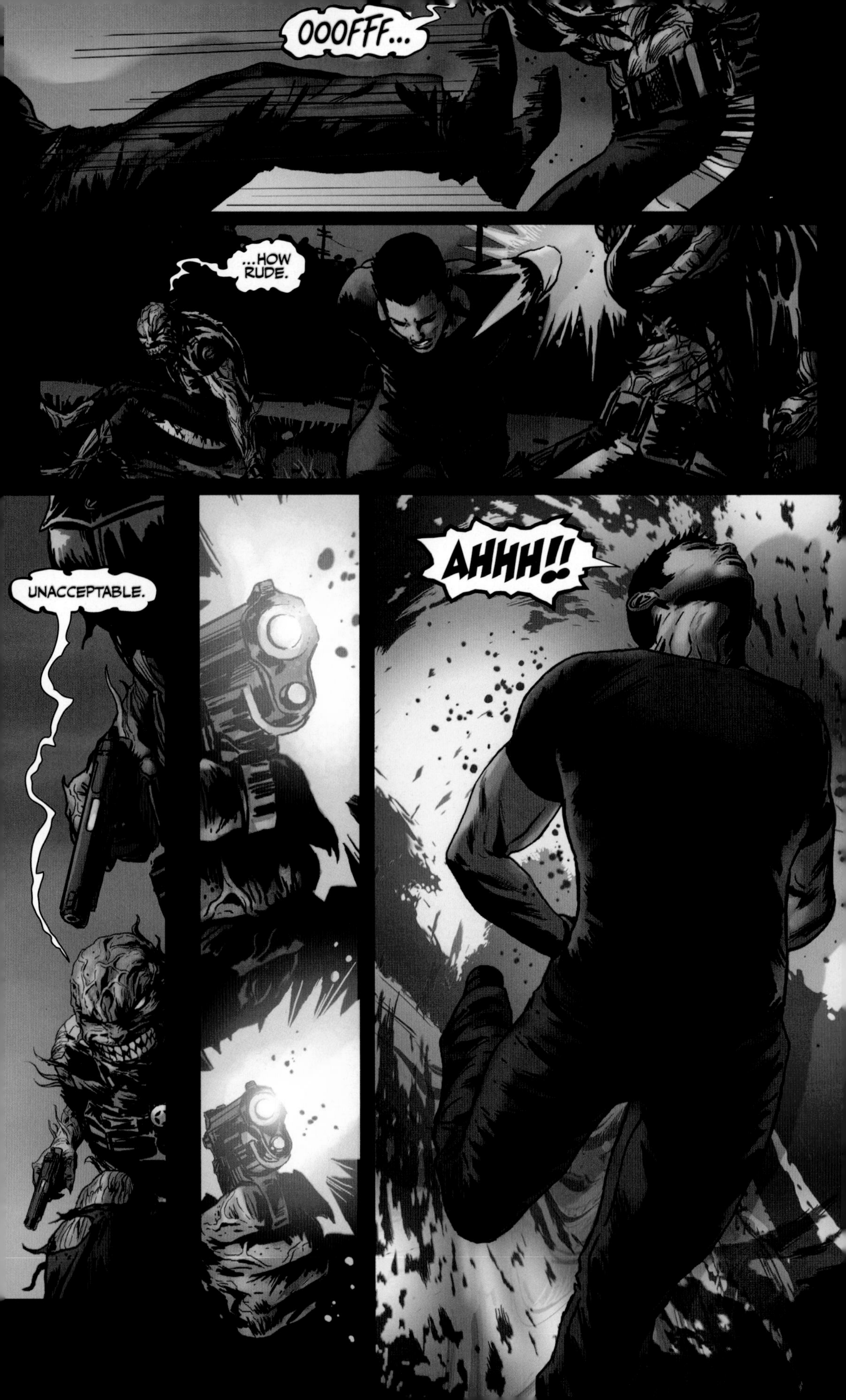
OOOFFF...
...HOW RUDE.
UNACCEPTABLE.
AHHH!!

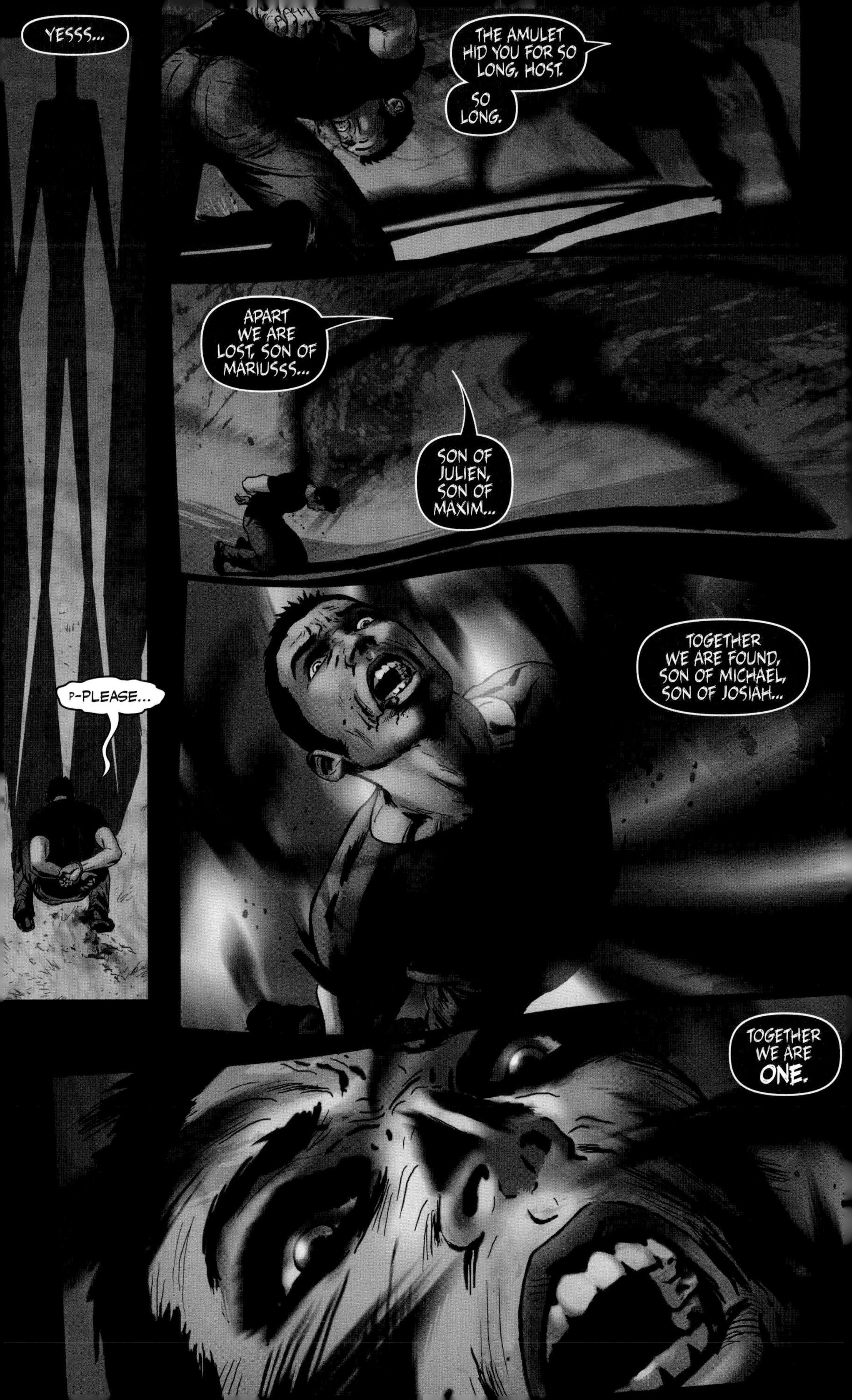
YESSS...
THE AMULET HID YOU FOR SO LONG, HOST.
SO LONG.
APART WE ARE LOST, SON OF MARIUSSS...
SON OF JULIEN, SON OF MAXIM...
P-PLEASE...
TOGETHER WE ARE FOUND, SON OF MICHAEL, SON OF JOSIAH...
TOGETHER WE ARE ONE.

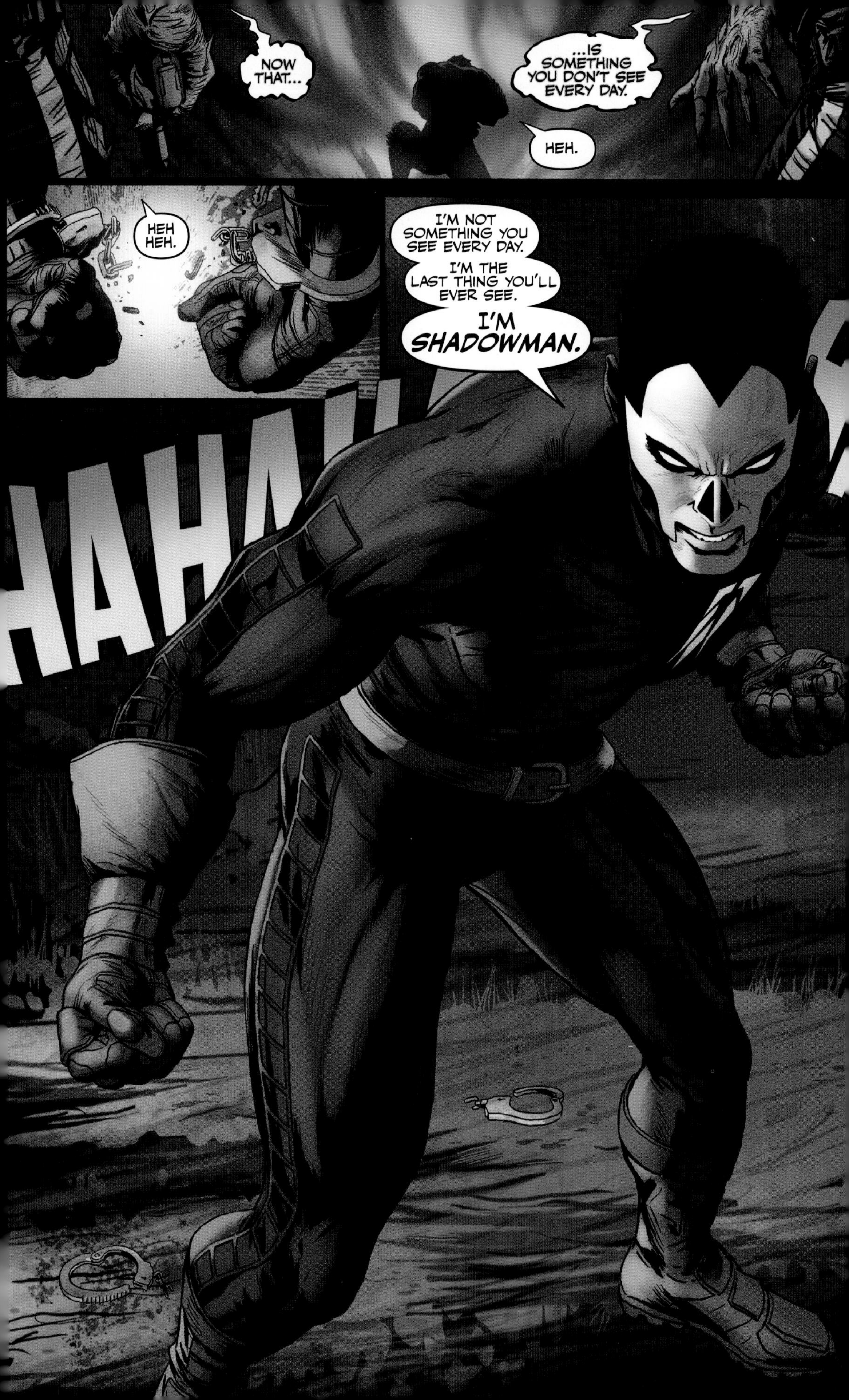
NOW THAT...
...IS SOMETHING YOU DON'T SEE EVERY DAY.
HEH.
HEH HEH.
I'M NOT SOMETHING YOU SEE EVERY DAY.
I'M THE LAST THING YOU'LL EVER SEE.
I'M SHADOWMAN.
HAHAHA

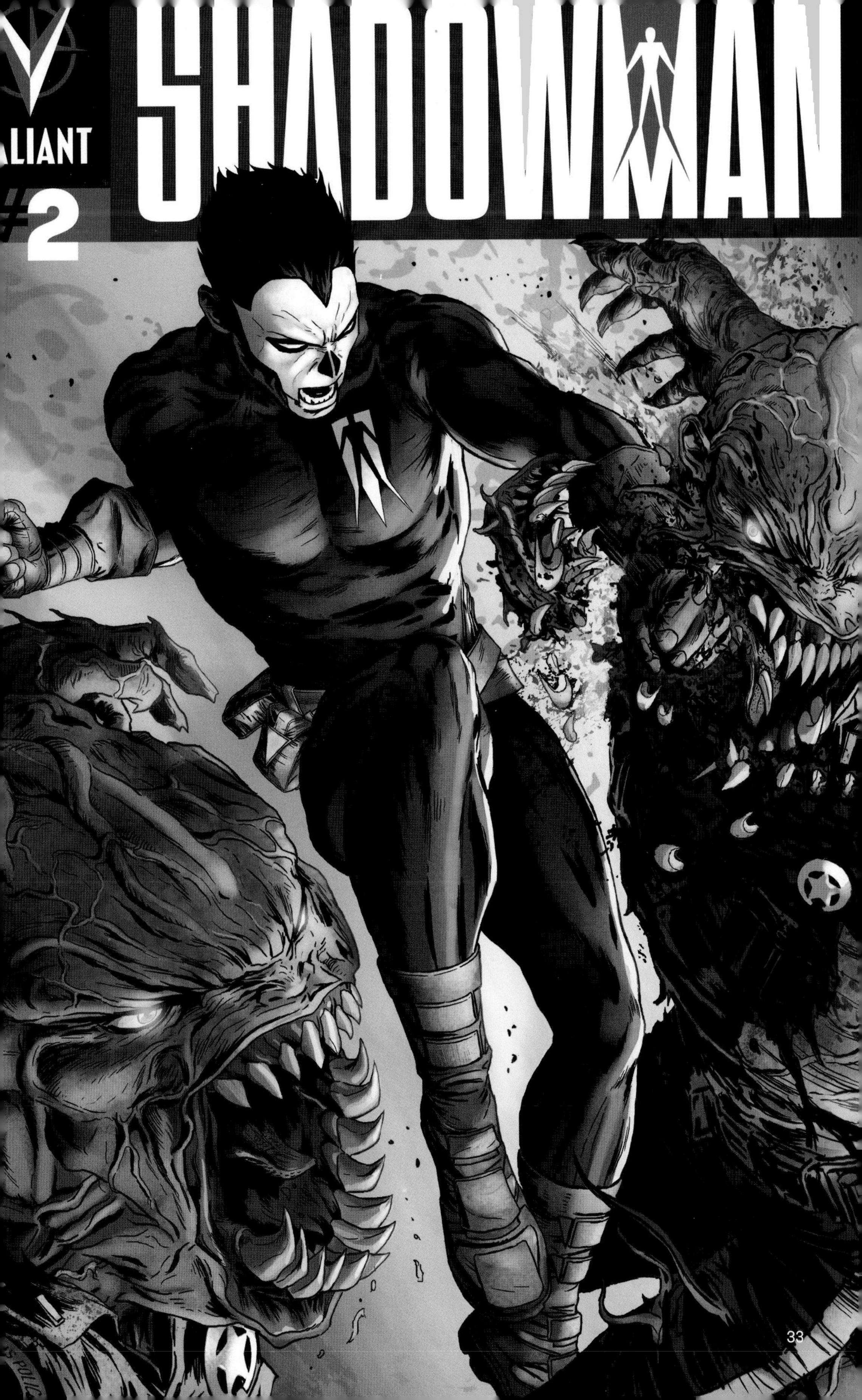
ALIANT
SHADOWMAN
#2

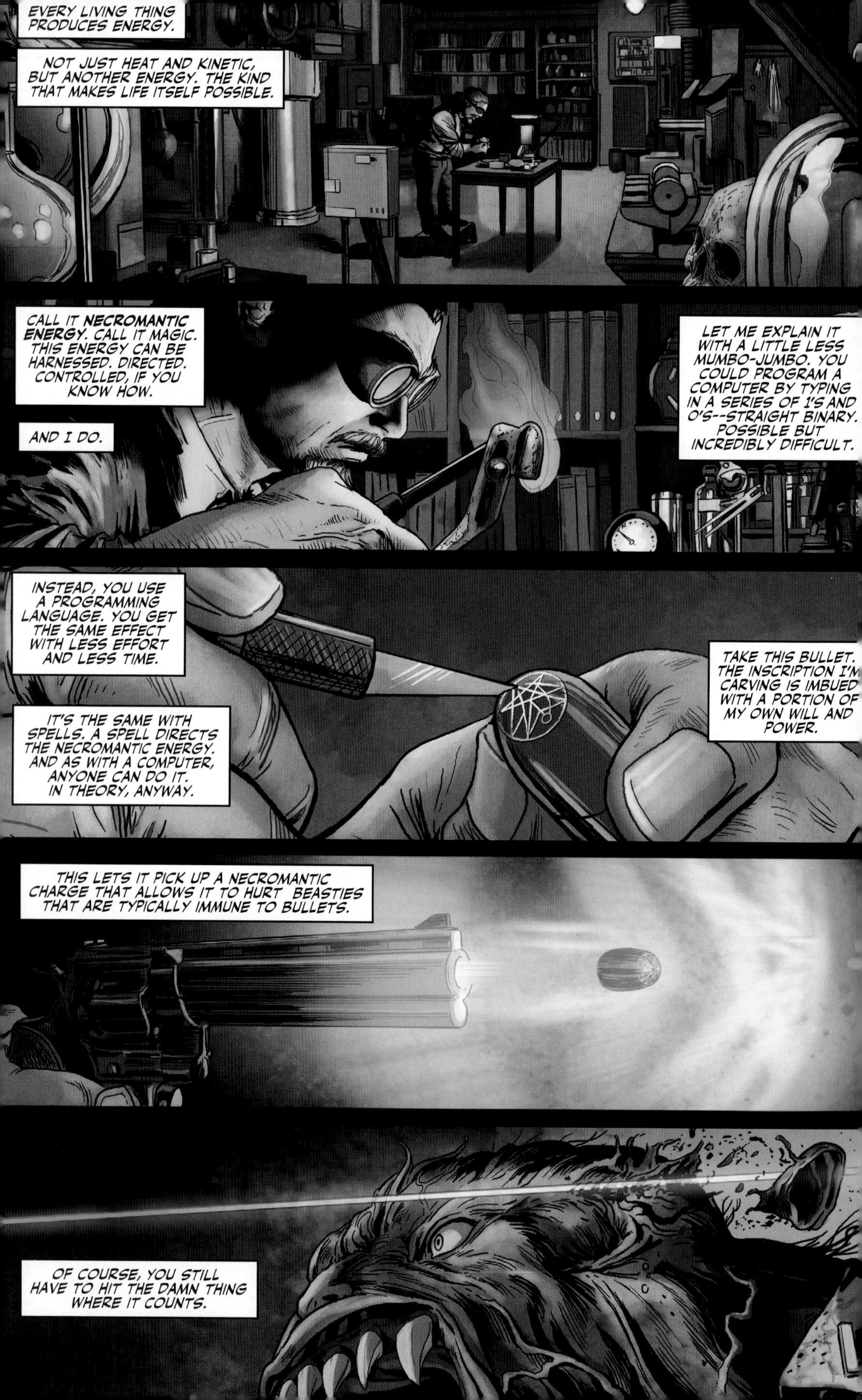
EVERY LIVING THING PRODUCES ENERGY.
NOT JUST HEAT AND KINETIC, BUT ANOTHER ENERGY. THE KIND THAT MAKES LIFE ITSELF POSSIBLE.
CALL IT **NECROMANTIC ENERGY**. CALL IT MAGIC. THIS ENERGY CAN BE HARNESSED. DIRECTED. CONTROLLED, IF YOU KNOW HOW.
AND I DO.
LET ME EXPLAIN IT WITH A LITTLE LESS MUMBO-JUMBO. YOU COULD PROGRAM A COMPUTER BY TYPING IN A SERIES OF 1'S AND O'S--STRAIGHT BINARY. POSSIBLE BUT INCREDIBLY DIFFICULT.
INSTEAD, YOU USE A PROGRAMMING LANGUAGE. YOU GET THE SAME EFFECT WITH LESS EFFORT AND LESS TIME.
IT'S THE SAME WITH SPELLS. A SPELL DIRECTS THE NECROMANTIC ENERGY. AND AS WITH A COMPUTER, ANYONE CAN DO IT. IN THEORY, ANYWAY.
TAKE THIS BULLET. THE INSCRIPTION I'M CARVING IS IMBUED WITH A PORTION OF MY OWN WILL AND POWER.
THIS LETS IT PICK UP A NECROMANTIC CHARGE THAT ALLOWS IT TO HURT BEASTIES THAT ARE TYPICALLY IMMUNE TO BULLETS.
OF COURSE, YOU STILL HAVE TO HIT THE DAMN THING WHERE IT COUNTS.

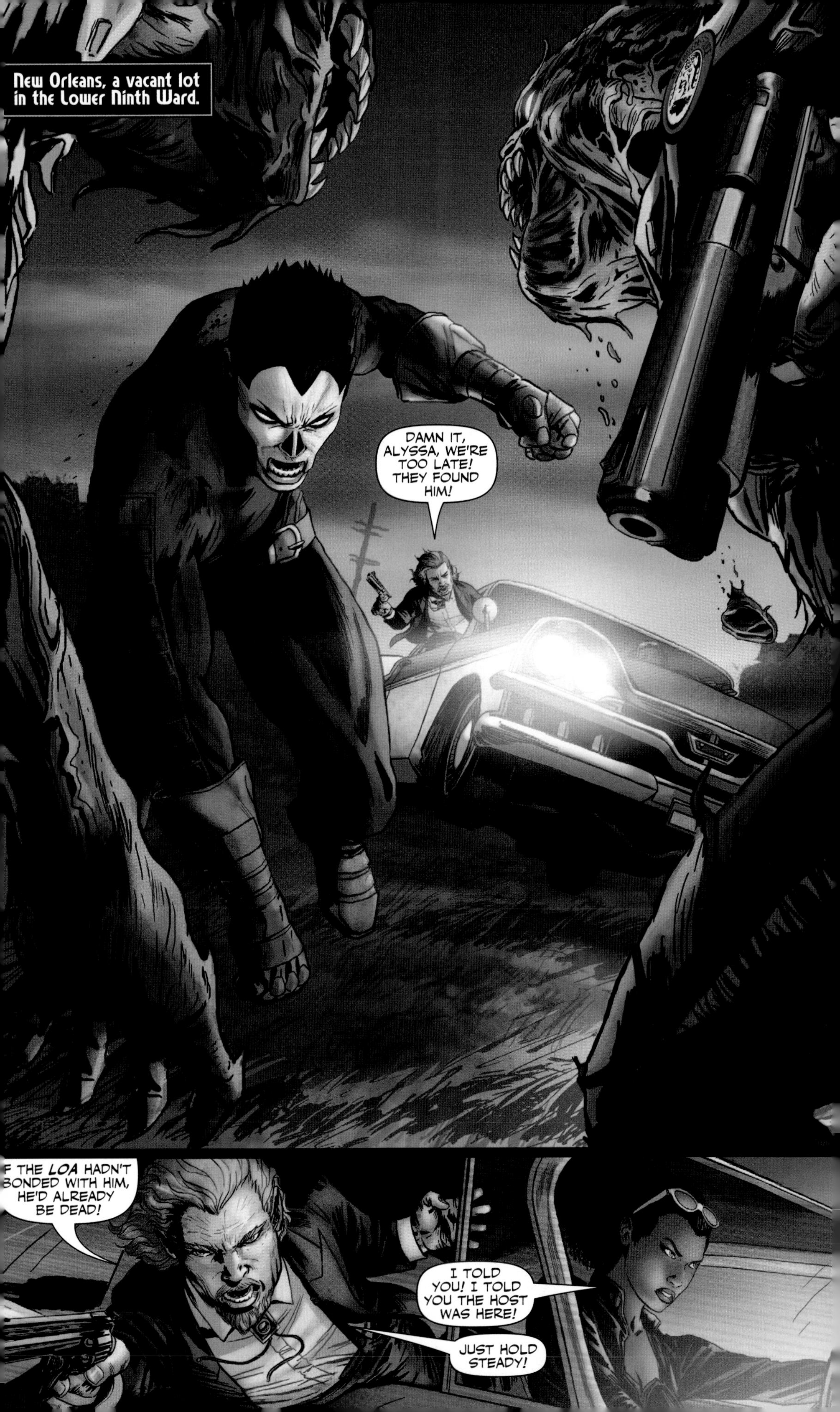
New Orleans, a vacant lot in the Lower Ninth Ward.
DAMN IT, ALYSSA, WE'RE TOO LATE! THEY FOUND HIM!
F THE LOA HADN'T BONDED WITH HIM, HE'D ALREADY BE DEAD!
I TOLD YOU! I TOLD YOU THE HOST WAS HERE!
JUST HOLD STEADY!

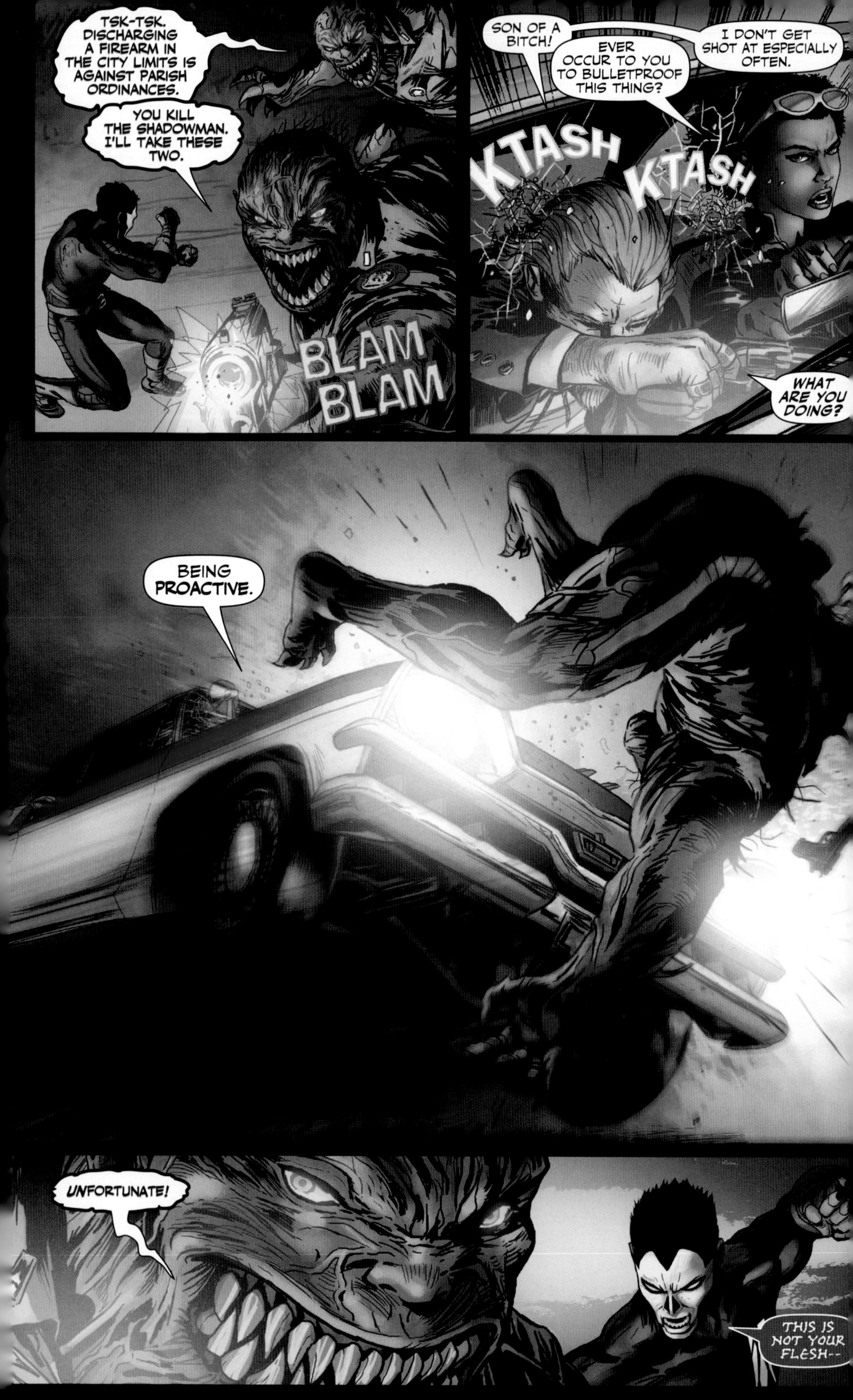
TSK-TSK. DISCHARGING A FIREARM IN THE CITY LIMITS IS AGAINST PARISH ORDINANCES.
YOU KILL THE SHADOWMAN. I'LL TAKE THESE TWO.
BLAM BLAM
SON OF A BITCH!
EVER OCCUR TO YOU TO BULLETPROOF THIS THING?
I DON'T GET SHOT AT ESPECIALLY OFTEN.
KTASH
KTASH
WHAT ARE YOU DOING?
BEING PROACTIVE.
UNFORTUNATE!
THIS IS NOT YOUR FLESH--

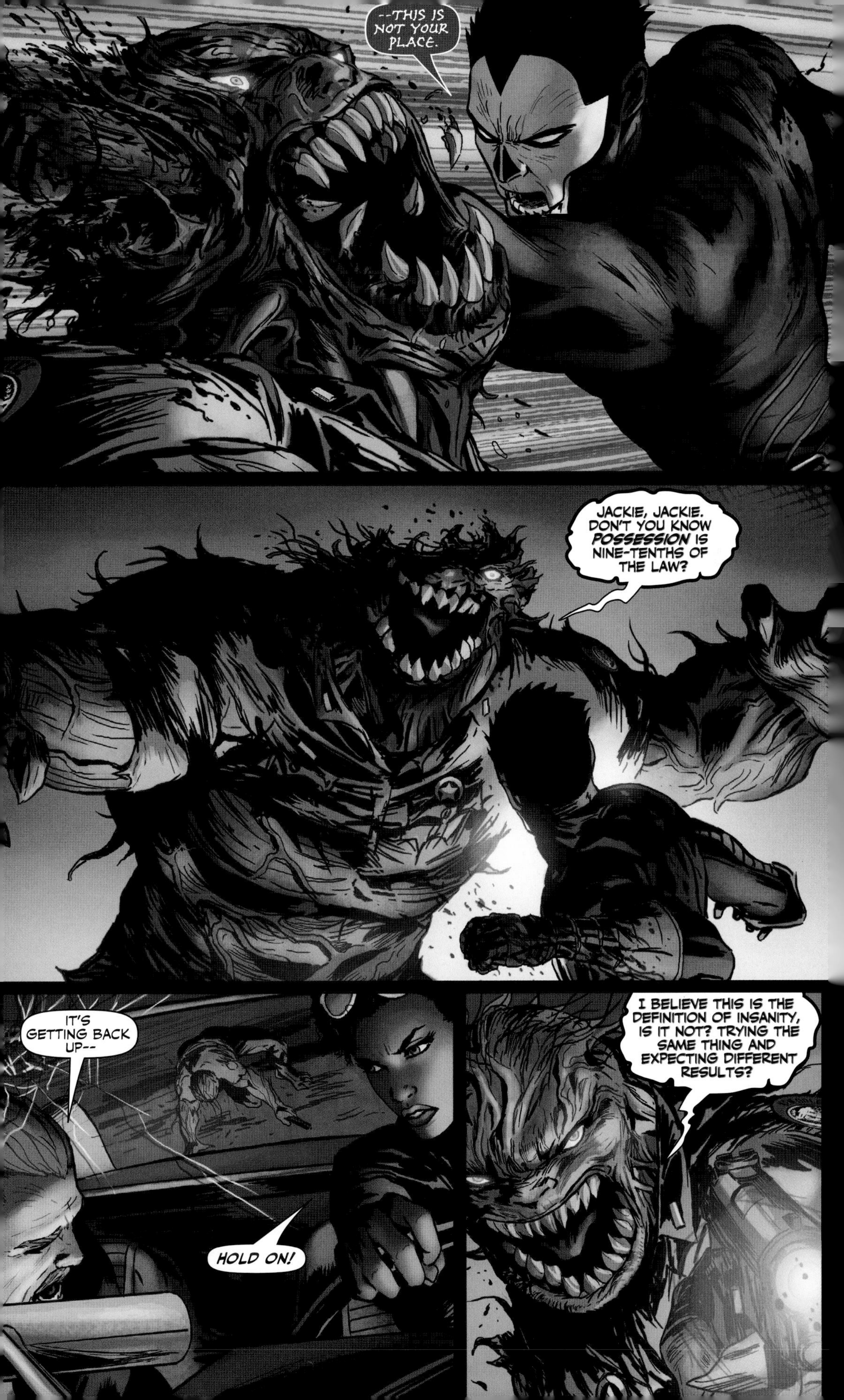
--THIS IS NOT YOUR PLACE.
JACKIE, JACKIE. DON'T YOU KNOW *POSSESSION* IS NINE-TENTHS OF THE LAW?
IT'S GETTING BACK UP--
HOLD ON!
I BELIEVE THIS IS THE DEFINITION OF INSANITY, IS IT NOT? TRYING THE SAME THING AND EXPECTING DIFFERENT RESULTS?

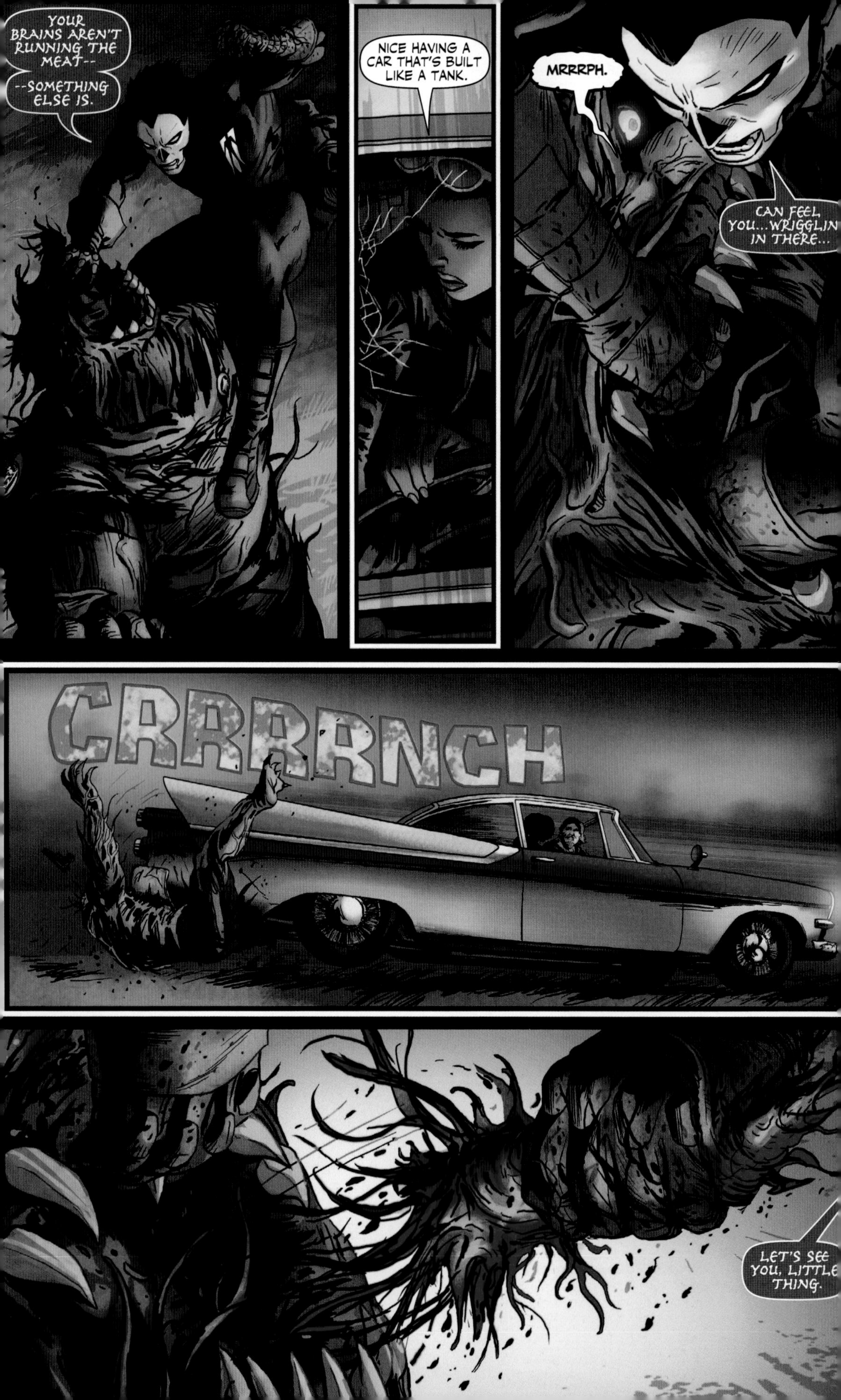
YOUR BRAINS AREN'T RUNNING THE MEAT--
--SOMETHING ELSE IS.
NICE HAVING A CAR THAT'S BUILT LIKE A TANK.
MRRRPH.
CAN FEEL YOU...WRIGGLIN IN THERE...
CRRRRNCH
LET'S SEE YOU, LITTLE THING.

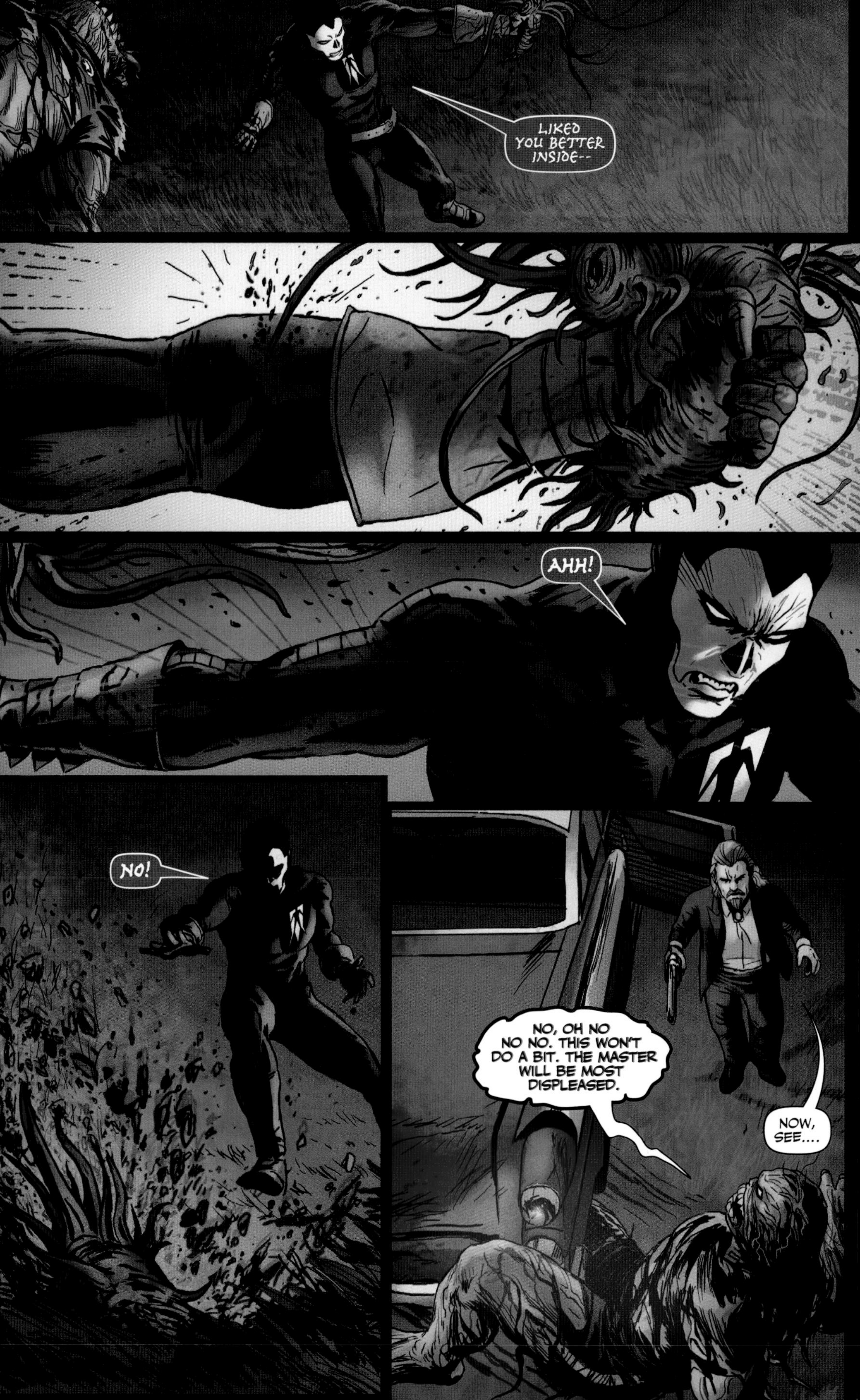
LIKED YOU BETTER INSIDE--
AHH!
NO!
NO, OH NO NO NO. THIS WON'T DO A BIT. THE MASTER WILL BE MOST DISPLEASED.
NOW, SEE....

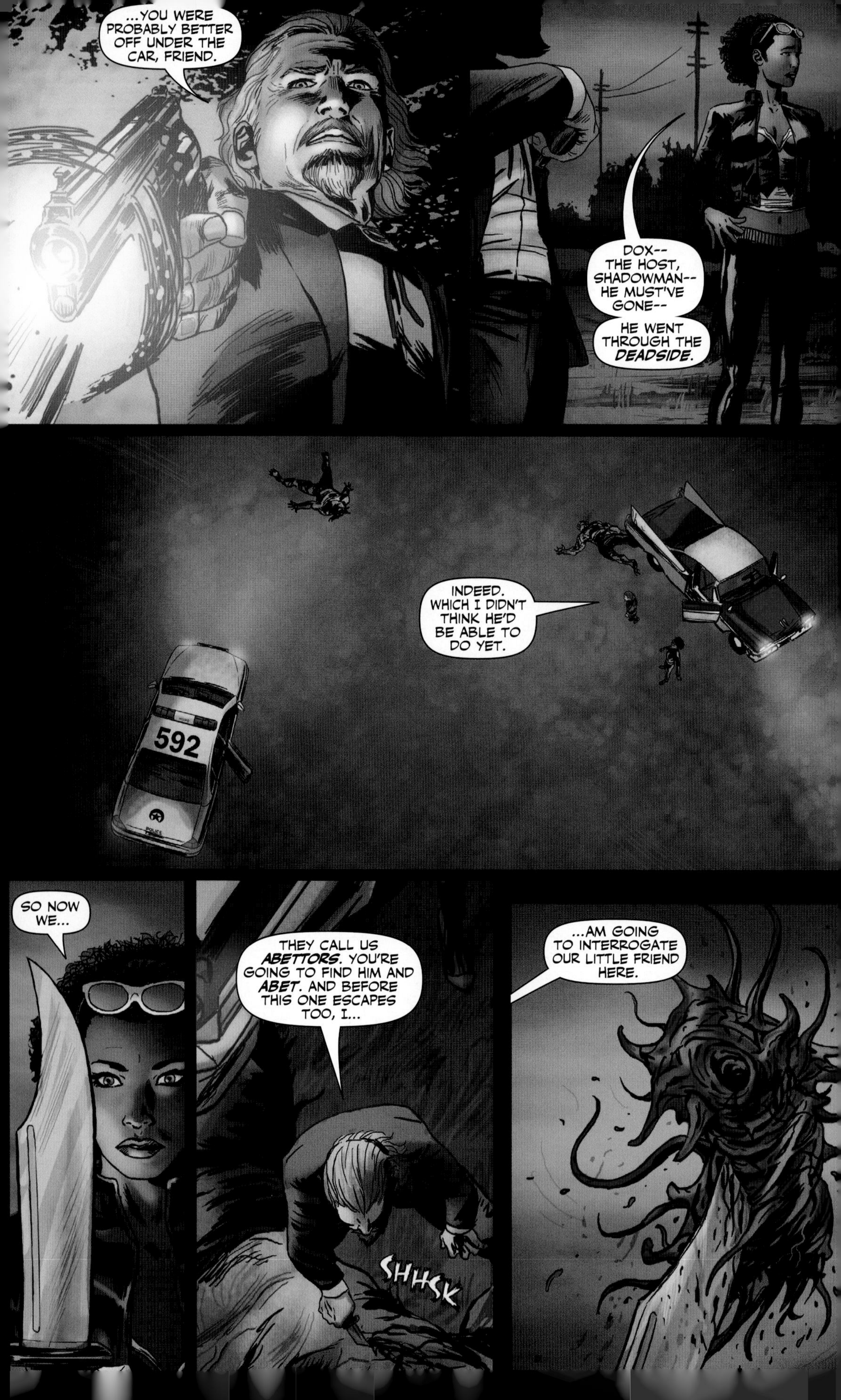
...YOU WERE PROBABLY BETTER OFF UNDER THE CAR, FRIEND.
DOX-- THE HOST, SHADOWMAN-- HE MUST'VE GONE--
HE WENT THROUGH THE DEADSIDE.
INDEED. WHICH I DIDN'T THINK HE'D BE ABLE TO DO YET.
592
SO NOW WE...
THEY CALL US ABETTORS. YOU'RE GOING TO FIND HIM AND ABET. AND BEFORE THIS ONE ESCAPES TOO, I...
SHHCK
...AM GOING TO INTERROGATE OUR LITTLE FRIEND HERE.

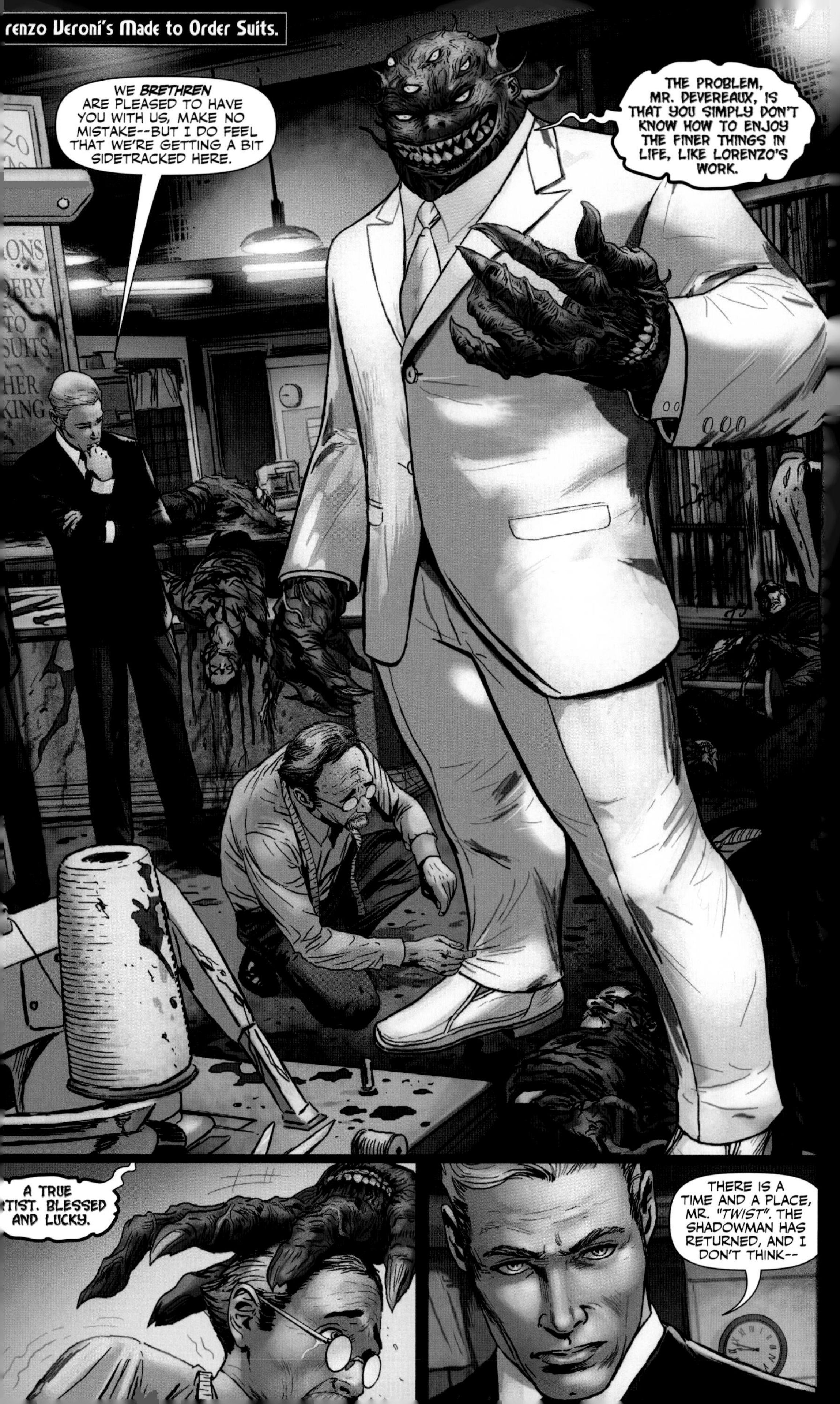
renzo Veroni's Made to Order Suits.
WE BRETHREN ARE PLEASED TO HAVE YOU WITH US, MAKE NO MISTAKE--BUT I DO FEEL THAT WE'RE GETTING A BIT SIDETRACKED HERE.
THE PROBLEM, MR. DEVEREAUX, IS THAT YOU SIMPLY DON'T KNOW HOW TO ENJOY THE FINER THINGS IN LIFE, LIKE LORENZO'S WORK.
A TRUE RTIST. BLESSED AND LUCKY.
THERE IS A TIME AND A PLACE, MR. "TWIST". THE SHADOWMAN HAS RETURNED, AND I DON'T THINK--

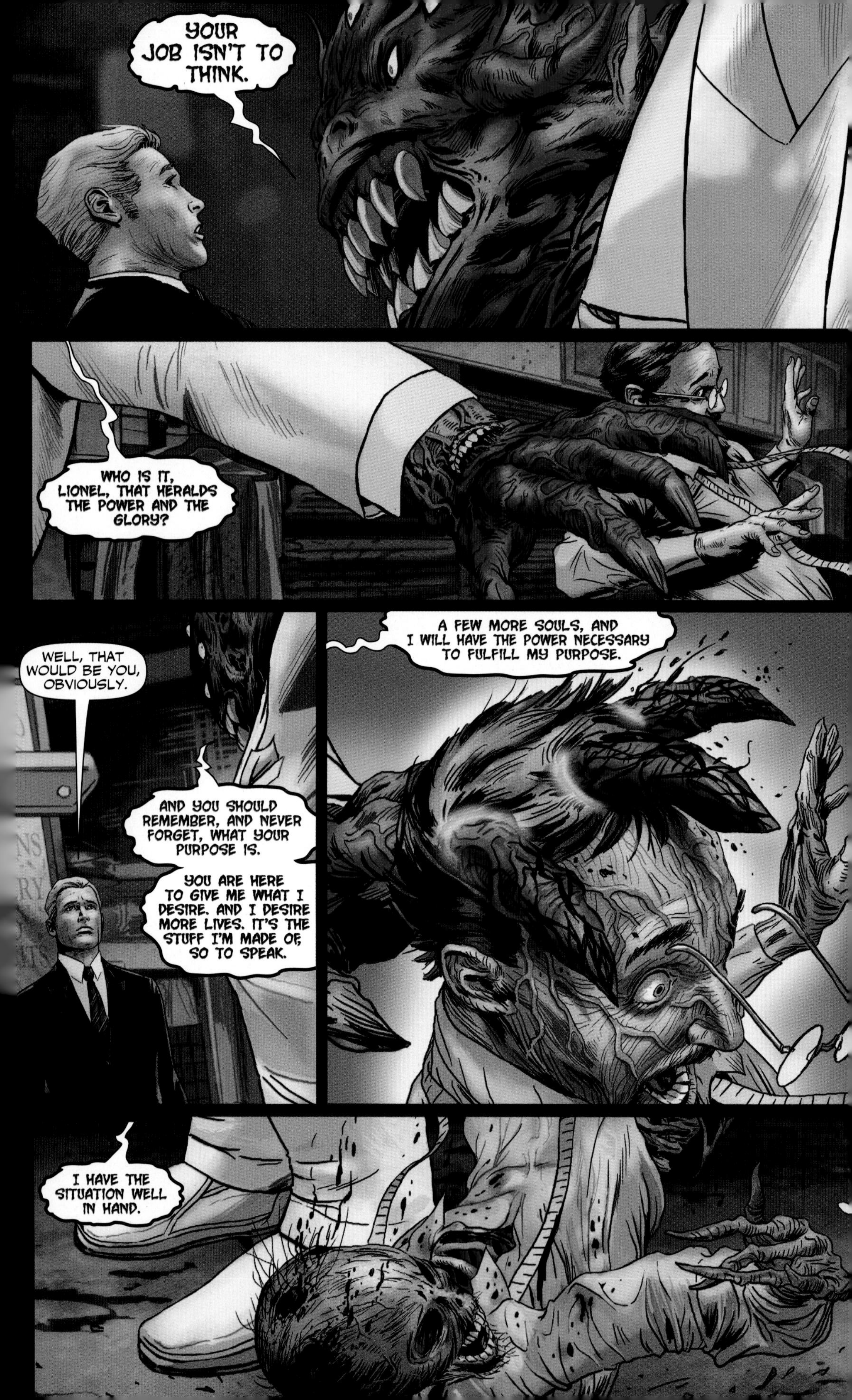
YOUR JOB ISN'T TO THINK.
WHO IS IT, LIONEL, THAT HERALDS THE POWER AND THE GLORY?
WELL, THAT WOULD BE YOU, OBVIOUSLY.
AND YOU SHOULD REMEMBER, AND NEVER FORGET, WHAT YOUR PURPOSE IS.
YOU ARE HERE TO GIVE ME WHAT I DESIRE. AND I DESIRE MORE LIVES. IT'S THE STUFF I'M MADE OF, SO TO SPEAK.
A FEW MORE SOULS, AND I WILL HAVE THE POWER NECESSARY TO FULFILL MY PURPOSE.
I HAVE THE SITUATION WELL IN HAND.

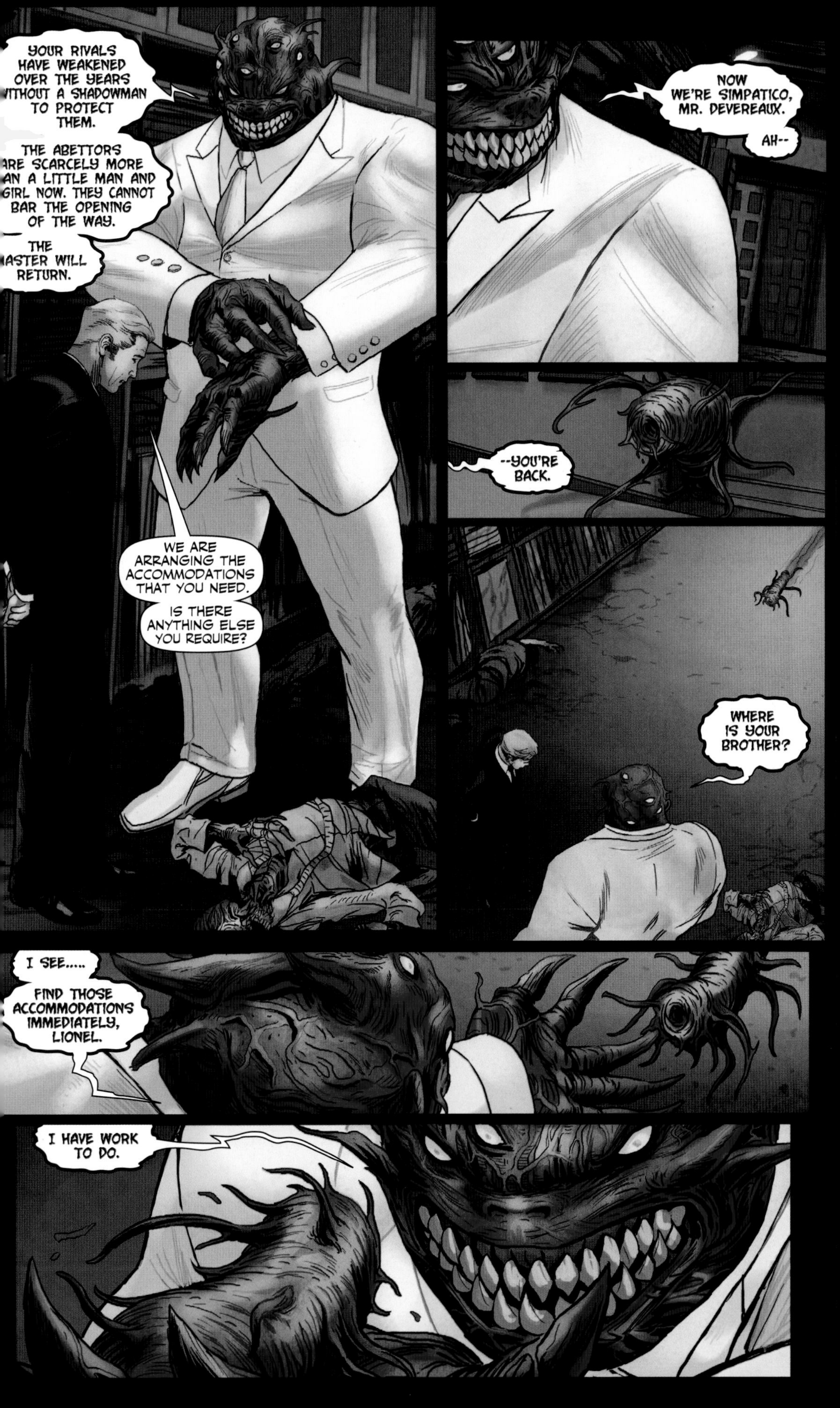
YOUR RIVALS HAVE WEAKENED OVER THE YEARS WITHOUT A SHADOWMAN TO PROTECT THEM.
THE ABETTORS ARE SCARCELY MORE THAN A LITTLE MAN AND GIRL NOW. THEY CANNOT BAR THE OPENING OF THE WAY.
THE MASTER WILL RETURN.
WE ARE ARRANGING THE ACCOMMODATIONS THAT YOU NEED.
IS THERE ANYTHING ELSE YOU REQUIRE?
NOW WE'RE SIMPATICO, MR. DEVEREAUX.
AH--
--YOU'RE BACK.
WHERE IS YOUR BROTHER?
I SEE.....
FIND THOSE ACCOMMODATIONS IMMEDIATELY, LIONEL.
I HAVE WORK TO DO.

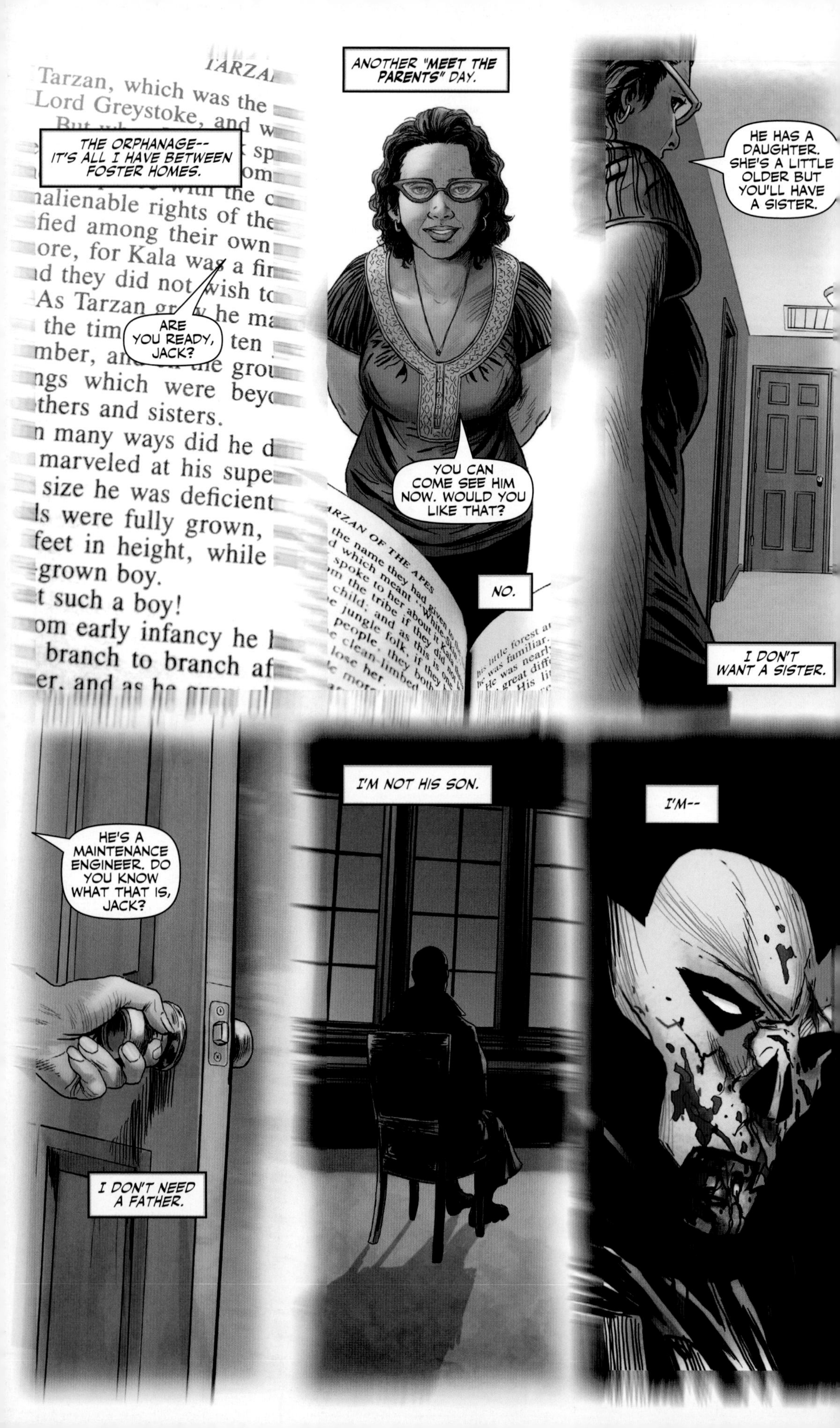
THE ORPHANAGE-- IT'S ALL I HAVE BETWEEN FOSTER HOMES.
ARE YOU READY, JACK?
ANOTHER "MEET THE PARENTS" DAY.
YOU CAN COME SEE HIM NOW. WOULD YOU LIKE THAT?
NO.
HE HAS A DAUGHTER. SHE'S A LITTLE OLDER BUT YOU'LL HAVE A SISTER.
I DON'T WANT A SISTER.
HE'S A MAINTENANCE ENGINEER. DO YOU KNOW WHAT THAT IS, JACK?
I DON'T NEED A FATHER.
I'M NOT HIS SON.
I'M--

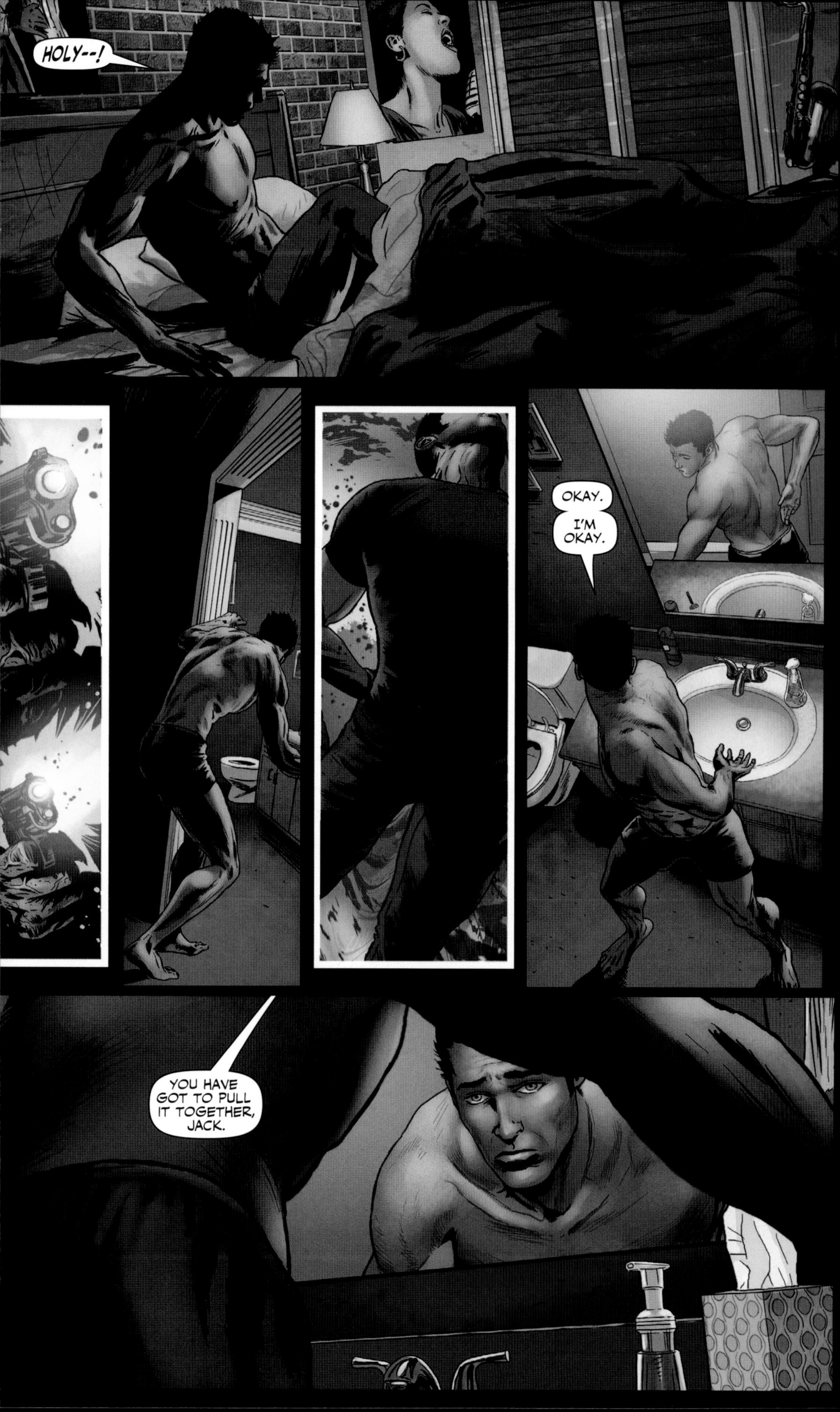
HOLY--!
OKAY.
I'M OKAY.
YOU HAVE GOT TO PULL IT TOGETHER, JACK.

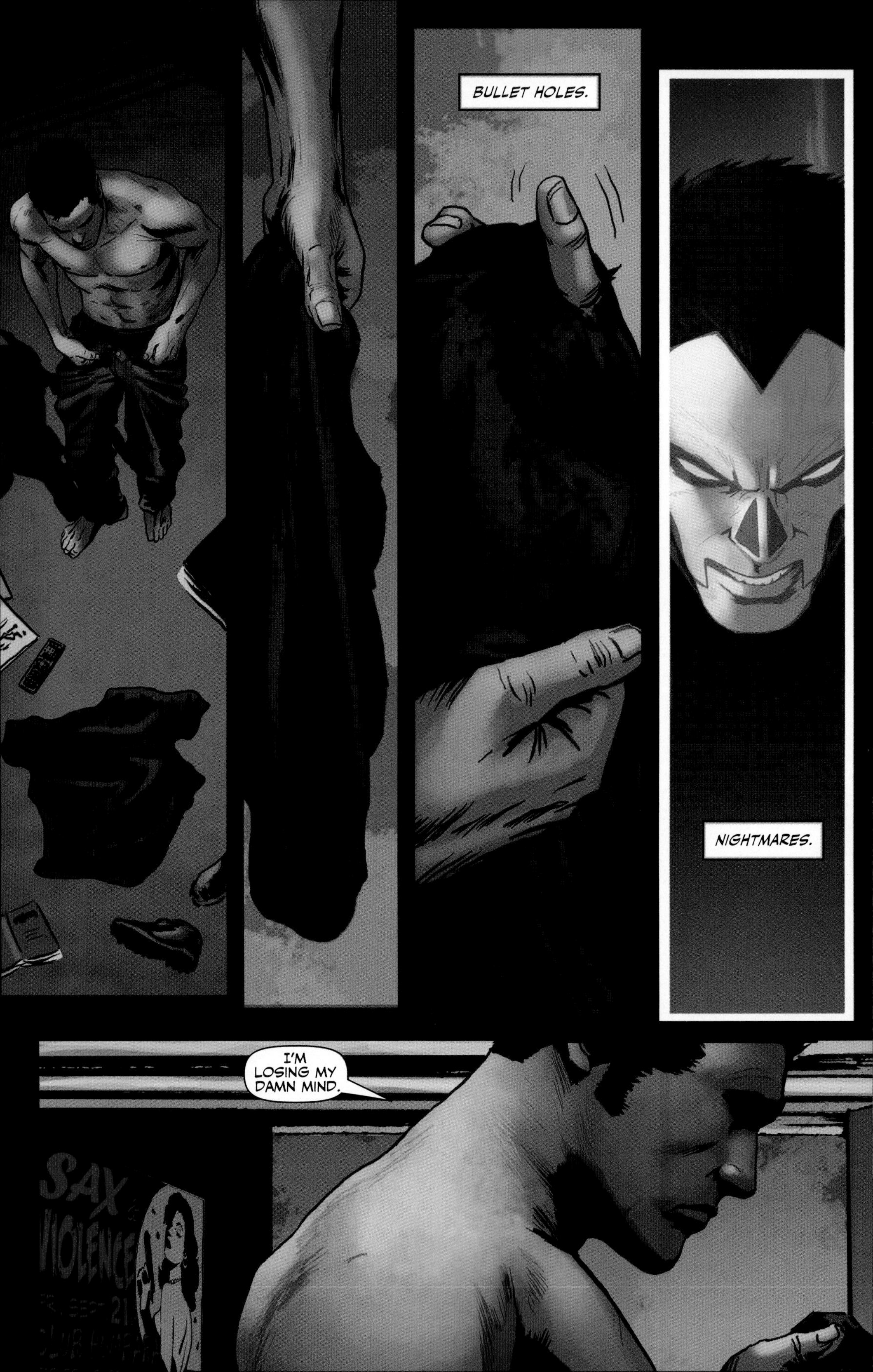
BULLET HOLES.
NIGHTMARES.
I'M LOSING MY DAMN MIND.
SAX
VIOLENCE

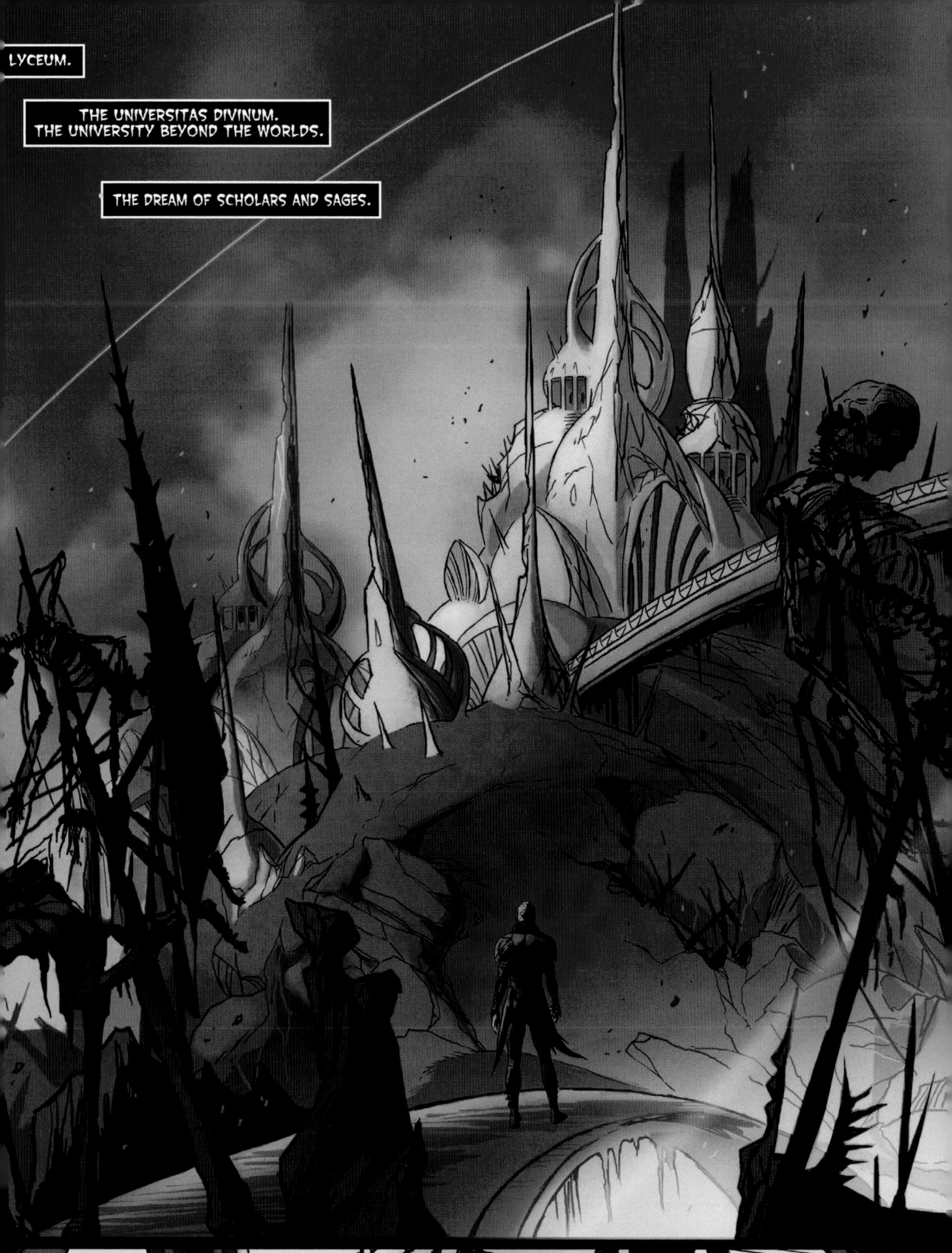
LYCEUM.
THE UNIVERSITAS DIVINUM. THE UNIVERSITY BEYOND THE WORLDS.
THE DREAM OF SCHOLARS AND SAGES.

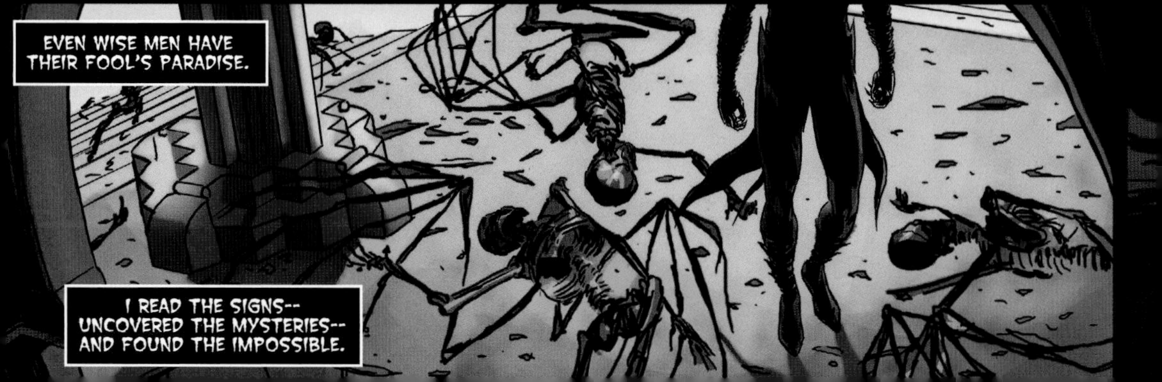
EVEN WISE MEN HAVE THEIR FOOL'S PARADISE.
I READ THE SIGNS-- UNCOVERED THE MYSTERIES-- AND FOUND THE IMPOSSIBLE.

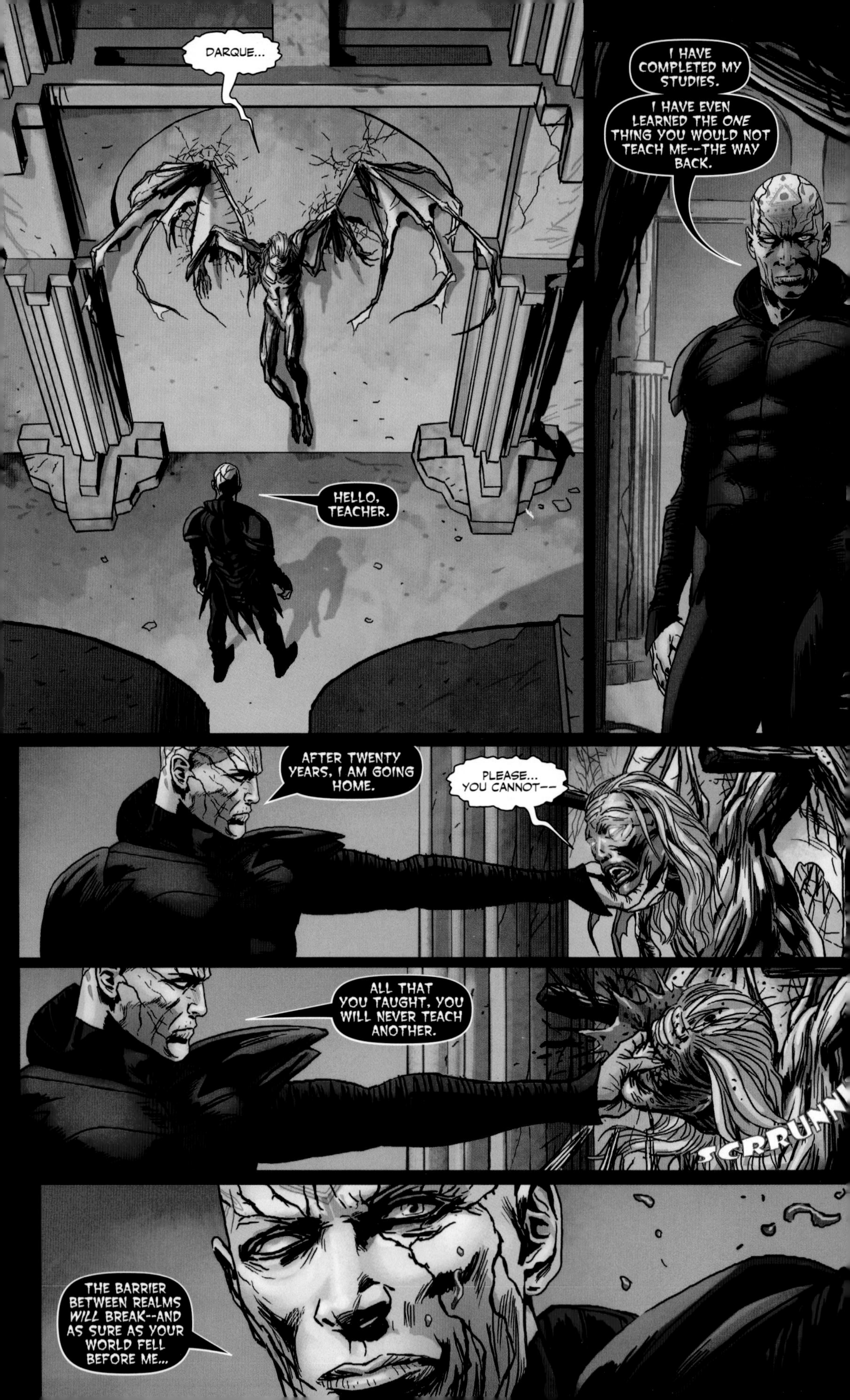
DARQUE...
HELLO, TEACHER.
I HAVE COMPLETED MY STUDIES.
I HAVE EVEN LEARNED THE ONE THING YOU WOULD NOT TEACH ME--THE WAY BACK.
AFTER TWENTY YEARS, I AM GOING HOME.
PLEASE... YOU CANNOT--
ALL THAT YOU TAUGHT, YOU WILL NEVER TEACH ANOTHER.
SCRRUNN
THE BARRIER BETWEEN REALMS WILL BREAK--AND AS SURE AS YOUR WORLD FELL BEFORE ME...

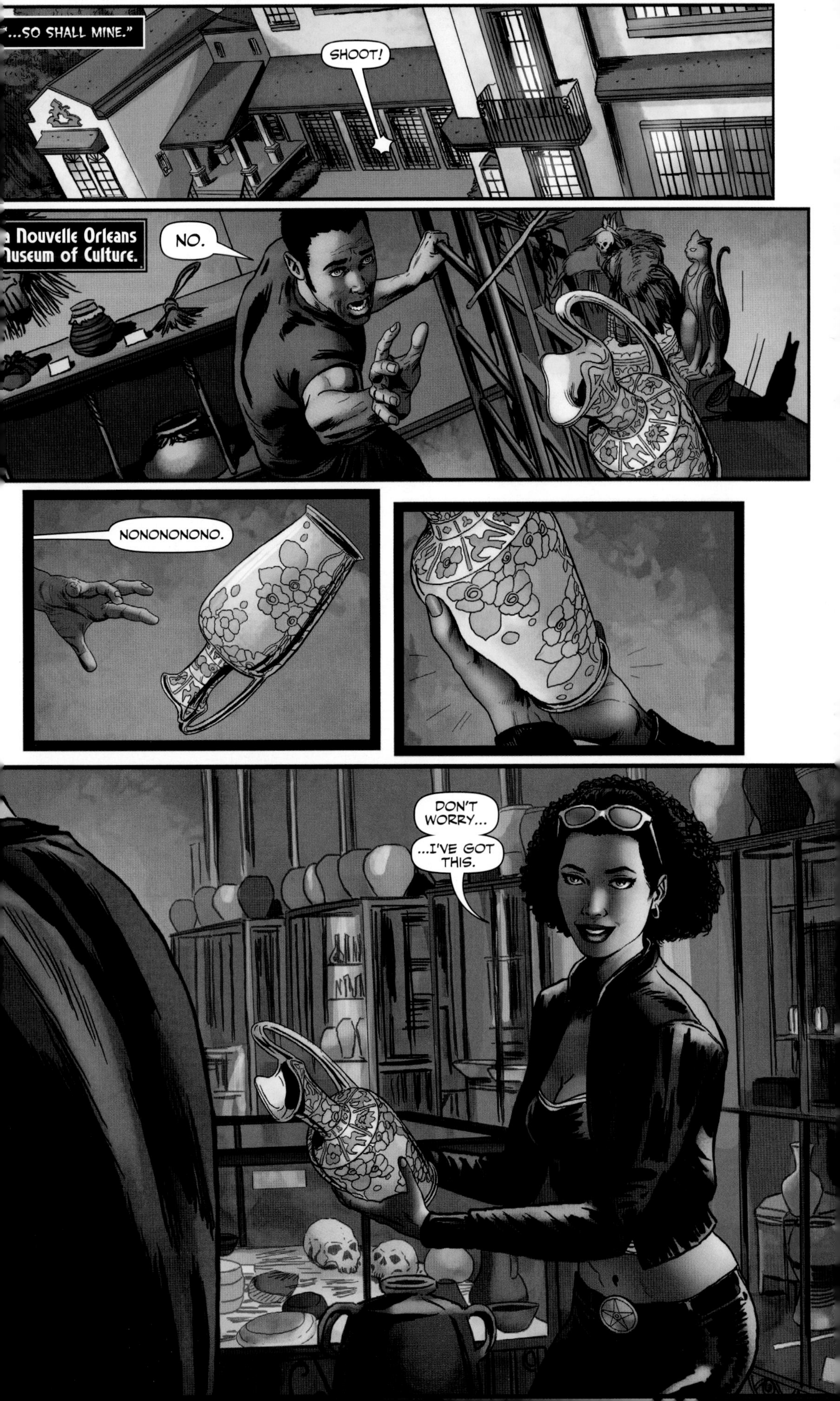
"...SO SHALL MINE."
SHOOT!
a Nouvelle Orleans Museum of Culture.
NO.
NONONONONO.
DON'T WORRY...
...I'VE GOT THIS.

GOOD HANDS.

BELIEVE ME, IT COMES WITH THE TERRITORY WHEN YOU WORK IN PLACES STUFFED WITH OLD CRAP. YOU'LL GET THEM IF YOU KEEP WORKING HERE.

I THOUGHT I ALREADY HAD THEM. DISTRACTED, I GUESS.

STRANGE NIGHT?

I...I'M SORRY...HAVE WE MET?

WHY WOULD YOU SAY THAT?

THAT'S NOT AN ANSWER, IS IT?

WELL, YOU GOT ME THERE. NO, WE HAVEN'T MET.

ALYSSA MYLES.

I'M--

JACK BONIFACE. SON OF JOSIAH BONIFACE AND HELENA LeBRETON. OH BELIEVE ME, I KNOW ALL ABOUT YOU.

SO TELL ME, WHY DID YOU THROW IT AWAY? SHE NEVER TOLD YOU, DID SHE? WHAT THE AMULET WAS? WHAT YOU ARE?

I... YOU...

YOU CAN'T POSSIBLY KNOW ALL THIS. WHOEVER YOU ARE, I DON'T--

I JUST TOLD YOU WHO I AM. THE REAL QUESTION IS, WHO ARE YOU? I HAVE ANSWERS.

I'M SURE, BUT I DON' ACTUALLY HA THE TIME TO GASLIGHTED STRANGER

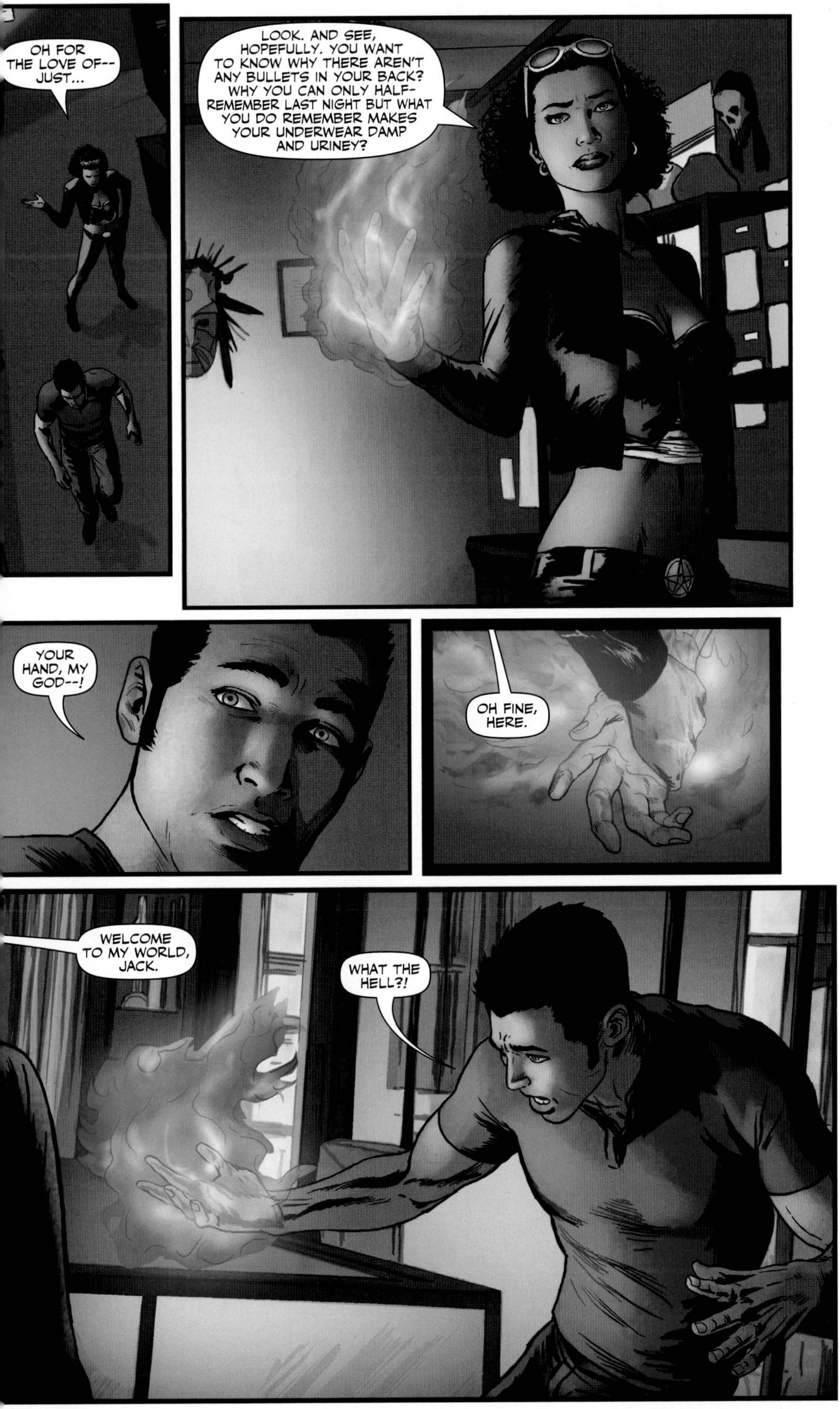
OH FOR THE LOVE OF-- JUST...
LOOK. AND SEE, HOPEFULLY. YOU WANT TO KNOW WHY THERE AREN'T ANY BULLETS IN YOUR BACK? WHY YOU CAN ONLY HALF-REMEMBER LAST NIGHT BUT WHAT YOU DO REMEMBER MAKES YOUR UNDERWEAR DAMP AND URINEY?
YOUR HAND, MY GOD--!
OH FINE, HERE.
WELCOME TO MY WORLD, JACK.
WHAT THE HELL?!

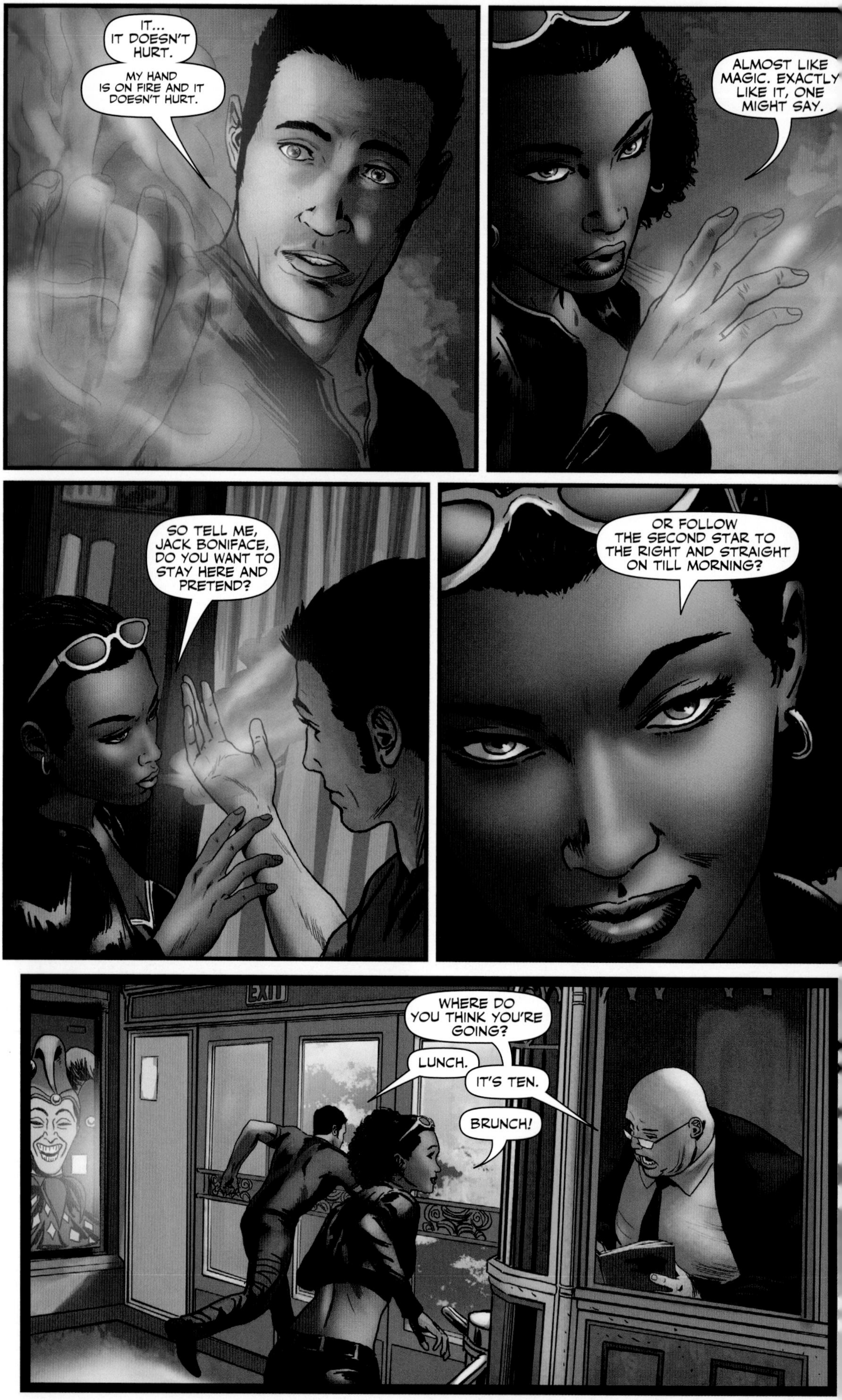
IT... IT DOESN'T HURT.
MY HAND IS ON FIRE AND IT DOESN'T HURT.
ALMOST LIKE MAGIC. EXACTLY LIKE IT, ONE MIGHT SAY.
SO TELL ME, JACK BONIFACE, DO YOU WANT TO STAY HERE AND PRETEND?
OR FOLLOW THE SECOND STAR TO THE RIGHT AND STRAIGHT ON TILL MORNING?
EXIT
WHERE DO YOU THINK YOU'RE GOING?
LUNCH.
IT'S TEN.
BRUNCH!

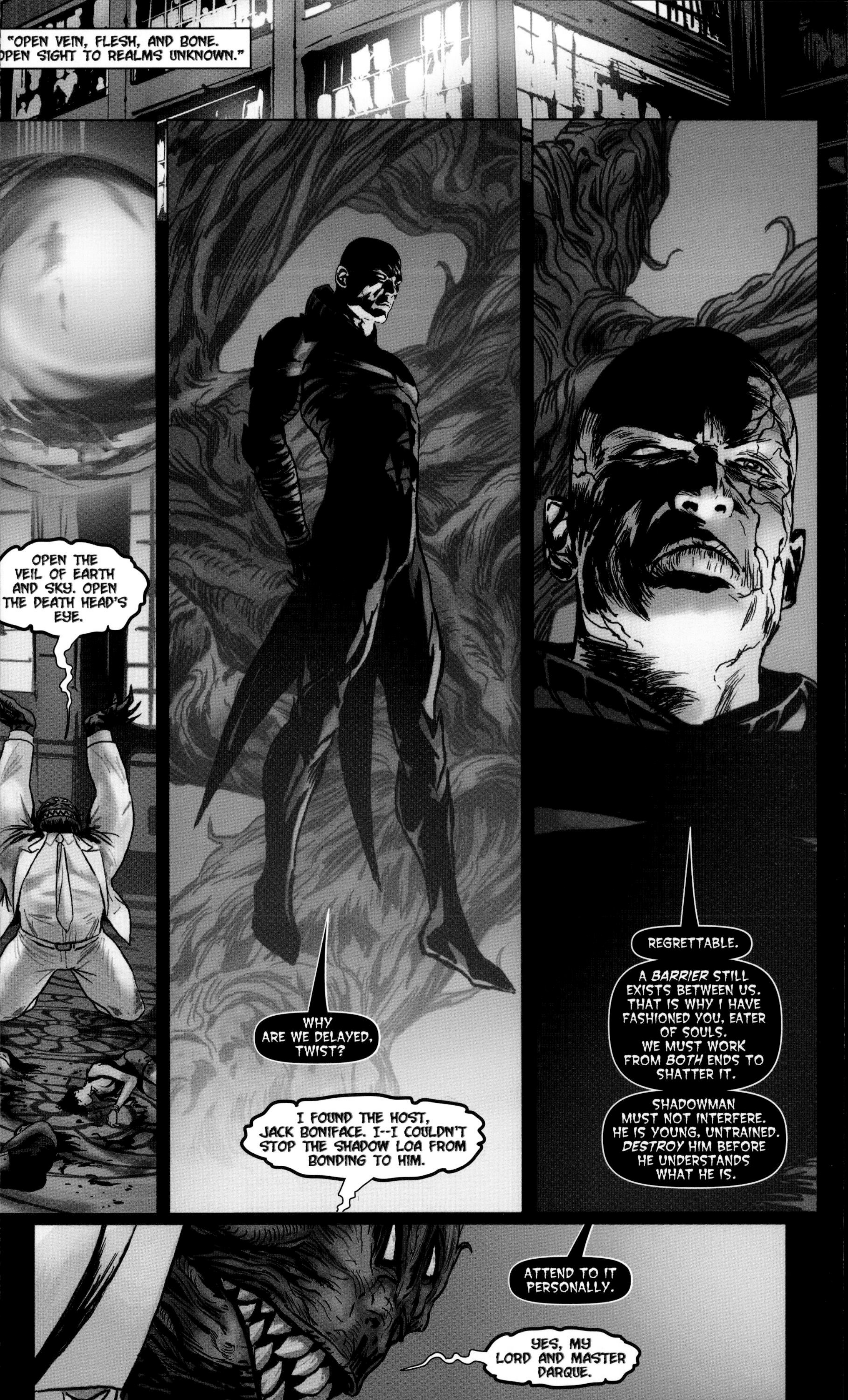
"OPEN VEIN, FLESH, AND BONE.
OPEN SIGHT TO REALMS UNKNOWN."
OPEN THE VEIL OF EARTH AND SKY. OPEN THE DEATH HEAD'S EYE.
WHY ARE WE DELAYED, TWIST?
I FOUND THE HOST, JACK BONIFACE. I--I COULDN'T STOP THE SHADOW LOA FROM BONDING TO HIM.
REGRETTABLE.
A *BARRIER* STILL EXISTS BETWEEN US. THAT IS WHY I HAVE FASHIONED YOU, EATER OF SOULS. WE MUST WORK FROM *BOTH* ENDS TO SHATTER IT.
SHADOWMAN MUST NOT INTERFERE. HE IS YOUNG, UNTRAINED. *DESTROY* HIM BEFORE HE UNDERSTANDS WHAT HE IS.
ATTEND TO IT PERSONALLY.
YES, MY LORD AND MASTER DARQUE.

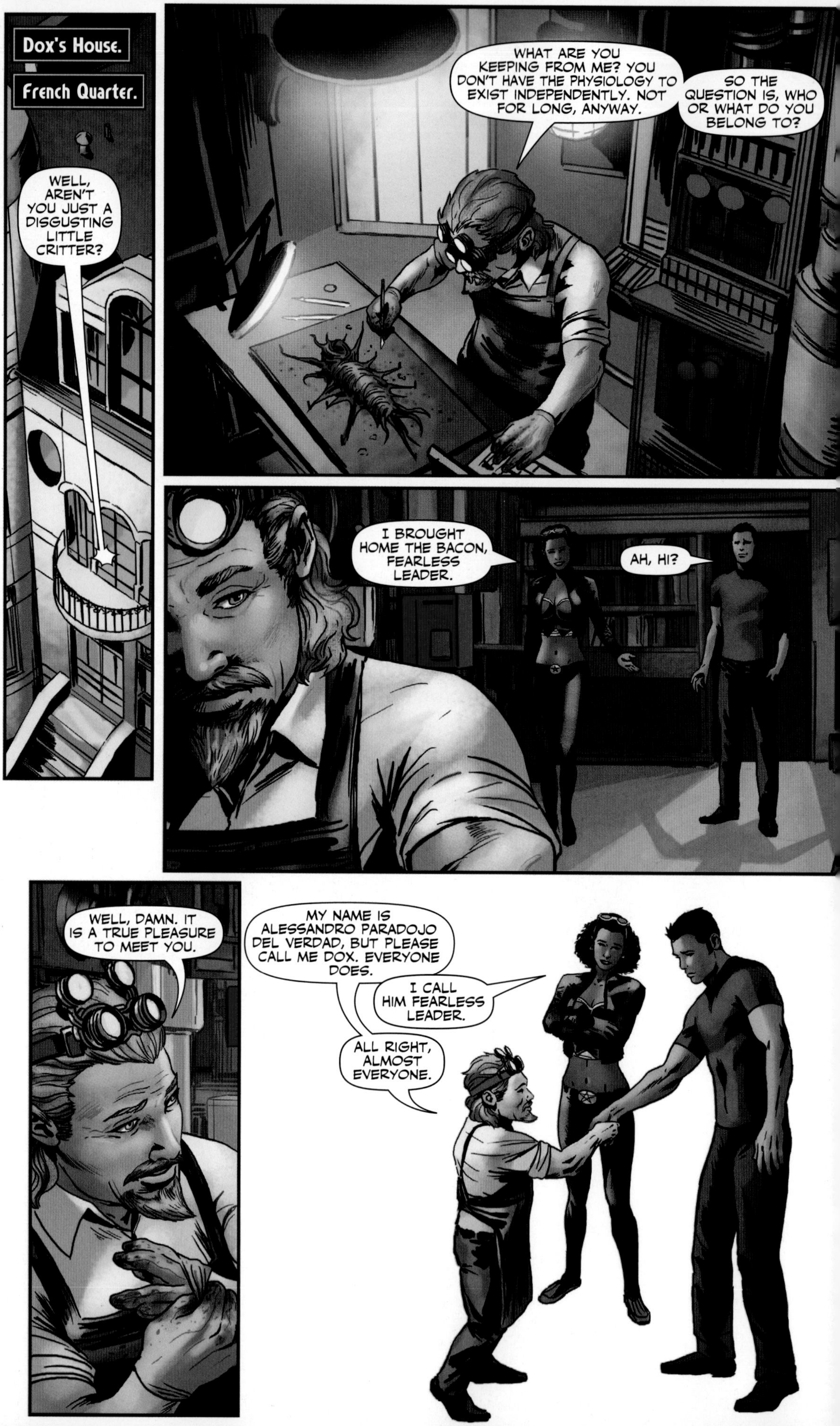
Dox's House.
French Quarter.
WELL, AREN'T YOU JUST A DISGUSTING LITTLE CRITTER?
WHAT ARE YOU KEEPING FROM ME? YOU DON'T HAVE THE PHYSIOLOGY TO EXIST INDEPENDENTLY. NOT FOR LONG, ANYWAY.
SO THE QUESTION IS, WHO OR WHAT DO YOU BELONG TO?
I BROUGHT HOME THE BACON, FEARLESS LEADER.
AH, HI?
WELL, DAMN. IT IS A TRUE PLEASURE TO MEET YOU.
MY NAME IS ALESSANDRO PARADOJO DEL VERDAD, BUT PLEASE CALL ME DOX. EVERYONE DOES.
I CALL HIM FEARLESS LEADER.
ALL RIGHT, ALMOST EVERYONE.

JACK. IT'S A PLEASURE. UMM, I'M NOT SURE I'M THE GUY YOU THINK--I MEAN, THINGS HAVE BEEN STRANGE--

LOOK, I JUST WORK IN A MUSEUM. I'M NOT EVEN THE CURATOR. ALYSSA SAID--

LOTS OF THINGS, I'M GUESSING. SHE SHOW YOU THE HAND OF FIRE TRICK?

WAS IT A TRICK?

SURE. BUT EVERYTHING'S A TRICK, WHEN YOU KNOW HOW IT'S DONE. BUT I GUESS YOUR QUESTION--SORRY, HOLD ON.

ALYSSA, EVIL IS NOT A TOY. DON'T POKE THAT.

YOUR QUESTION IS, WAS IT REAL? WAS IT MAGIC? AND THE ANSWER IS YES, ALTHOUGH I'M NOT MUCH FOND OF THE TERM.

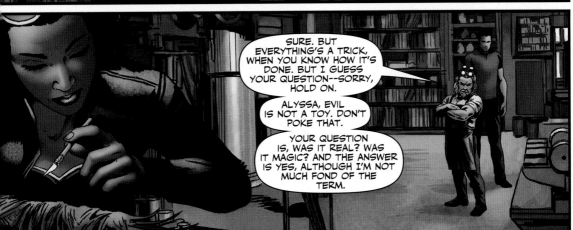

HERE, LOOK AT THIS. DO YOU KNOW WHAT THIS IS?

NAUSEATING?

IT IS THAT. BUT IT'S ALSO A CONSTRUCT.

I-I'VE SEEN ONE OF THESE BEFORE.

AS RECENTLY AS LAST NIGHT, NO DOUBT. WE'LL GET TO THAT.

IT'S A LIVING THING MADE FROM THE FLESH OF THE SACRIFICE. A THOUGHT FORM BROUGHT MONSTROUSLY TO LIFE. WHO THOUGHT IT TO LIFE IS WHAT I NEED TO DETERMINE.

THERE IS AN OCEAN OF ENERGY AROUND US. MOSTLY WE CAN'T SEE IT, TOUCH IT OR TASTE IT. BUT IT IS MEASURABLE AND IT IS REAL. AND IT CAN BE USED.

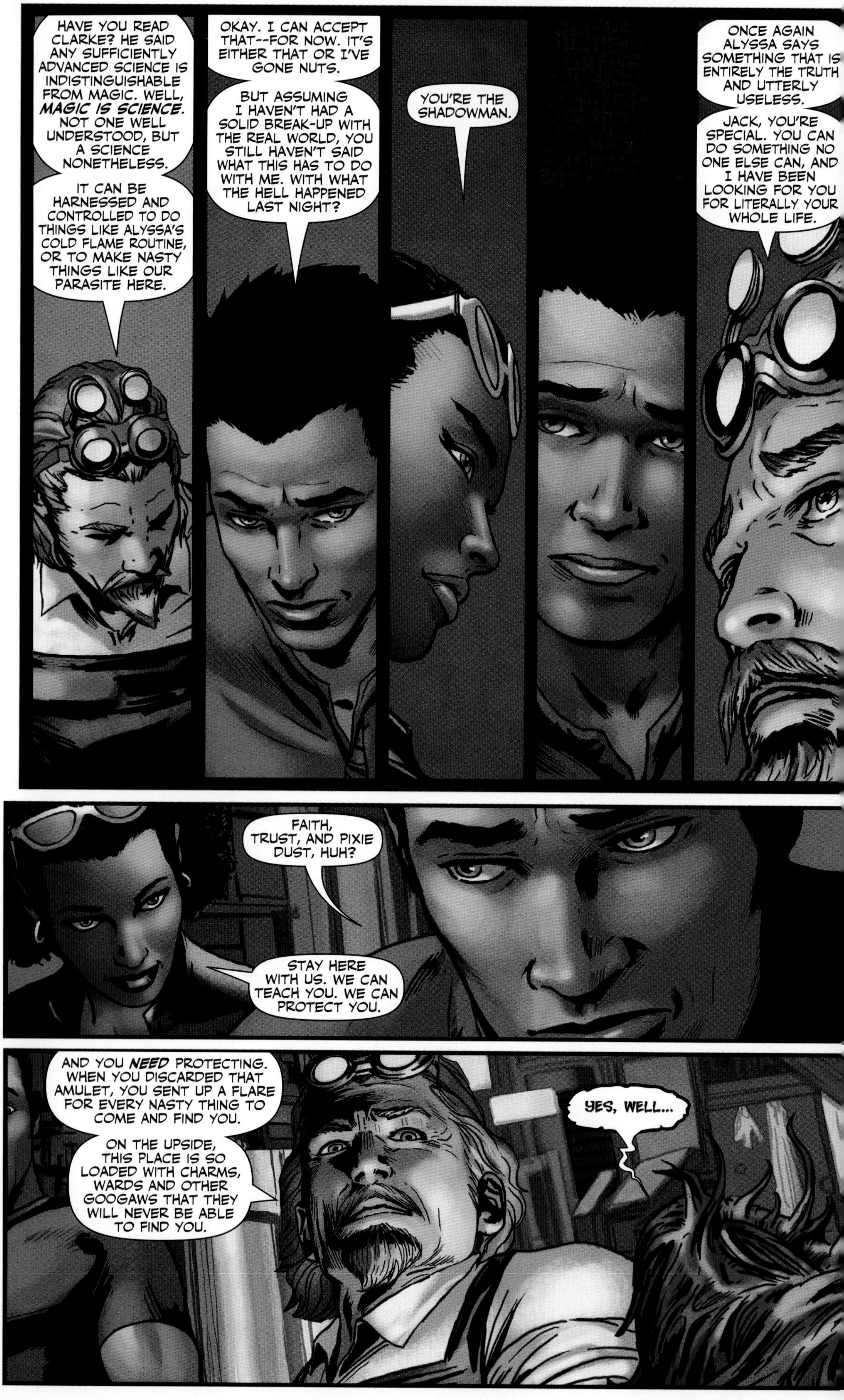
HAVE YOU READ CLARKE? HE SAID ANY SUFFICIENTLY ADVANCED SCIENCE IS INDISTINGUISHABLE FROM MAGIC. WELL, *MAGIC IS SCIENCE*. NOT ONE WELL UNDERSTOOD, BUT A SCIENCE NONETHELESS.
IT CAN BE HARNESSED AND CONTROLLED TO DO THINGS LIKE ALYSSA'S COLD FLAME ROUTINE, OR TO MAKE NASTY THINGS LIKE OUR PARASITE HERE.
OKAY. I CAN ACCEPT THAT--FOR NOW. IT'S EITHER THAT OR I'VE GONE NUTS.
BUT ASSUMING I HAVEN'T HAD A SOLID BREAK-UP WITH THE REAL WORLD, YOU STILL HAVEN'T SAID WHAT THIS HAS TO DO WITH ME. WITH WHAT THE HELL HAPPENED LAST NIGHT?
YOU'RE THE SHADOWMAN.
ONCE AGAIN ALYSSA SAYS SOMETHING THAT IS ENTIRELY THE TRUTH AND UTTERLY USELESS.
JACK, YOU'RE SPECIAL. YOU CAN DO SOMETHING NO ONE ELSE CAN, AND I HAVE BEEN LOOKING FOR YOU FOR LITERALLY YOUR WHOLE LIFE.
FAITH, TRUST, AND PIXIE DUST, HUH?
STAY HERE WITH US. WE CAN TEACH YOU. WE CAN PROTECT YOU.
AND YOU *NEED* PROTECTING. WHEN YOU DISCARDED THAT AMULET, YOU SENT UP A FLARE FOR EVERY NASTY THING TO COME AND FIND YOU.
ON THE UPSIDE, THIS PLACE IS SO LOADED WITH CHARMS, WARDS AND OTHER GOOGAWS THAT THEY WILL NEVER BE ABLE TO FIND YOU.
YES, WELL...

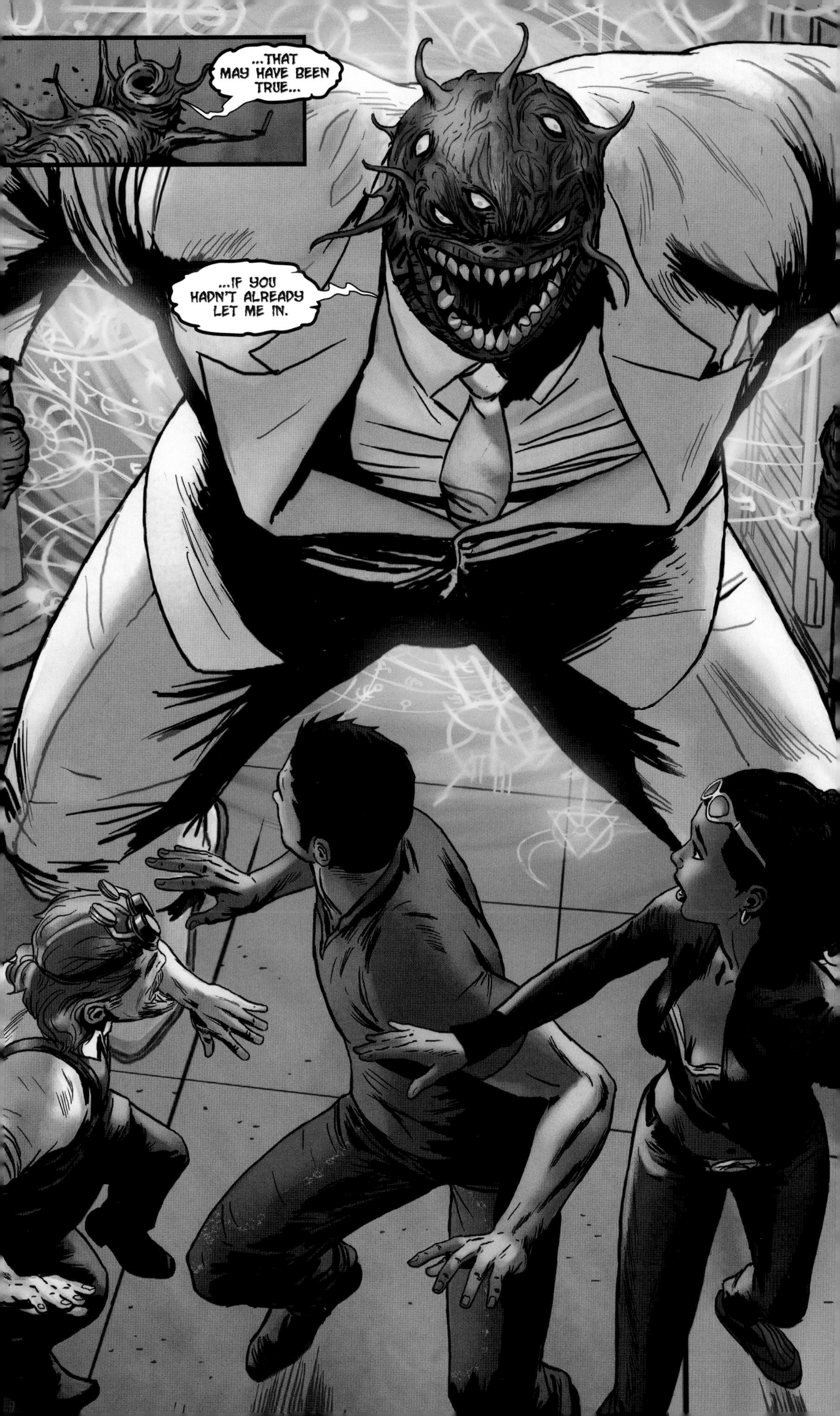
...THAT MAY HAVE BEEN TRUE...
...IF YOU HADN'T ALREADY LET ME IN.

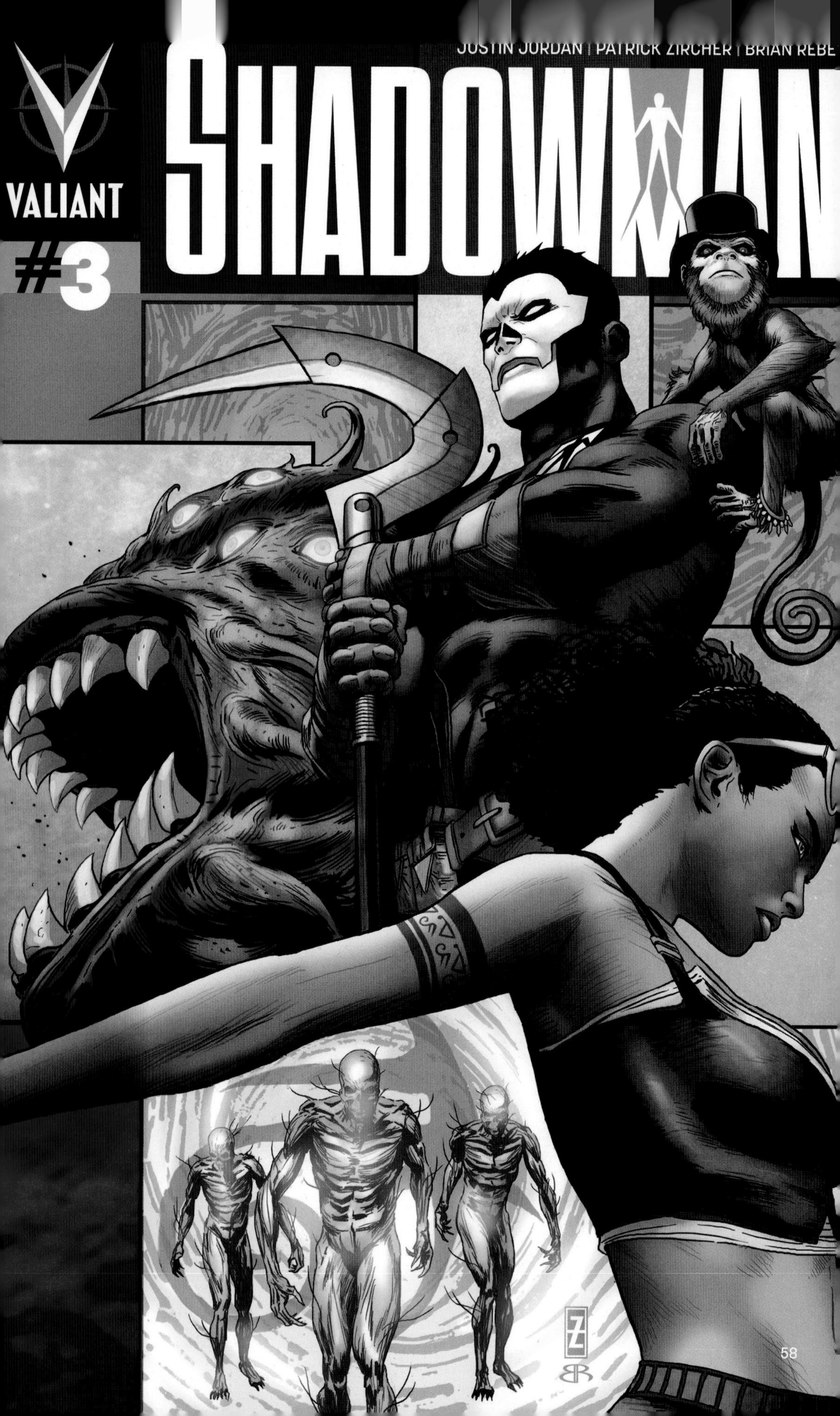
VALIANT
#3
JUSTIN JORDAN | PATRICK ZIRCHER | BRIAN REBE
SHADOWMAN

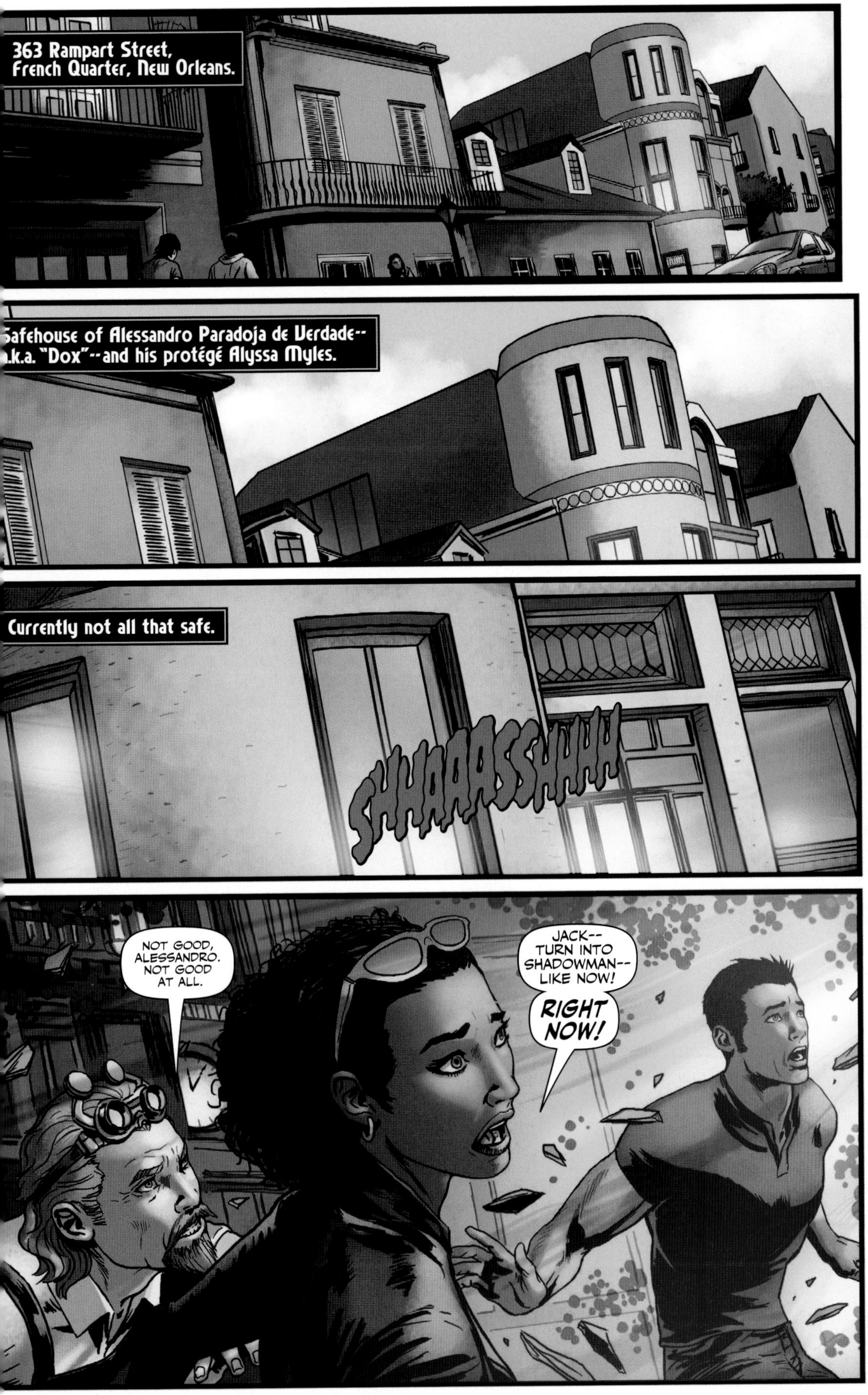

363 Rampart Street,
French Quarter, New Orleans.
Safehouse of Alessandro Paradoja de Verdade--
a.k.a. "Dox"--and his protégé Alyssa Myles.
Currently not all that safe.
SHHAAASSHHH
NOT GOOD, ALESSANDRO. NOT GOOD AT ALL.
JACK-- TURN INTO SHADOWMAN-- LIKE NOW!
RIGHT NOW!

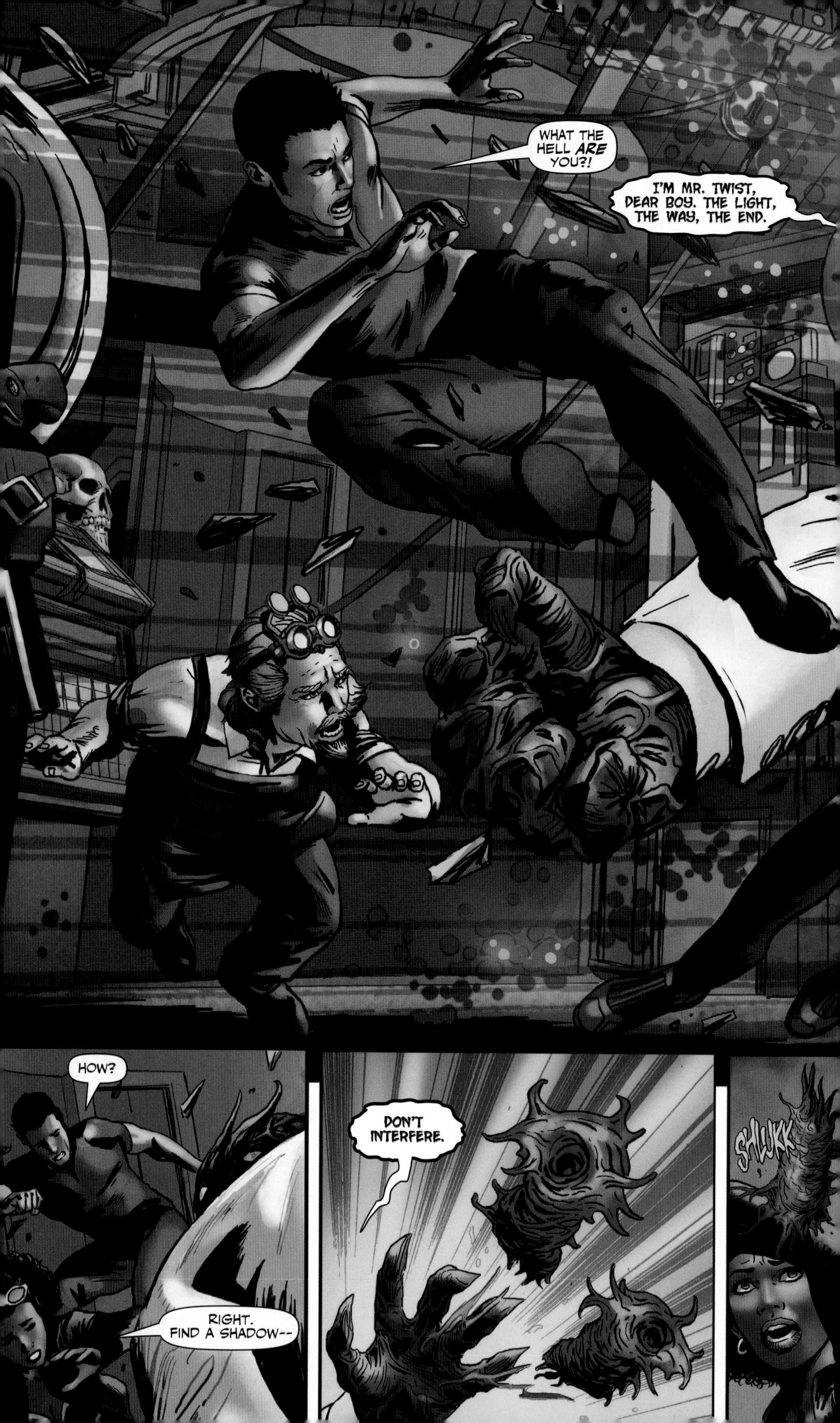
WHAT THE HELL *ARE* YOU?!
I'M MR. TWIST, DEAR BOY. THE LIGHT, THE WAY, THE END.
HOW?
RIGHT. FIND A SHADOW--
DON'T INTERFERE.
SHLUKK

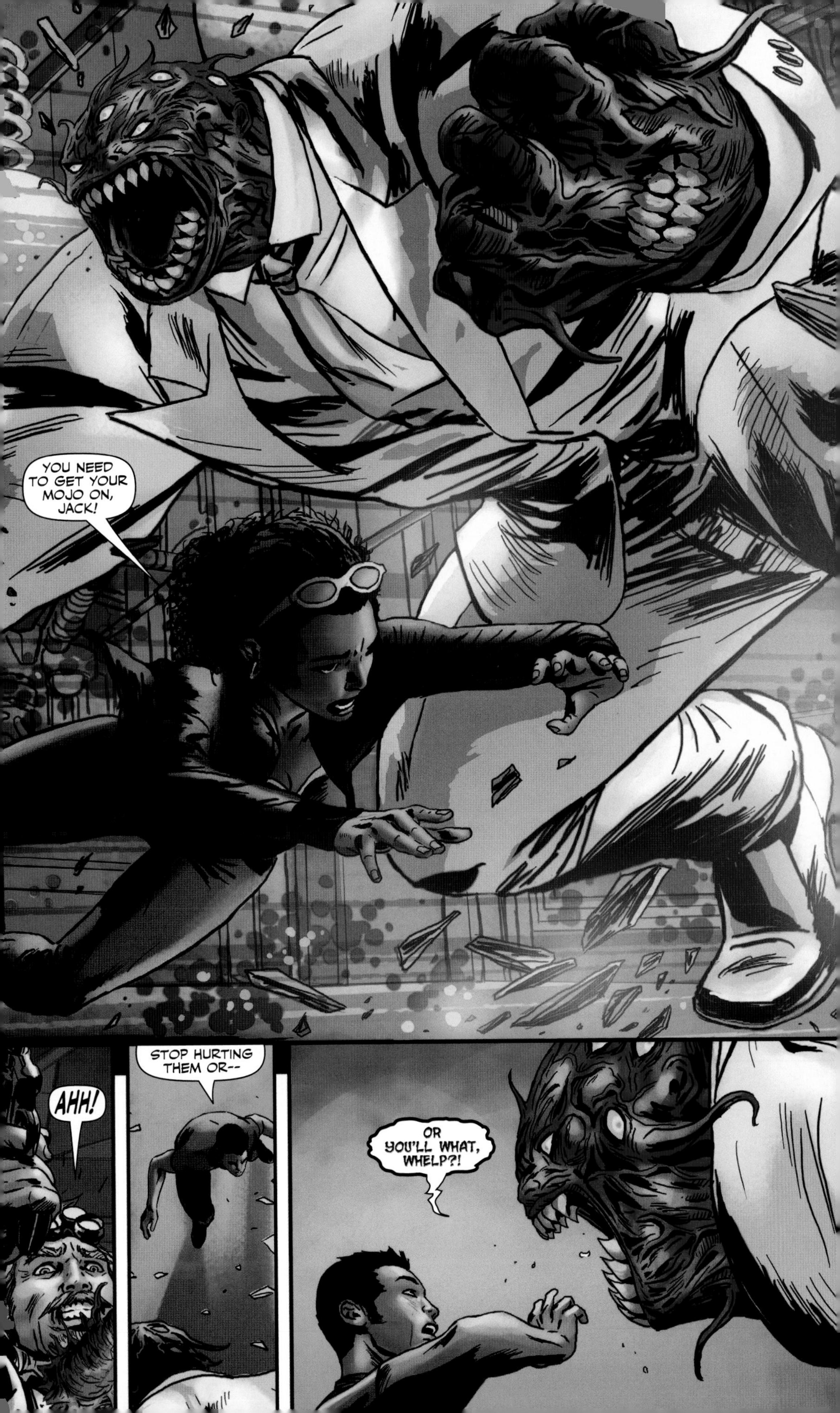
YOU NEED TO GET YOUR MOJO ON, JACK!
AHH!
STOP HURTING THEM OR--
OR YOU'LL WHAT, WHELP?!

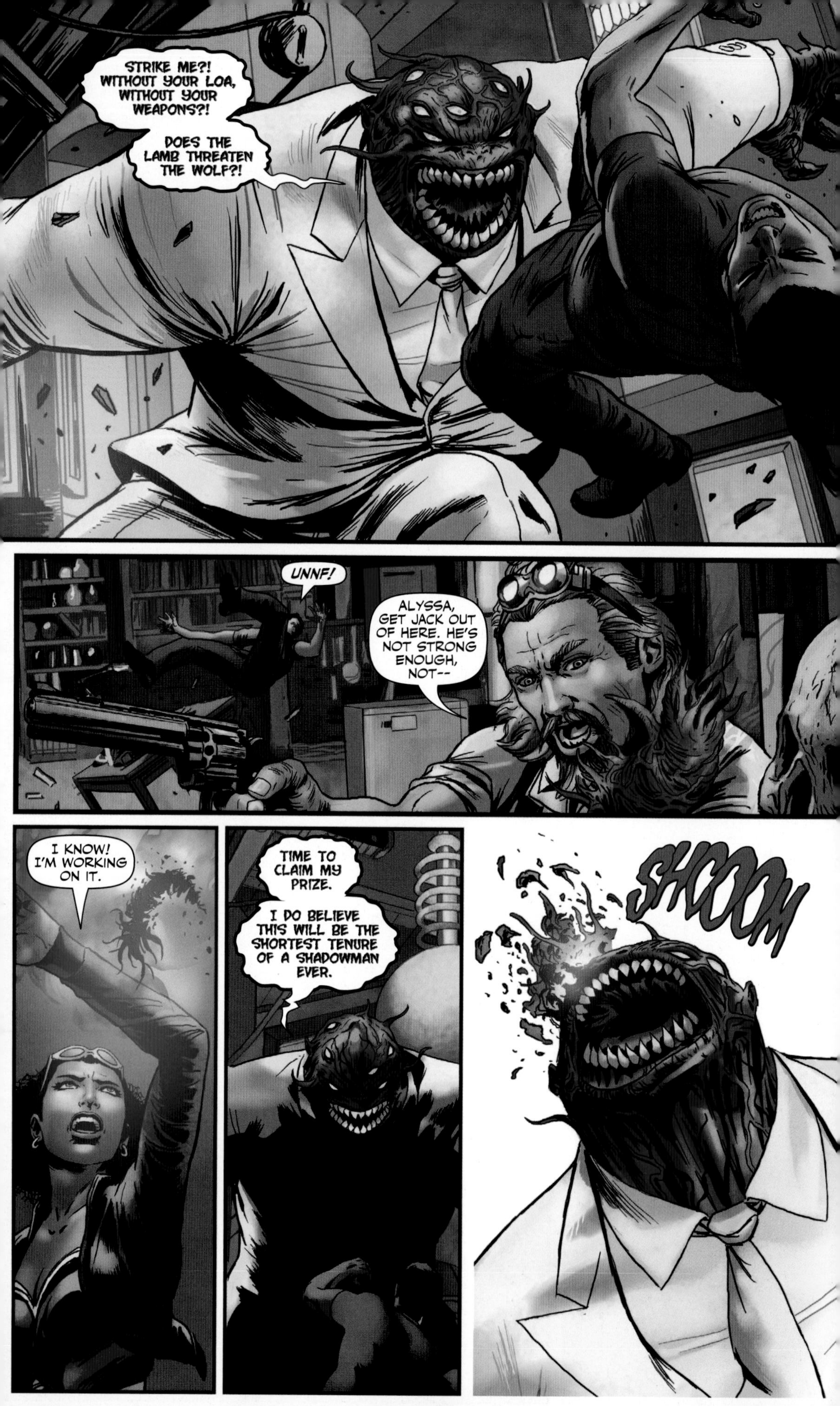
STRIKE ME?! WITHOUT YOUR LOA, WITHOUT YOUR WEAPONS?!
DOES THE LAMB THREATEN THE WOLF?!
UNNF!
ALYSSA, GET JACK OUT OF HERE. HE'S NOT STRONG ENOUGH, NOT--
I KNOW! I'M WORKING ON IT.
TIME TO CLAIM MY PRIZE.
I DO BELIEVE THIS WILL BE THE SHORTEST TENURE OF A SHADOWMAN EVER.
SHOOOM

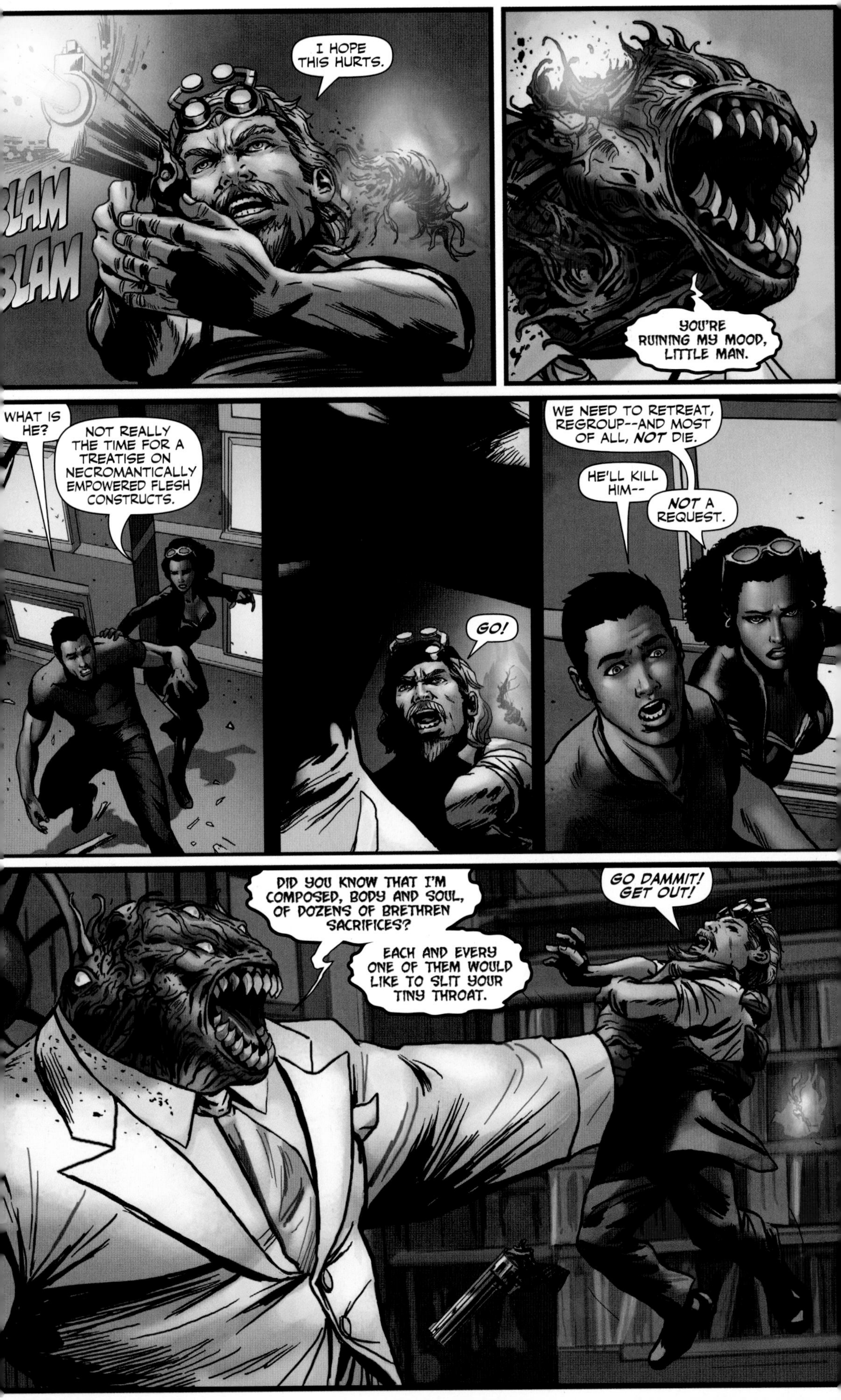
I HOPE THIS HURTS.
BLAM
BLAM
YOU'RE RUINING MY MOOD, LITTLE MAN.
WHAT IS HE?
NOT REALLY THE TIME FOR A TREATISE ON NECROMANTICALLY EMPOWERED FLESH CONSTRUCTS.
GO!
WE NEED TO RETREAT, REGROUP--AND MOST OF ALL, *NOT* DIE.
HE'LL KILL HIM--
NOT A REQUEST.
DID YOU KNOW THAT I'M COMPOSED, BODY AND SOUL, OF DOZENS OF BRETHREN SACRIFICES?
EACH AND EVERY ONE OF THEM WOULD LIKE TO SLIT YOUR TINY THROAT.
GO DAMMIT! GET OUT!

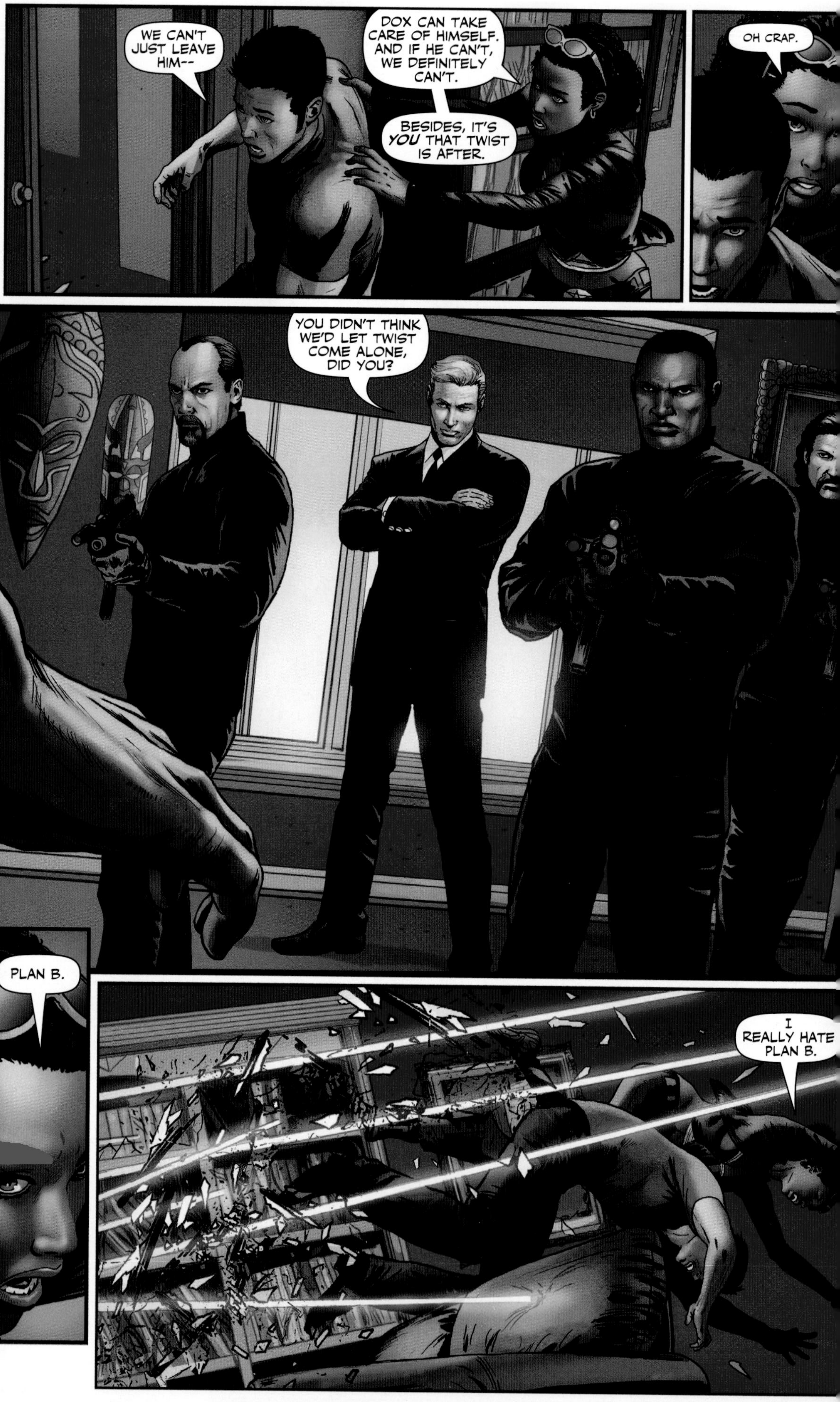
WE CAN'T JUST LEAVE HIM--
DOX CAN TAKE CARE OF HIMSELF. AND IF HE CAN'T, WE DEFINITELY CAN'T.
BESIDES, IT'S *YOU* THAT TWIST IS AFTER.
OH CRAP.
YOU DIDN'T THINK WE'D LET TWIST COME ALONE, DID YOU?
PLAN B.
I REALLY HATE PLAN B.

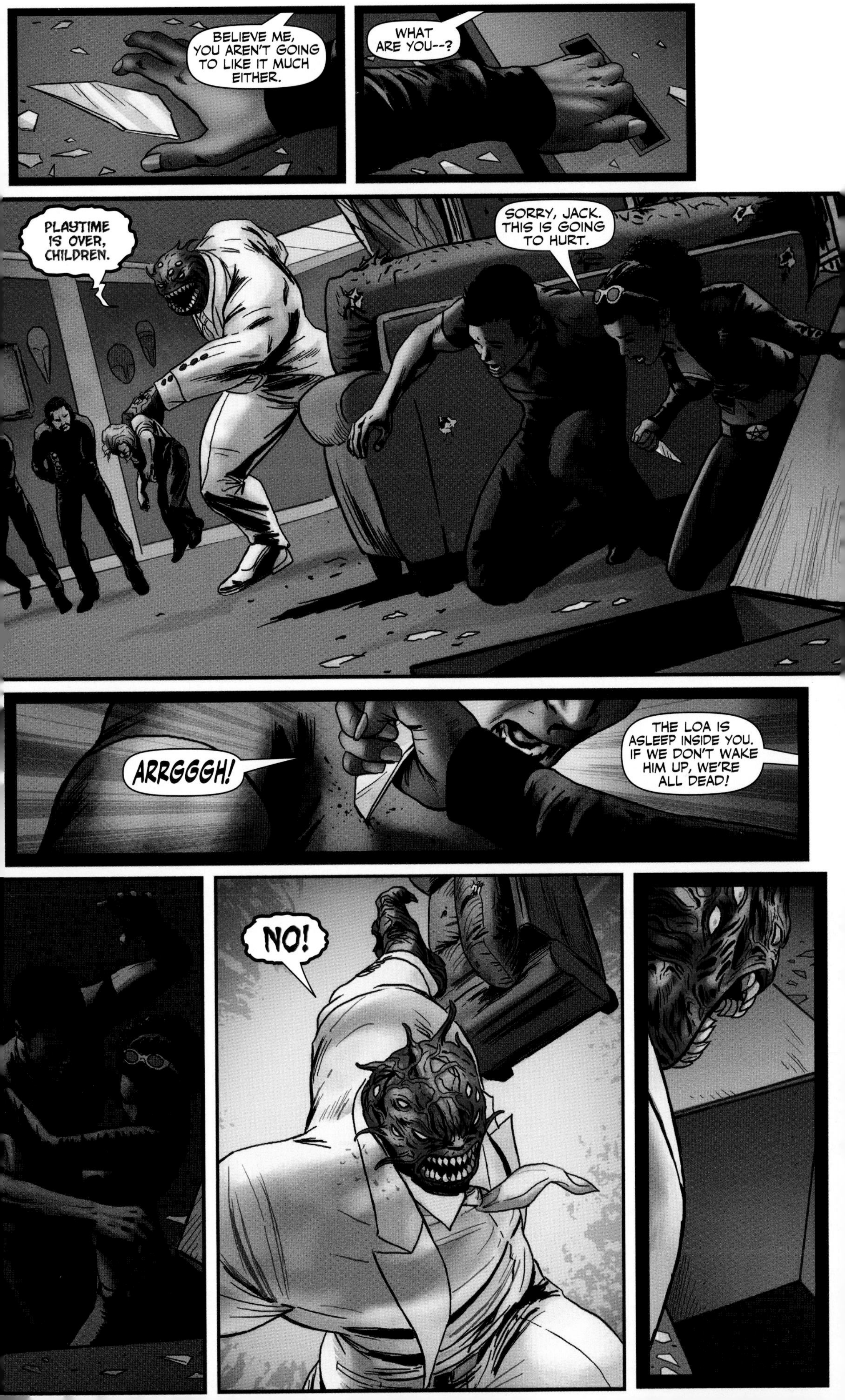

BELIEVE ME, YOU AREN'T GOING TO LIKE IT MUCH EITHER.
WHAT ARE YOU--?
PLAYTIME IS OVER, CHILDREN.
SORRY, JACK. THIS IS GOING TO HURT.
ARRGGGH!
THE LOA IS ASLEEP INSIDE YOU. IF WE DON'T WAKE HIM UP, WE'RE ALL DEAD!
NO!

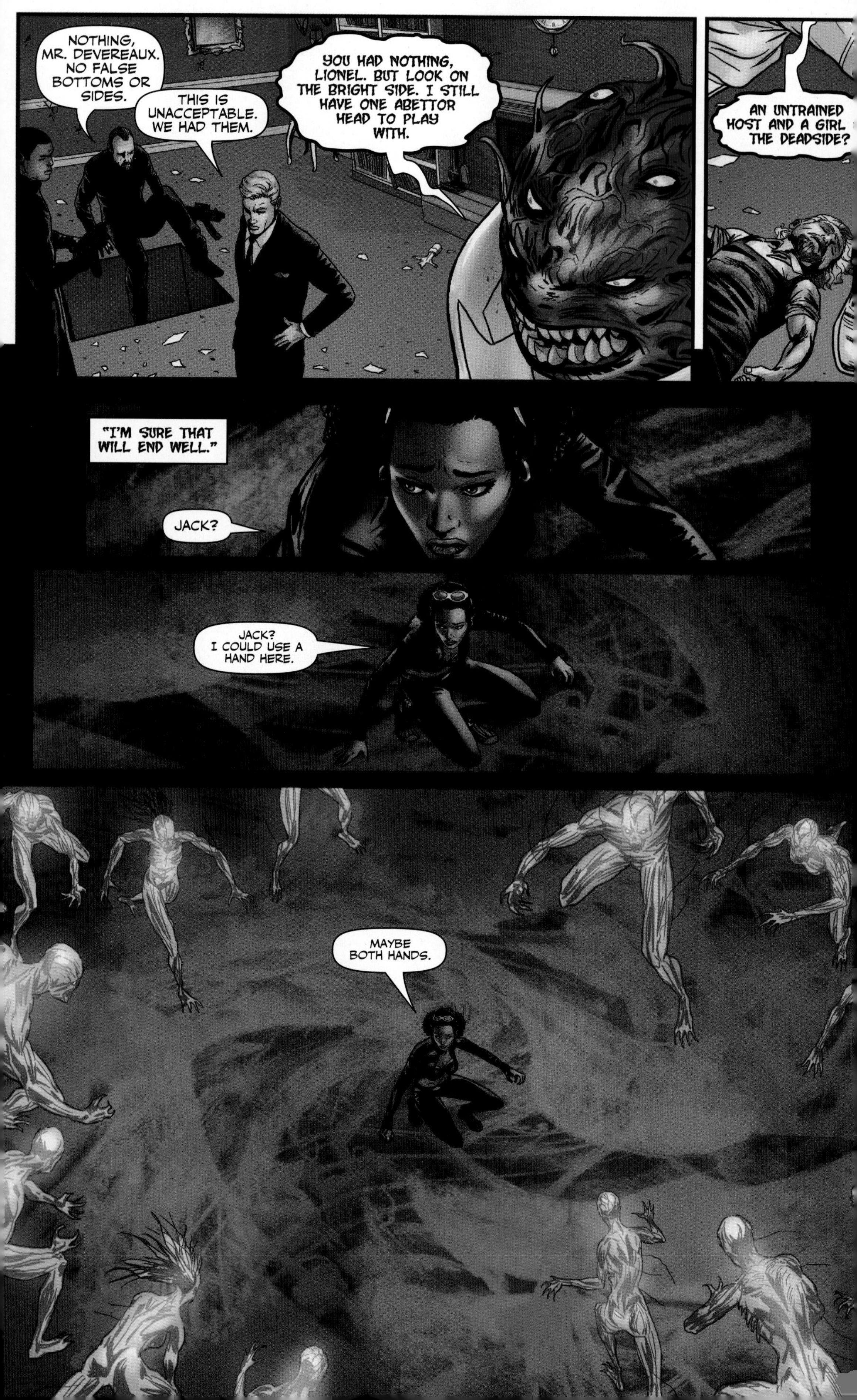
NOTHING, MR. DEVEREAUX. NO FALSE BOTTOMS OR SIDES.
THIS IS UNACCEPTABLE. WE HAD THEM.
YOU HAD NOTHING, LIONEL. BUT LOOK ON THE BRIGHT SIDE. I STILL HAVE ONE ABETTOR HEAD TO PLAY WITH.
AN UNTRAINED HOST AND A GIRL THE DEADSIDE?
"I'M SURE THAT WILL END WELL."
JACK?
JACK? I COULD USE A HAND HERE.
MAYBE BOTH HANDS.

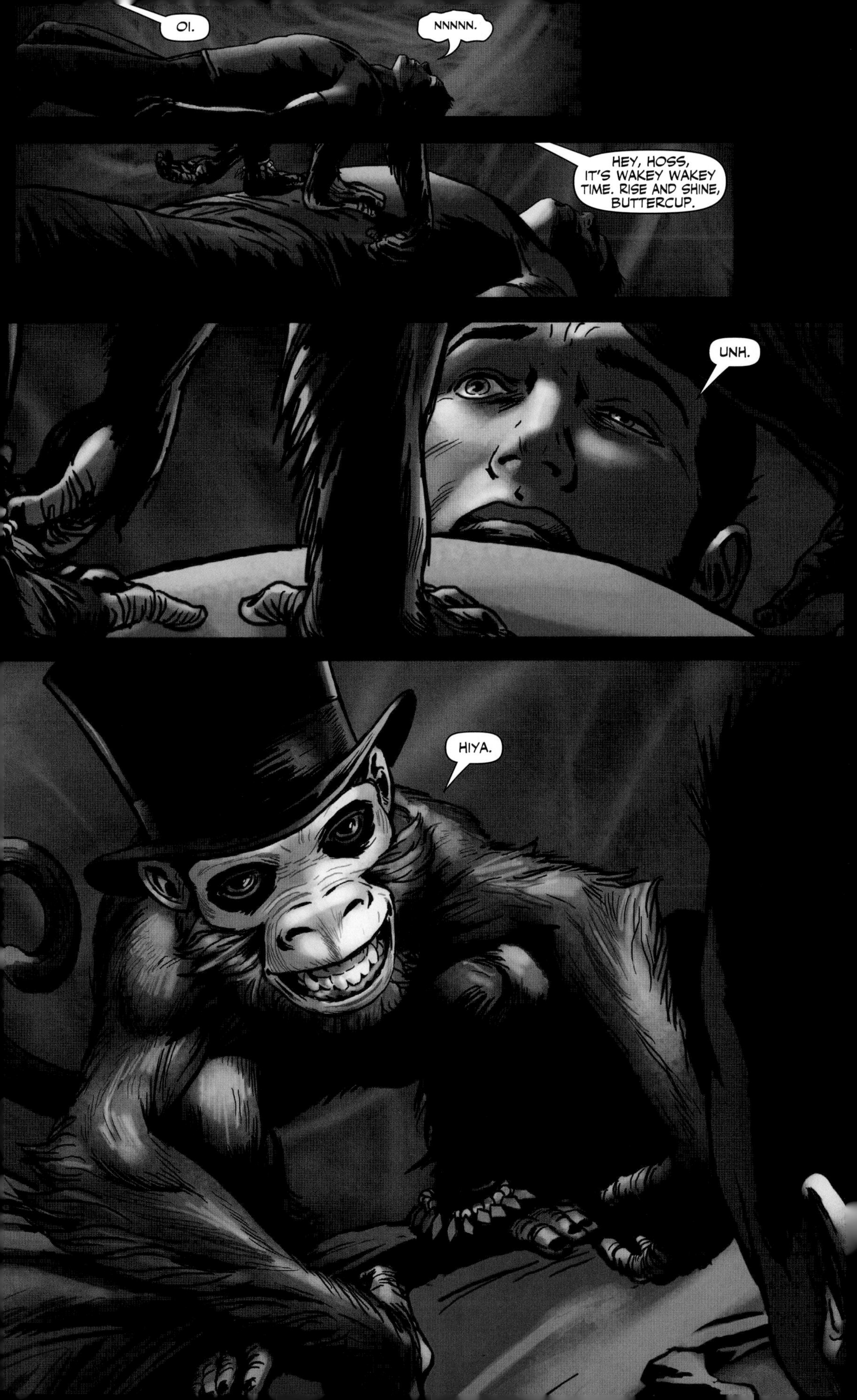
OI.
NNNNN.
HEY, HOSS, IT'S WAKEY WAKEY TIME. RISE AND SHINE, BUTTERCUP.
UNH.
HIYA.

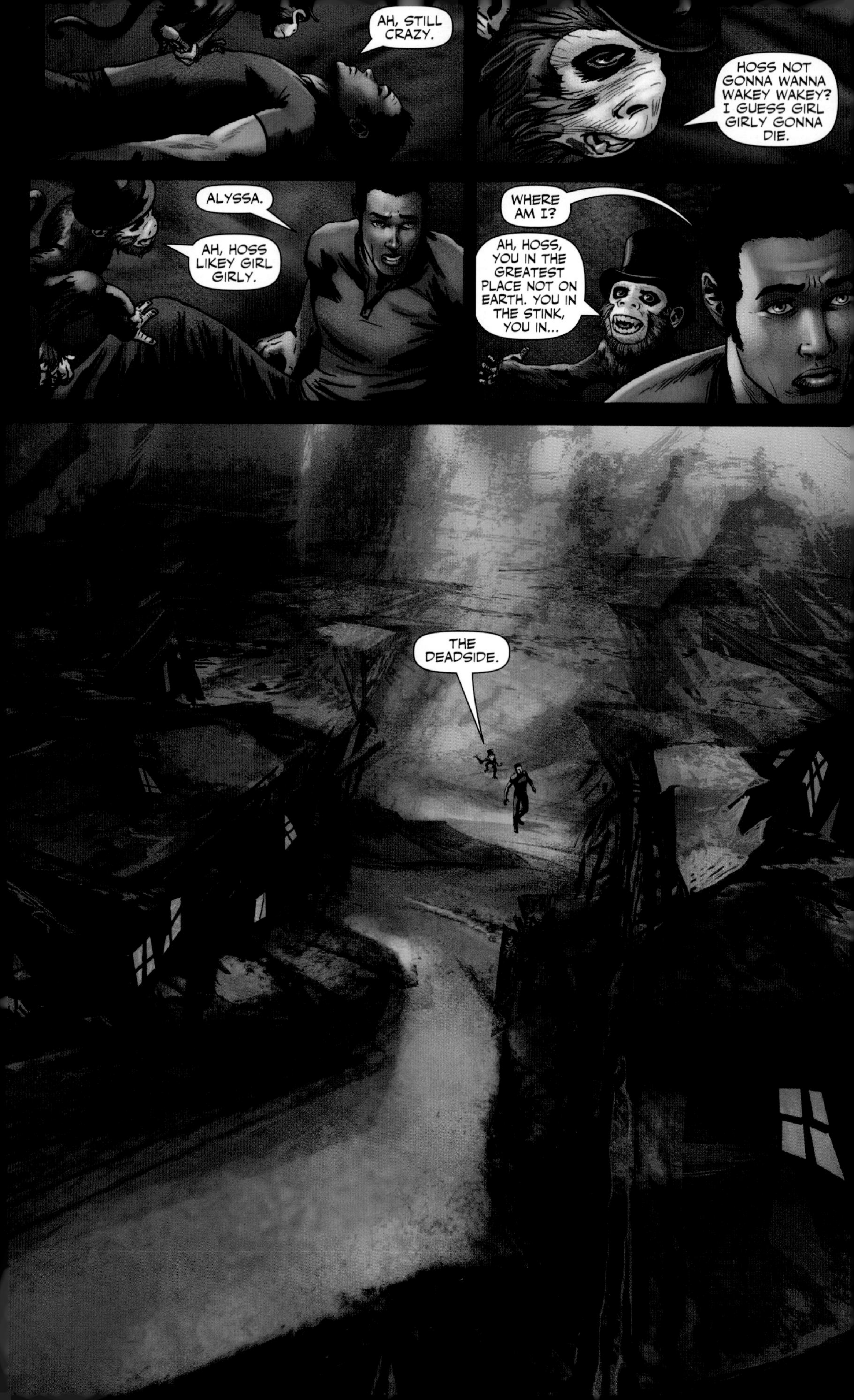
AH, STILL CRAZY.
HOSS NOT GONNA WANNA WAKEY WAKEY? I GUESS GIRL GIRLY GONNA DIE.
ALYSSA.
AH, HOSS LIKEY GIRL GIRLY.
WHERE AM I?
AH, HOSS, YOU IN THE GREATEST PLACE NOT ON EARTH. YOU IN THE STINK, YOU IN...
THE DEADSIDE.

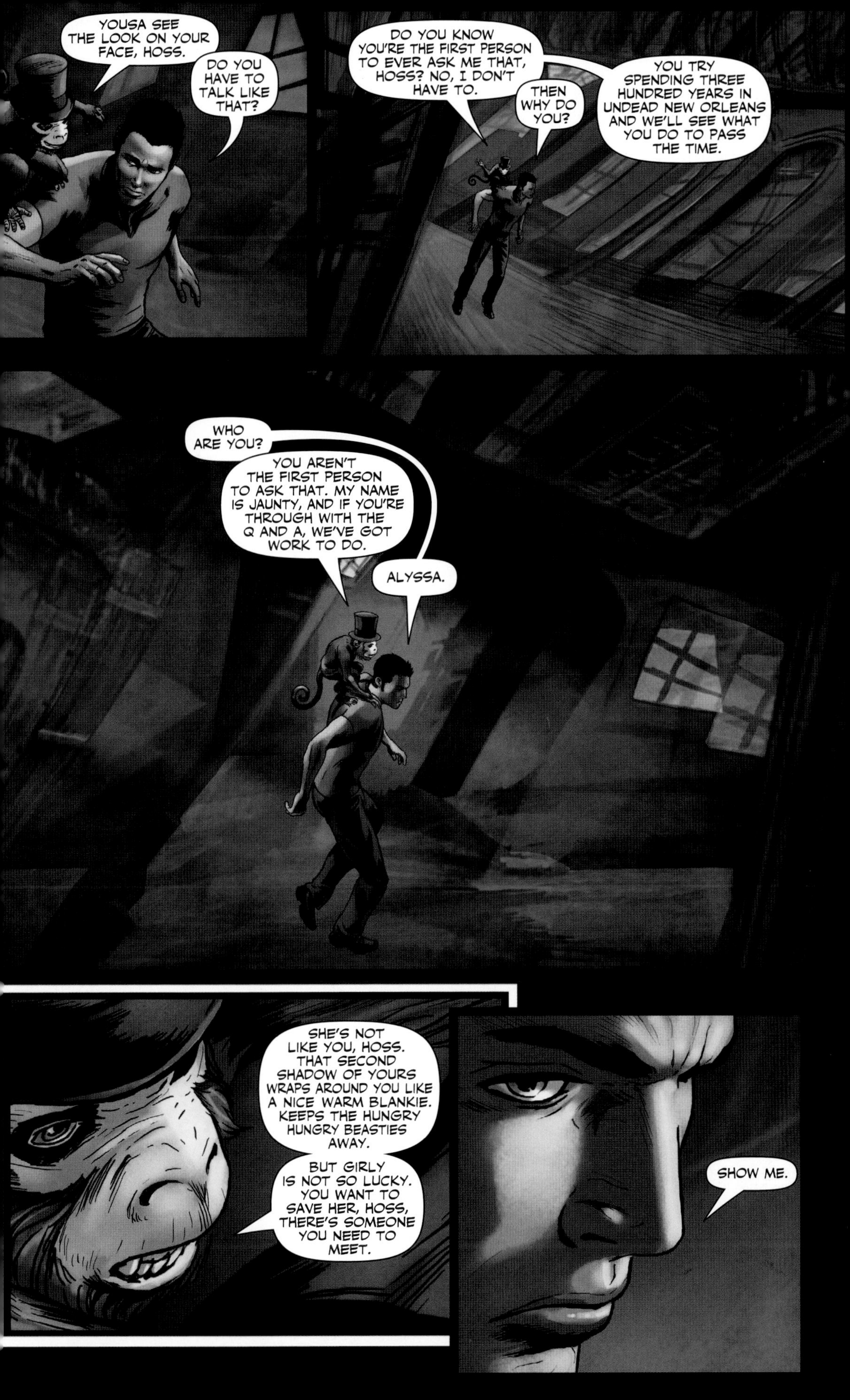
YOUSA SEE THE LOOK ON YOUR FACE, HOSS.
DO YOU HAVE TO TALK LIKE THAT?
DO YOU KNOW YOU'RE THE FIRST PERSON TO EVER ASK ME THAT, HOSS? NO, I DON'T HAVE TO.
THEN WHY DO YOU?
YOU TRY SPENDING THREE HUNDRED YEARS IN UNDEAD NEW ORLEANS AND WE'LL SEE WHAT YOU DO TO PASS THE TIME.
WHO ARE YOU?
YOU AREN'T THE FIRST PERSON TO ASK THAT. MY NAME IS JAUNTY, AND IF YOU'RE THROUGH WITH THE Q AND A, WE'VE GOT WORK TO DO.
ALYSSA.
SHE'S NOT LIKE YOU, HOSS. THAT SECOND SHADOW OF YOURS WRAPS AROUND YOU LIKE A NICE WARM BLANKIE. KEEPS THE HUNGRY HUNGRY BEASTIES AWAY.
BUT GIRLY IS NOT SO LUCKY. YOU WANT TO SAVE HER, HOSS, THERE'S SOMEONE YOU NEED TO MEET.
SHOW ME.

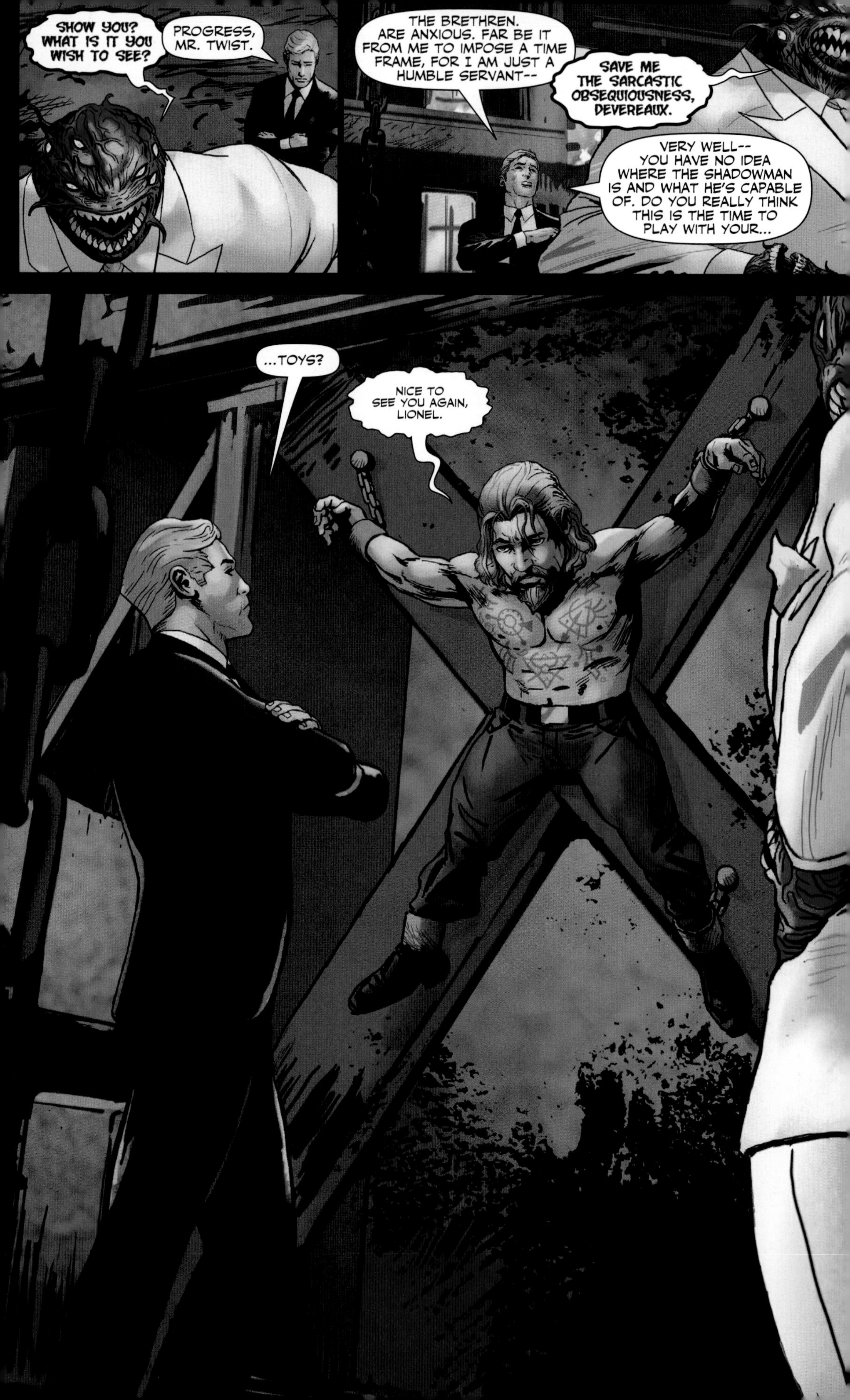
SHOW YOU? WHAT IS IT YOU WISH TO SEE?
PROGRESS, MR. TWIST.
THE BRETHREN. ARE ANXIOUS. FAR BE IT FROM ME TO IMPOSE A TIME FRAME, FOR I AM JUST A HUMBLE SERVANT--
SAVE ME THE SARCASTIC OBSEQUIOUSNESS, DEVEREAUX.
VERY WELL-- YOU HAVE NO IDEA WHERE THE SHADOWMAN IS AND WHAT HE'S CAPABLE OF. DO YOU REALLY THINK THIS IS THE TIME TO PLAY WITH YOUR...
...TOYS?
NICE TO SEE YOU AGAIN, LIONEL.

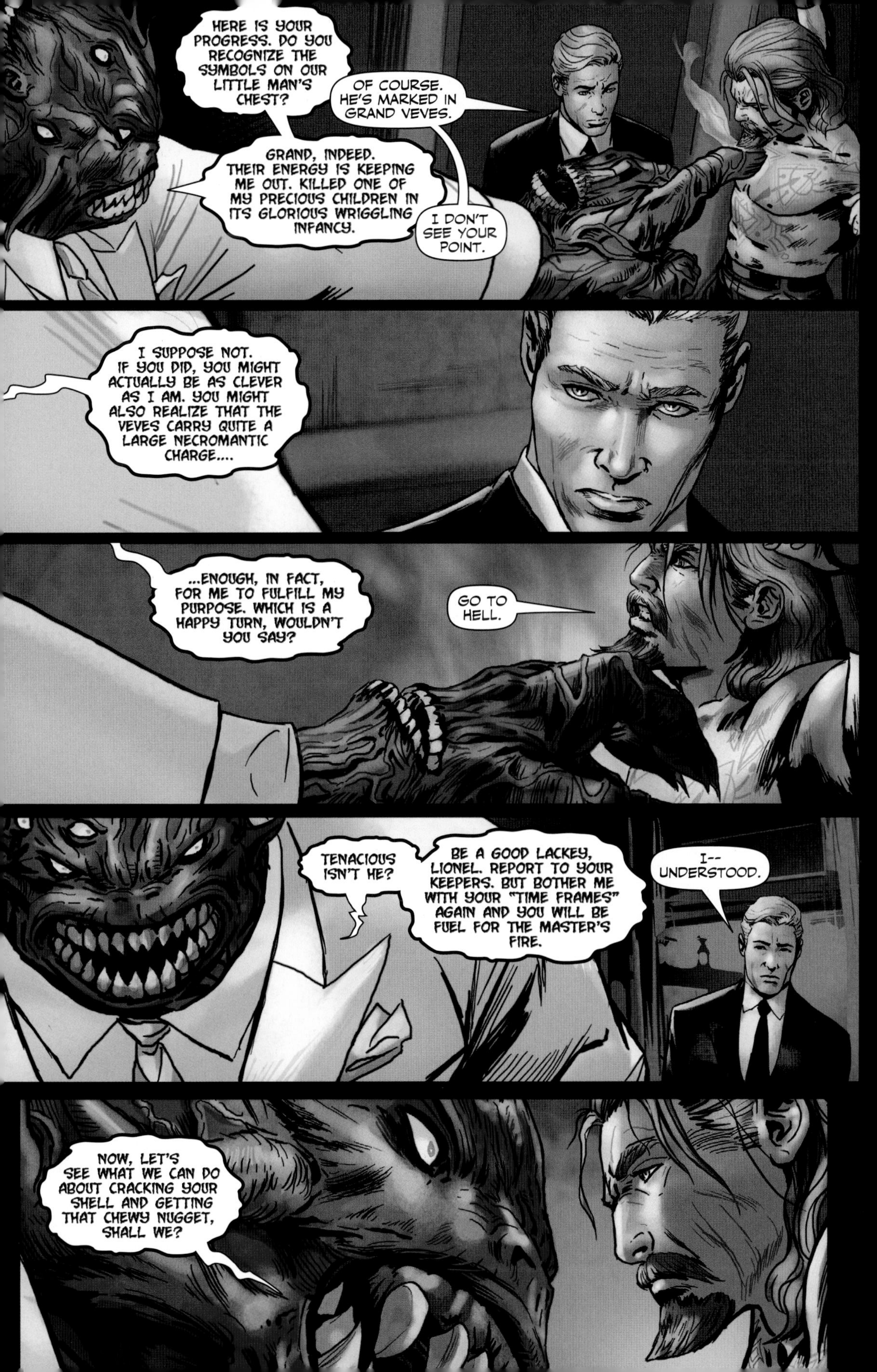
HERE IS YOUR PROGRESS. DO YOU RECOGNIZE THE SYMBOLS ON OUR LITTLE MAN'S CHEST?
OF COURSE. HE'S MARKED IN GRAND VEVES.
GRAND, INDEED. THEIR ENERGY IS KEEPING ME OUT. KILLED ONE OF MY PRECIOUS CHILDREN IN ITS GLORIOUS WRIGGLING INFANCY.
I DON'T SEE YOUR POINT.
I SUPPOSE NOT. IF YOU DID, YOU MIGHT ACTUALLY BE AS CLEVER AS I AM. YOU MIGHT ALSO REALIZE THAT THE VEVES CARRY QUITE A LARGE NECROMANTIC CHARGE....
...ENOUGH, IN FACT, FOR ME TO FULFILL MY PURPOSE. WHICH IS A HAPPY TURN, WOULDN'T YOU SAY?
GO TO HELL.
TENACIOUS ISN'T HE?
BE A GOOD LACKEY, LIONEL. REPORT TO YOUR KEEPERS. BUT BOTHER ME WITH YOUR "TIME FRAMES" AGAIN AND YOU WILL BE FUEL FOR THE MASTER'S FIRE.
I-- UNDERSTOOD.
NOW, LET'S SEE WHAT WE CAN DO ABOUT CRACKING YOUR SHELL AND GETTING THAT CHEWY NUGGET, SHALL WE?

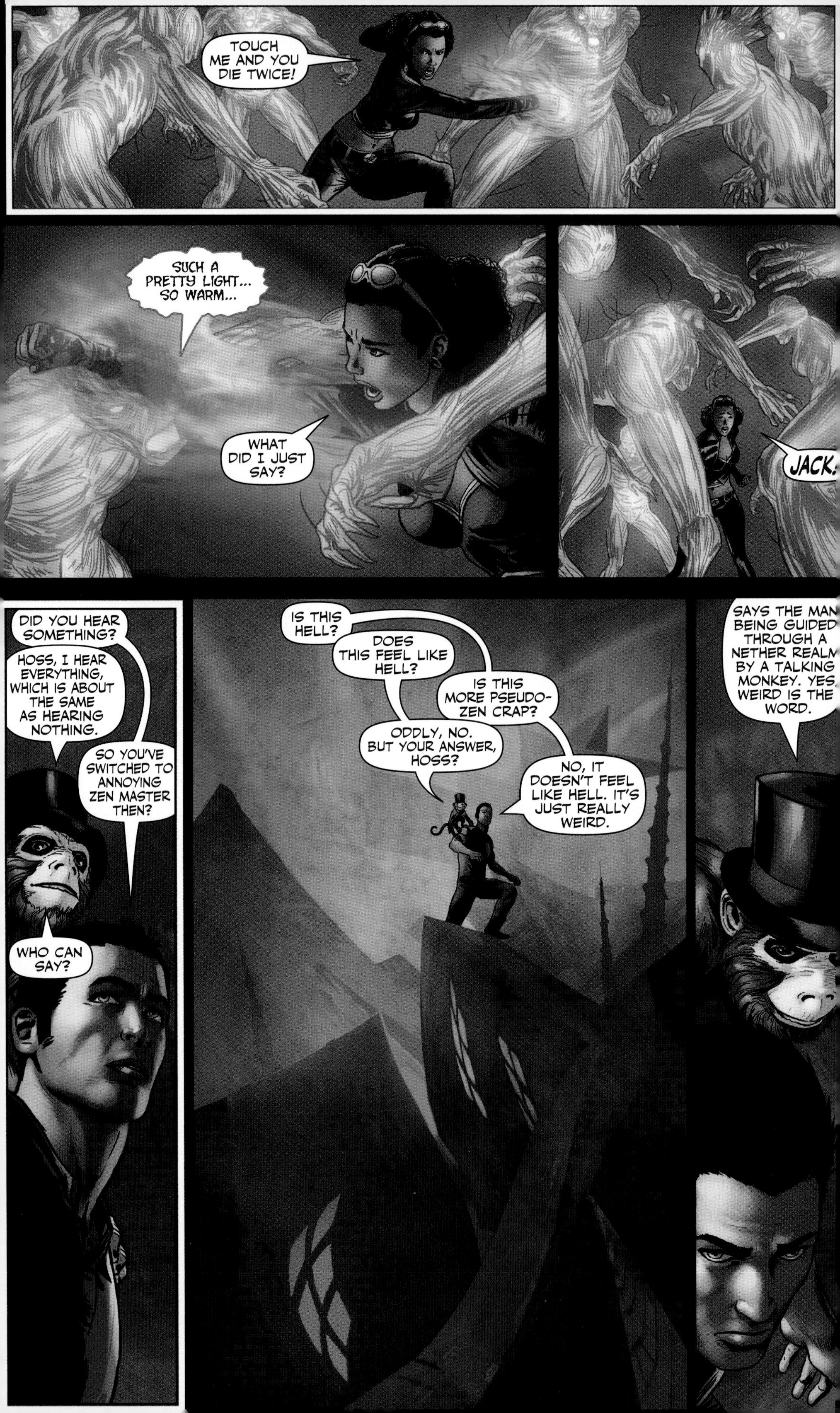
TOUCH ME AND YOU DIE TWICE!
SUCH A PRETTY LIGHT... SO WARM...
WHAT DID I JUST SAY?
JACK!
DID YOU HEAR SOMETHING?
HOSS, I HEAR EVERYTHING, WHICH IS ABOUT THE SAME AS HEARING NOTHING.
SO YOU'VE SWITCHED TO ANNOYING ZEN MASTER THEN?
WHO CAN SAY?
IS THIS HELL?
DOES THIS FEEL LIKE HELL?
IS THIS MORE PSEUDO-ZEN CRAP?
ODDLY, NO. BUT YOUR ANSWER, HOSS?
NO, IT DOESN'T FEEL LIKE HELL. IT'S JUST REALLY WEIRD.
SAYS THE MAN BEING GUIDED THROUGH A NETHER REALM BY A TALKING MONKEY. YES, WEIRD IS THE WORD.

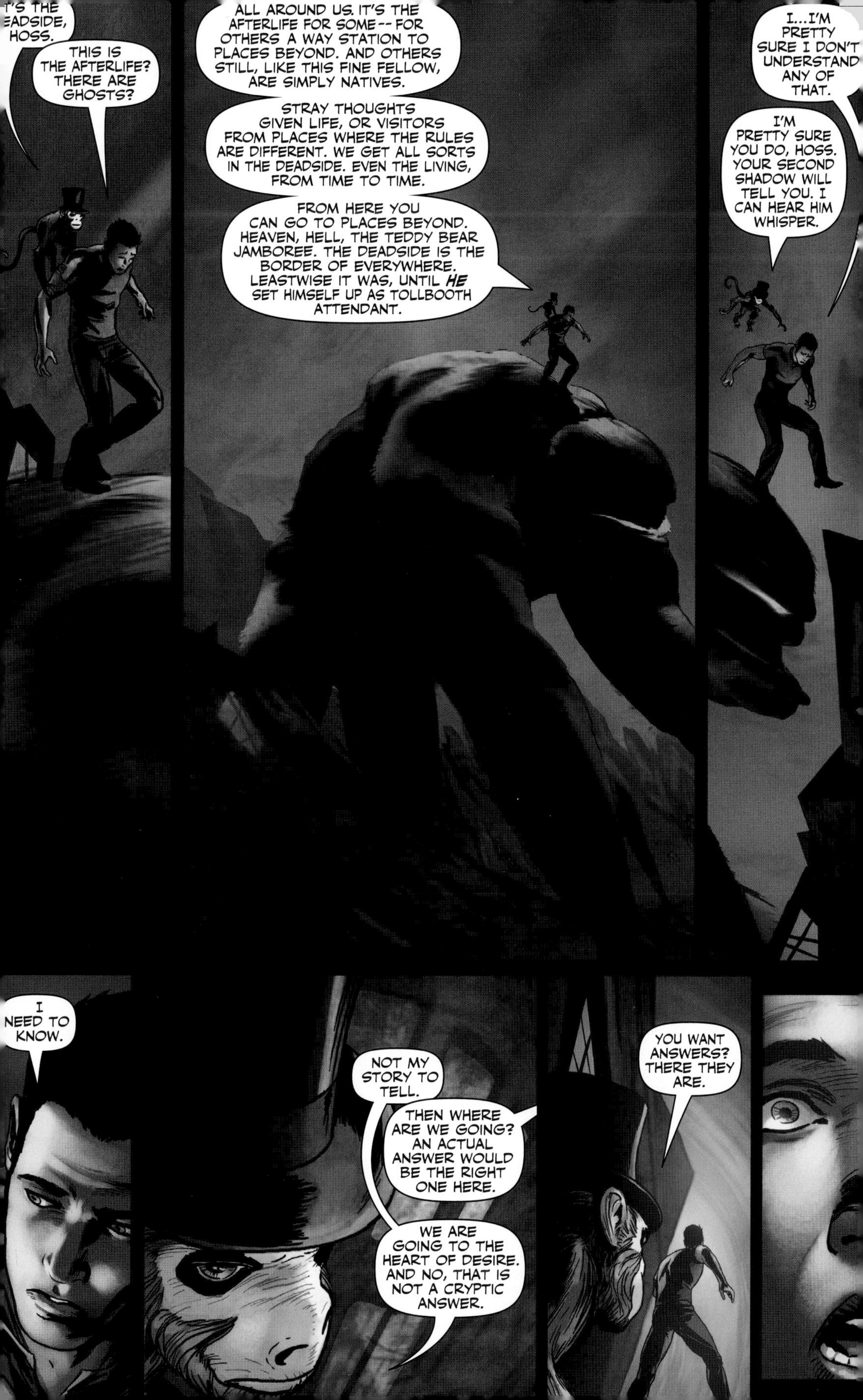

IT'S THE DEADSIDE, HOSS.
THIS IS THE AFTERLIFE? THERE ARE GHOSTS?
ALL AROUND US. IT'S THE AFTERLIFE FOR SOME-- FOR OTHERS A WAY STATION TO PLACES BEYOND. AND OTHERS STILL, LIKE THIS FINE FELLOW, ARE SIMPLY NATIVES.
STRAY THOUGHTS GIVEN LIFE, OR VISITORS FROM PLACES WHERE THE RULES ARE DIFFERENT. WE GET ALL SORTS IN THE DEADSIDE. EVEN THE LIVING, FROM TIME TO TIME.
FROM HERE YOU CAN GO TO PLACES BEYOND. HEAVEN, HELL, THE TEDDY BEAR JAMBOREE. THE DEADSIDE IS THE BORDER OF EVERYWHERE. LEASTWISE IT WAS, UNTIL ***HE*** SET HIMSELF UP AS TOLLBOOTH ATTENDANT.
I...I'M PRETTY SURE I DON'T UNDERSTAND ANY OF THAT.
I'M PRETTY SURE YOU DO, HOSS. YOUR SECOND SHADOW WILL TELL YOU. I CAN HEAR HIM WHISPER.
I NEED TO KNOW.
NOT MY STORY TO TELL.
THEN WHERE ARE WE GOING? AN ACTUAL ANSWER WOULD BE THE RIGHT ONE HERE.
WE ARE GOING TO THE HEART OF DESIRE. AND NO, THAT IS NOT A CRYPTIC ANSWER.
YOU WANT ANSWERS? THERE THEY ARE.

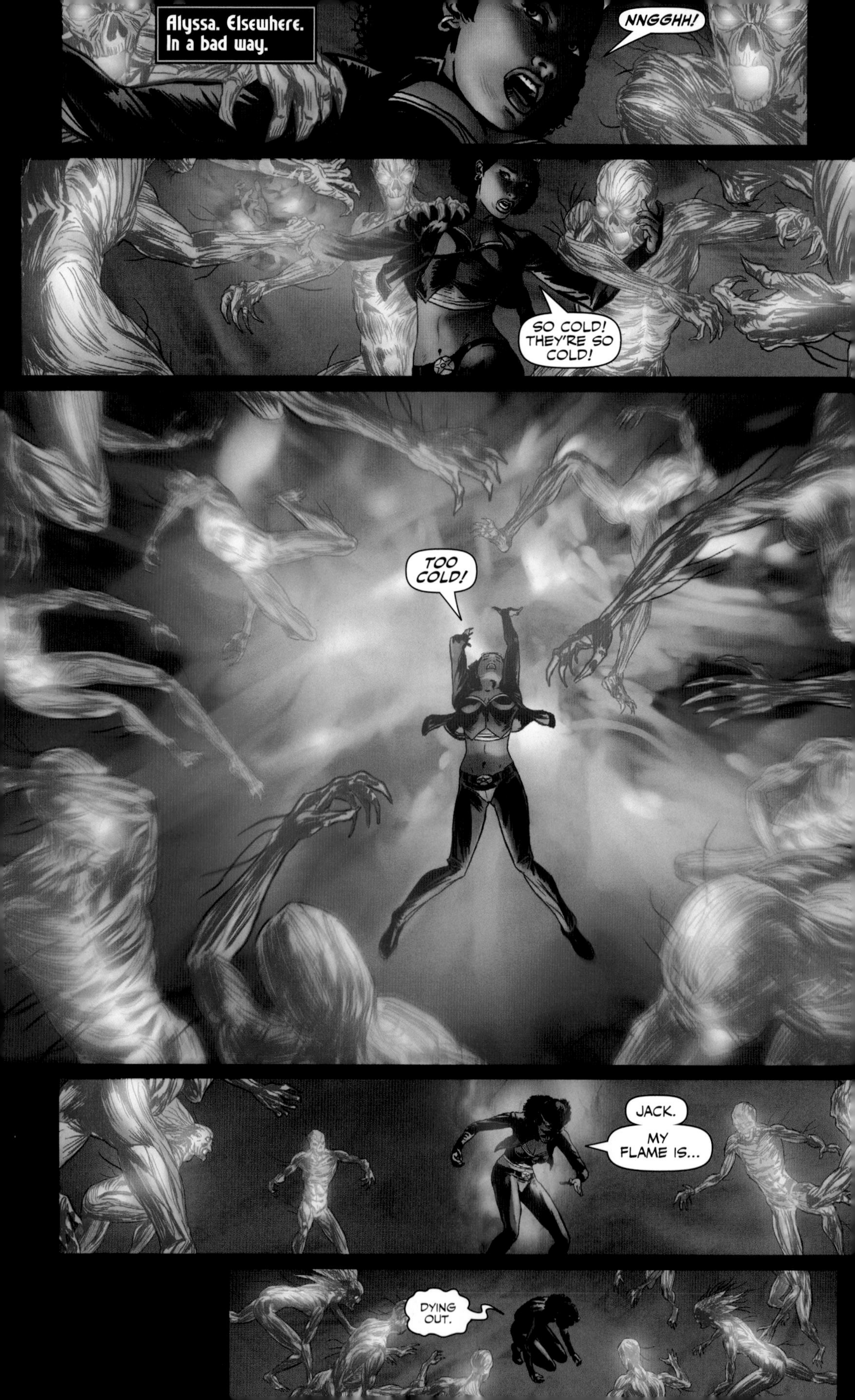
Alyssa. Elsewhere.
In a bad way.
NNGGHH!
SO COLD! THEY'RE SO COLD!
TOO COLD!
JACK.
MY FLAME IS...
DYING OUT.

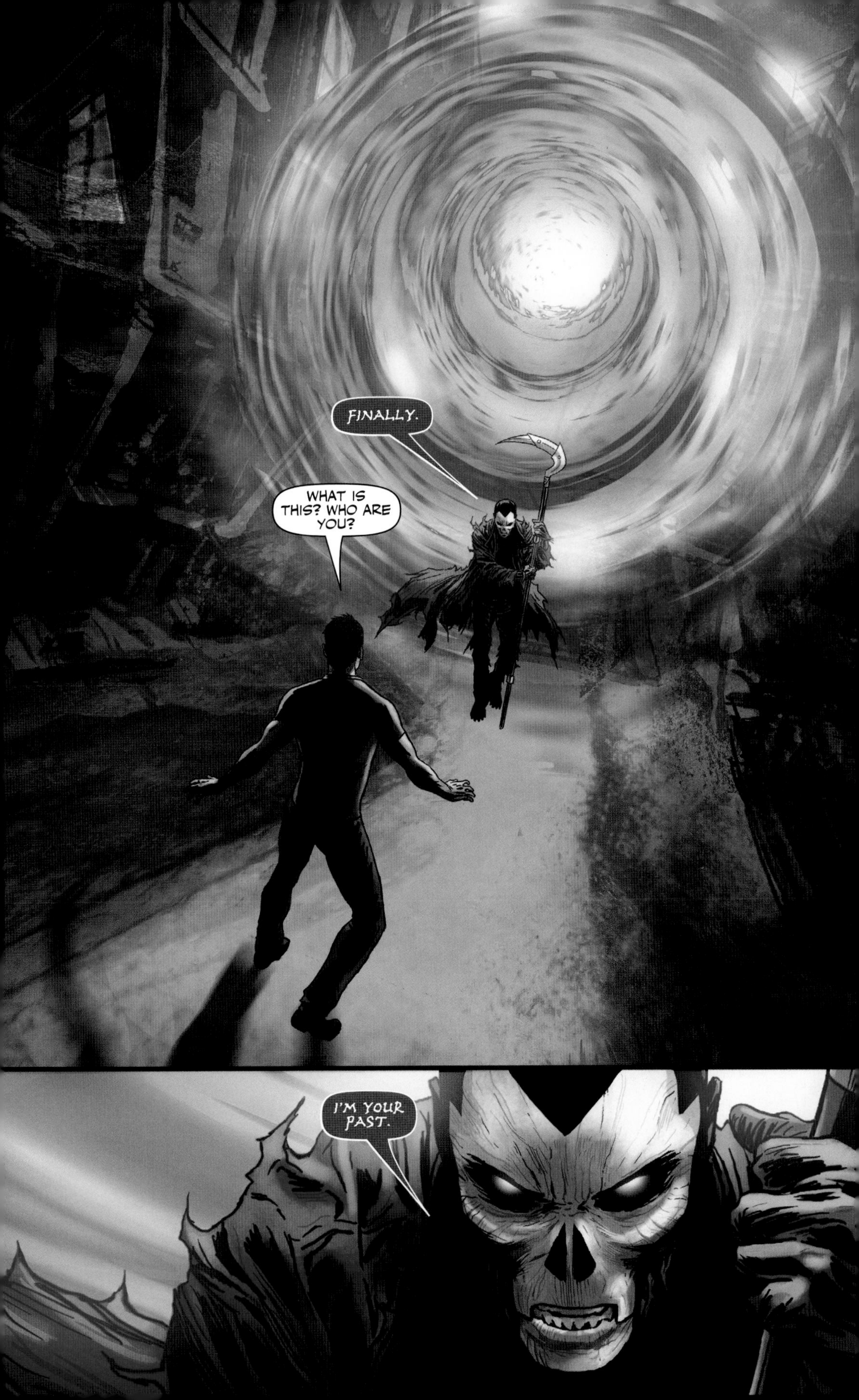
FINALLY.
WHAT IS THIS? WHO ARE YOU?
I'M YOUR PAST.

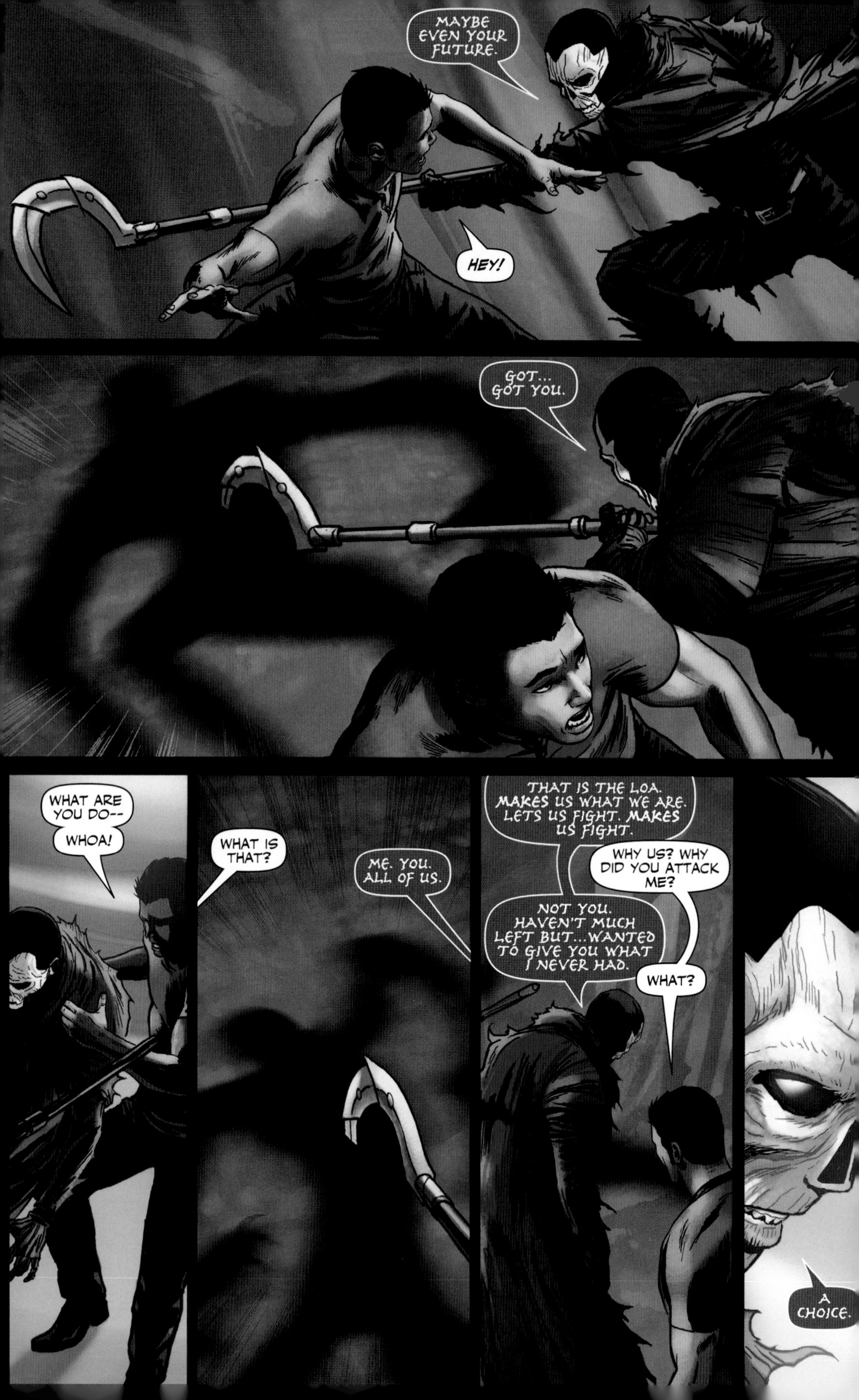
MAYBE EVEN YOUR FUTURE.
HEY!
GOT... GOT YOU.
WHAT ARE YOU DO--
WHOA!
WHAT IS THAT?
ME. YOU. ALL OF US.
THAT IS THE LOA. MAKES US WHAT WE ARE. LETS US FIGHT. MAKES US FIGHT.
WHY US? WHY DID YOU ATTACK ME?
NOT YOU. HAVEN'T MUCH LEFT BUT...WANTED TO GIVE YOU WHAT I NEVER HAD.
WHAT?
A CHOICE.

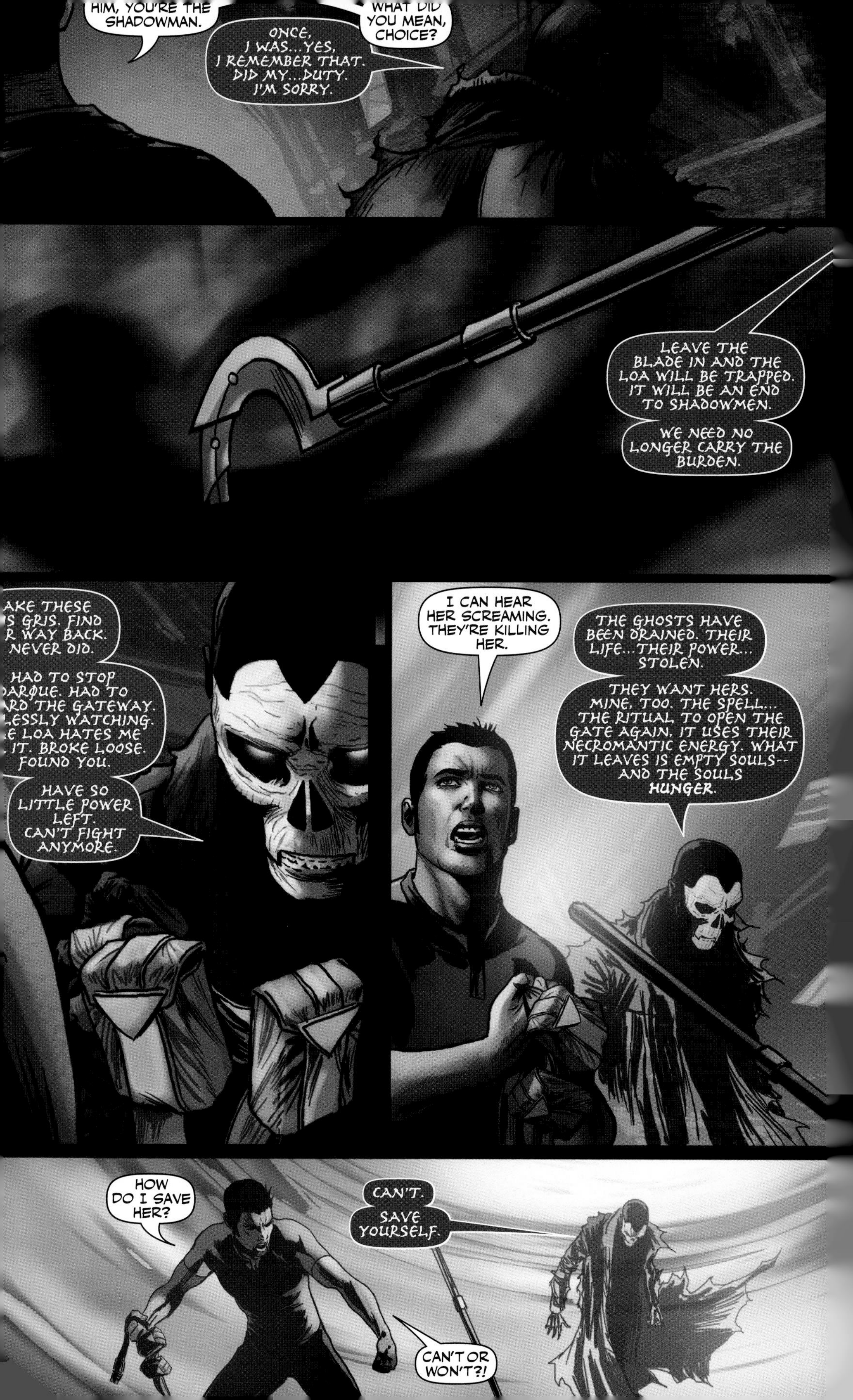
HIM, YOU'RE THE SHADOWMAN.
WHAT DID YOU MEAN, CHOICE?
ONCE, I WAS...YES, I REMEMBER THAT. DID MY...DUTY. I'M SORRY.
LEAVE THE BLADE IN AND THE LOA WILL BE TRAPPED. IT WILL BE AN END TO SHADOWMEN.
WE NEED NO LONGER CARRY THE BURDEN.
AKE THESE S GRIS. FIND R WAY BACK. NEVER DID.
HAD TO STOP ARQUE. HAD TO ARD THE GATEWAY. LESSLY WATCHING. E LOA HATES ME IT. BROKE LOOSE. FOUND YOU.
HAVE SO LITTLE POWER LEFT. CAN'T FIGHT ANYMORE.
I CAN HEAR HER SCREAMING. THEY'RE KILLING HER.
THE GHOSTS HAVE BEEN DRAINED. THEIR LIFE...THEIR POWER... STOLEN.
THEY WANT HERS. MINE, TOO. THE SPELL... THE RITUAL TO OPEN THE GATE AGAIN, IT USES THEIR NECROMANTIC ENERGY. WHAT IT LEAVES IS EMPTY SOULS-- AND THE SOULS **HUNGER**.
HOW DO I SAVE HER?
CAN'T.
SAVE YOURSELF.
CAN'T OR WON'T?!

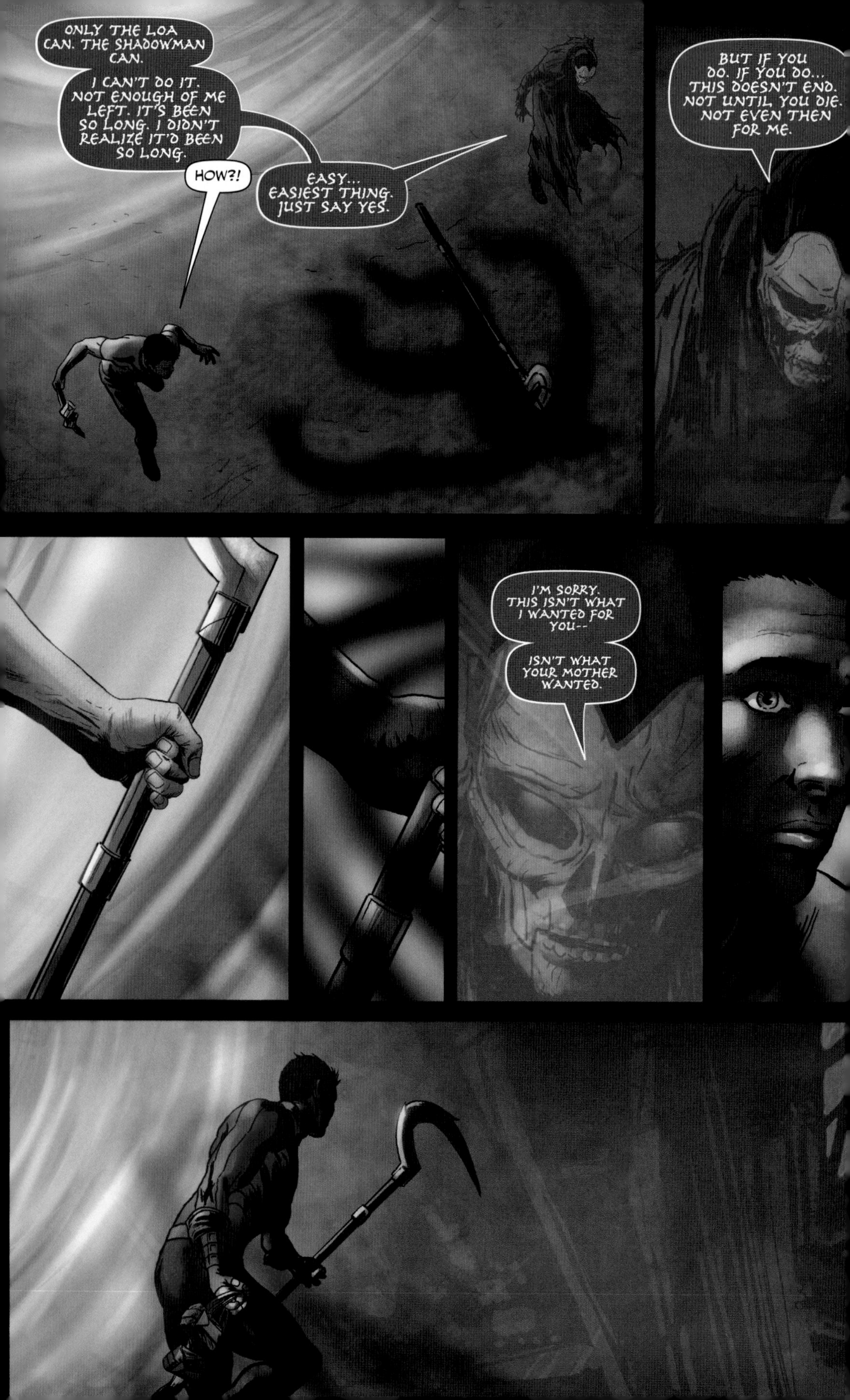
ONLY THE LOA CAN. THE SHADOWMAN CAN.
I CAN'T DO IT. NOT ENOUGH OF ME LEFT. IT'S BEEN SO LONG. I DIDN'T REALIZE IT'D BEEN SO LONG.
HOW?!
EASY... EASIEST THING. JUST SAY YES.
BUT IF YOU DO. IF YOU DO... THIS DOESN'T END. NOT UNTIL YOU DIE. NOT EVEN THEN FOR ME.
I'M SORRY. THIS ISN'T WHAT I WANTED FOR YOU--
ISN'T WHAT YOUR MOTHER WANTED.

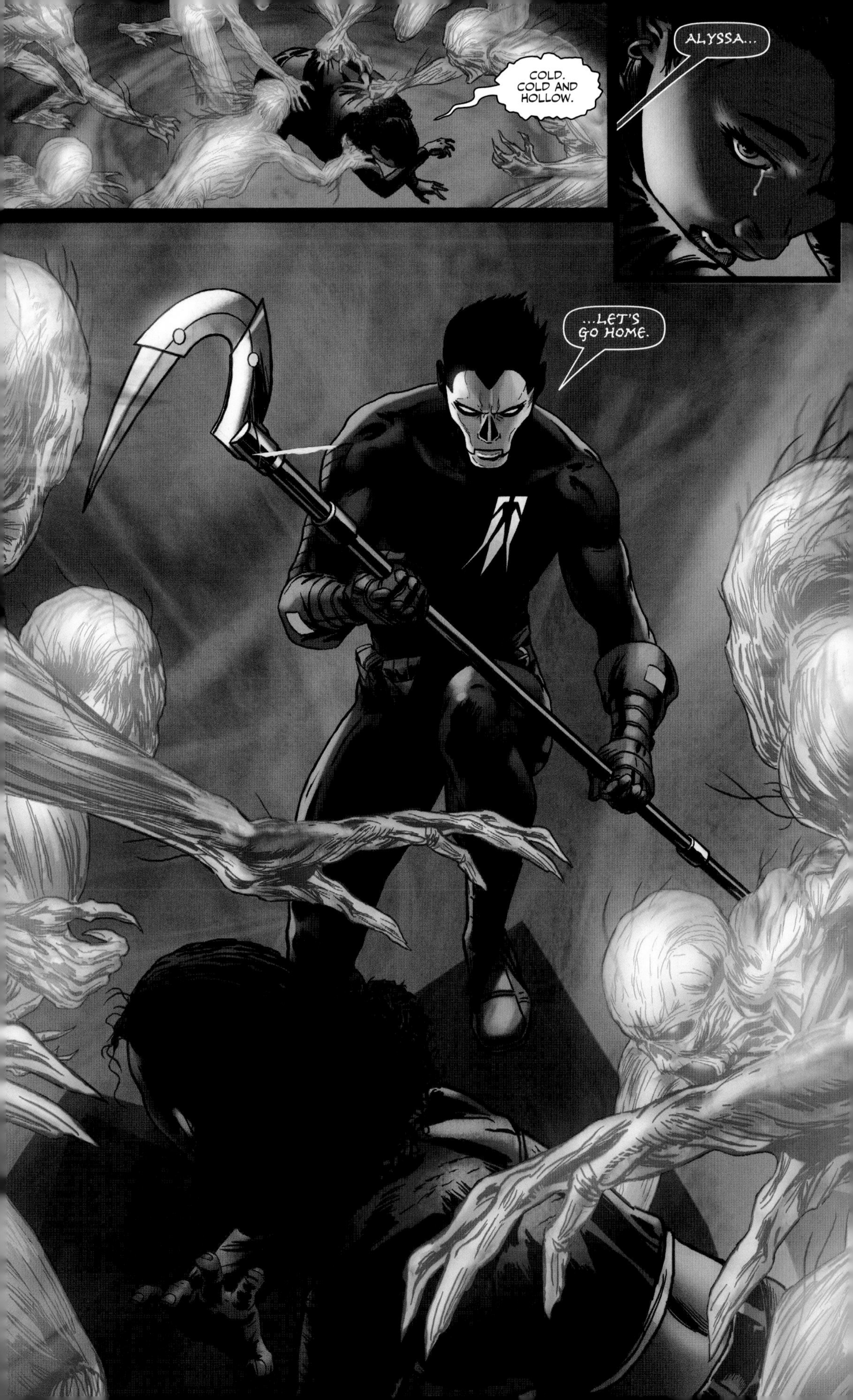
COLD. COLD AND HOLLOW.
ALYSSA...
...LET'S GO HOME.

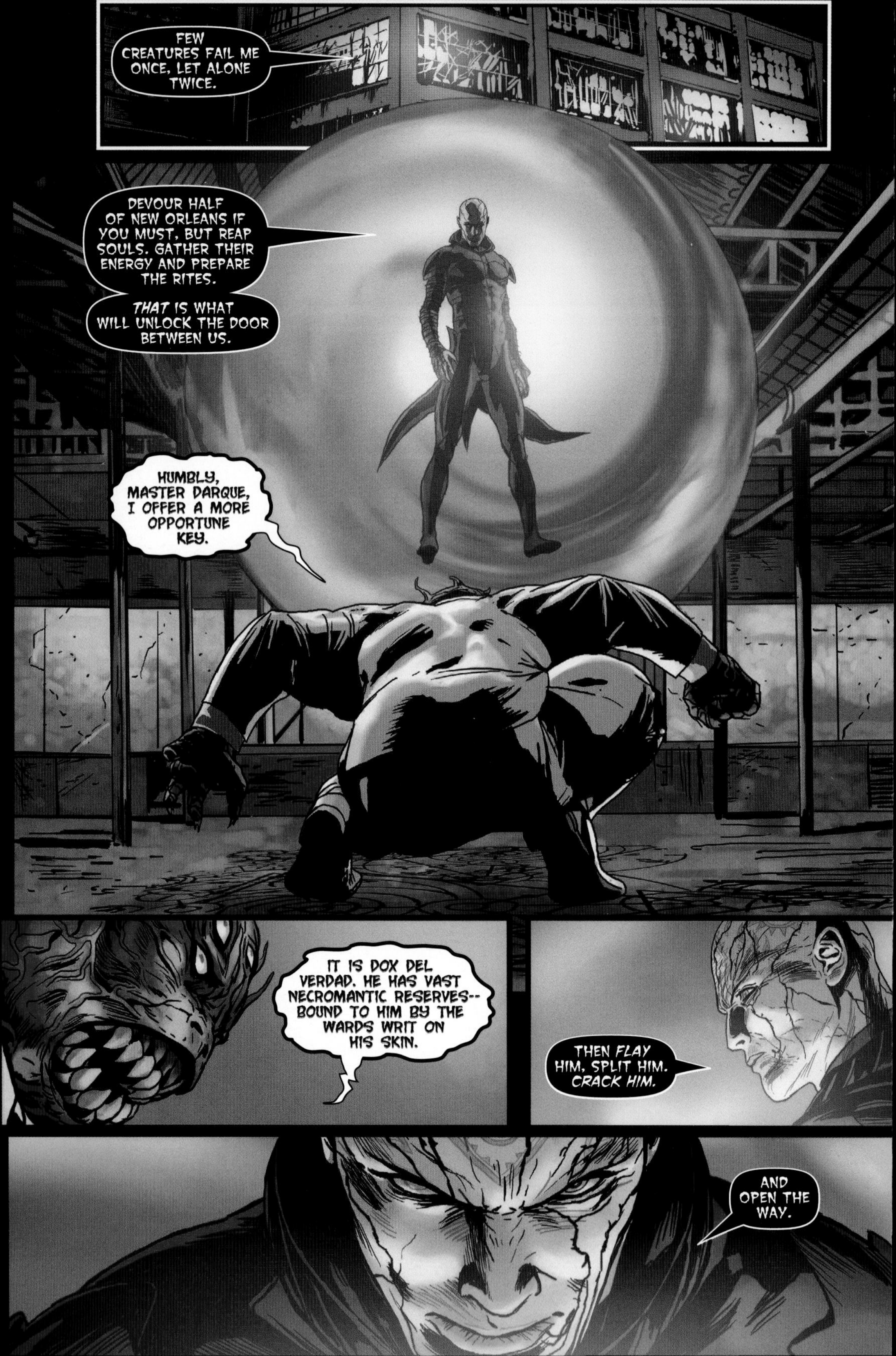
FEW CREATURES FAIL ME ONCE, LET ALONE TWICE.
DEVOUR HALF OF NEW ORLEANS IF YOU MUST, BUT REAP SOULS. GATHER THEIR ENERGY AND PREPARE THE RITES.
THAT IS WHAT WILL UNLOCK THE DOOR BETWEEN US.
HUMBLY, MASTER DARQUE, I OFFER A MORE OPPORTUNE KEY.
IT IS DOX DEL VERDAD. HE HAS VAST NECROMANTIC RESERVES--BOUND TO HIM BY THE WARDS WRIT ON HIS SKIN.
THEN *FLAY* HIM, SPLIT HIM. *CRACK HIM.*
AND OPEN THE WAY.

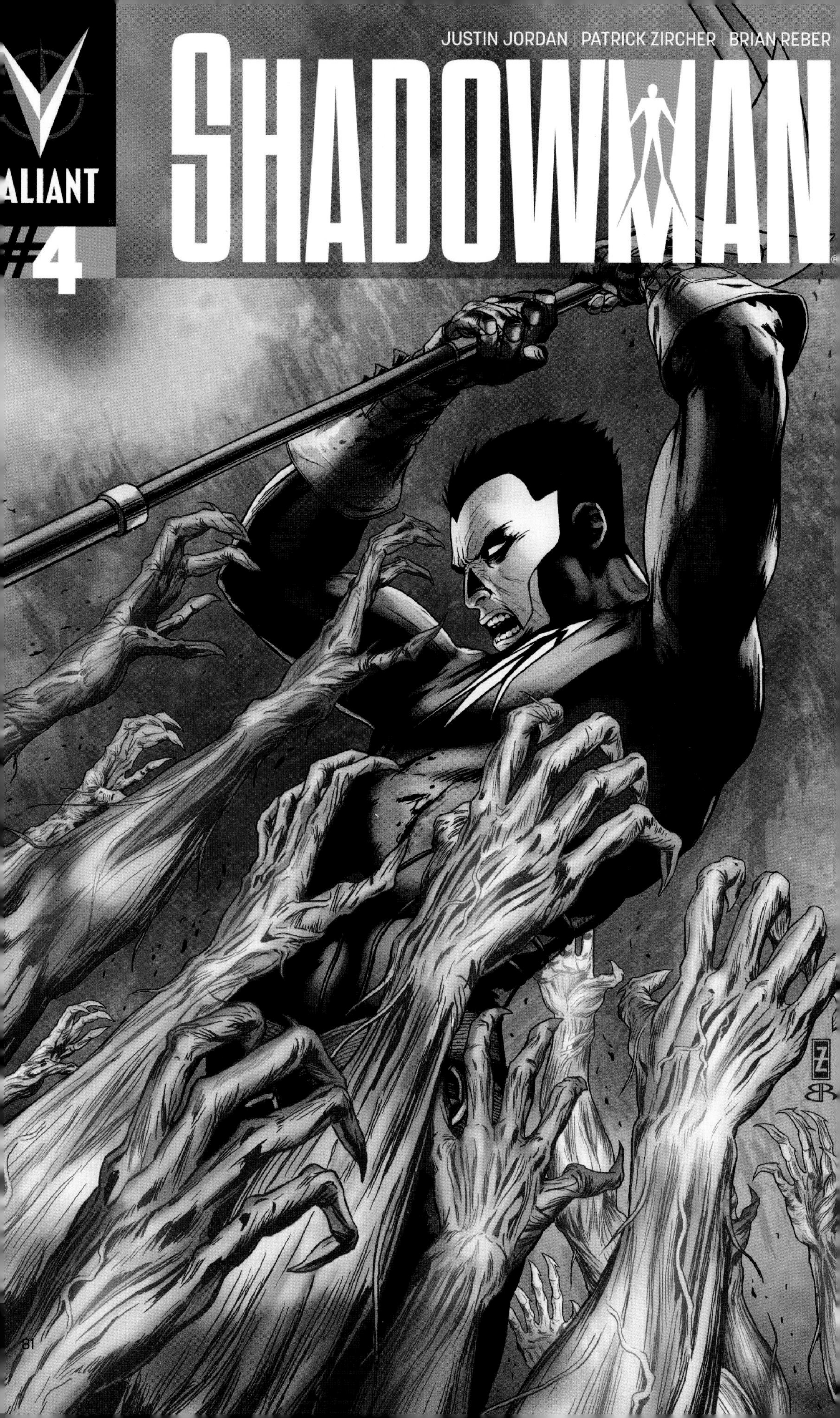
VALIANT
#4
JUSTIN JORDAN | PATRICK ZIRCHER | BRIAN REBER
SHADOWMAN

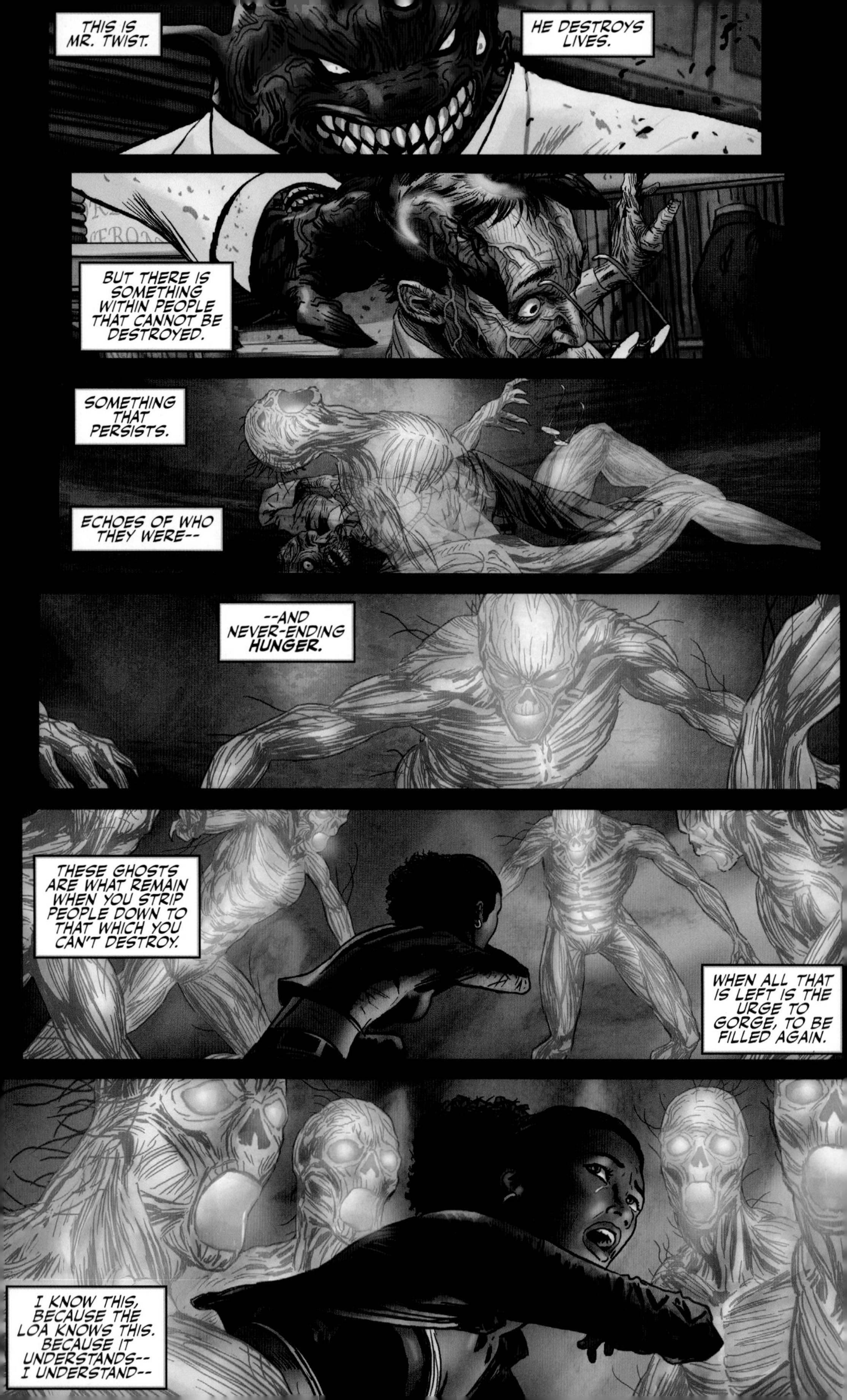
THIS IS MR. TWIST.
HE DESTROYS LIVES.
BUT THERE IS SOMETHING WITHIN PEOPLE THAT CANNOT BE DESTROYED.
SOMETHING THAT PERSISTS.
ECHOES OF WHO THEY WERE--
--AND NEVER-ENDING HUNGER.
THESE GHOSTS ARE WHAT REMAIN WHEN YOU STRIP PEOPLE DOWN TO THAT WHICH YOU CAN'T DESTROY.
WHEN ALL THAT IS LEFT IS THE URGE TO GORGE, TO BE FILLED AGAIN.
I KNOW THIS, BECAUSE THE LOA KNOWS THIS. BECAUSE IT UNDERSTANDS-- I UNDERSTAND--

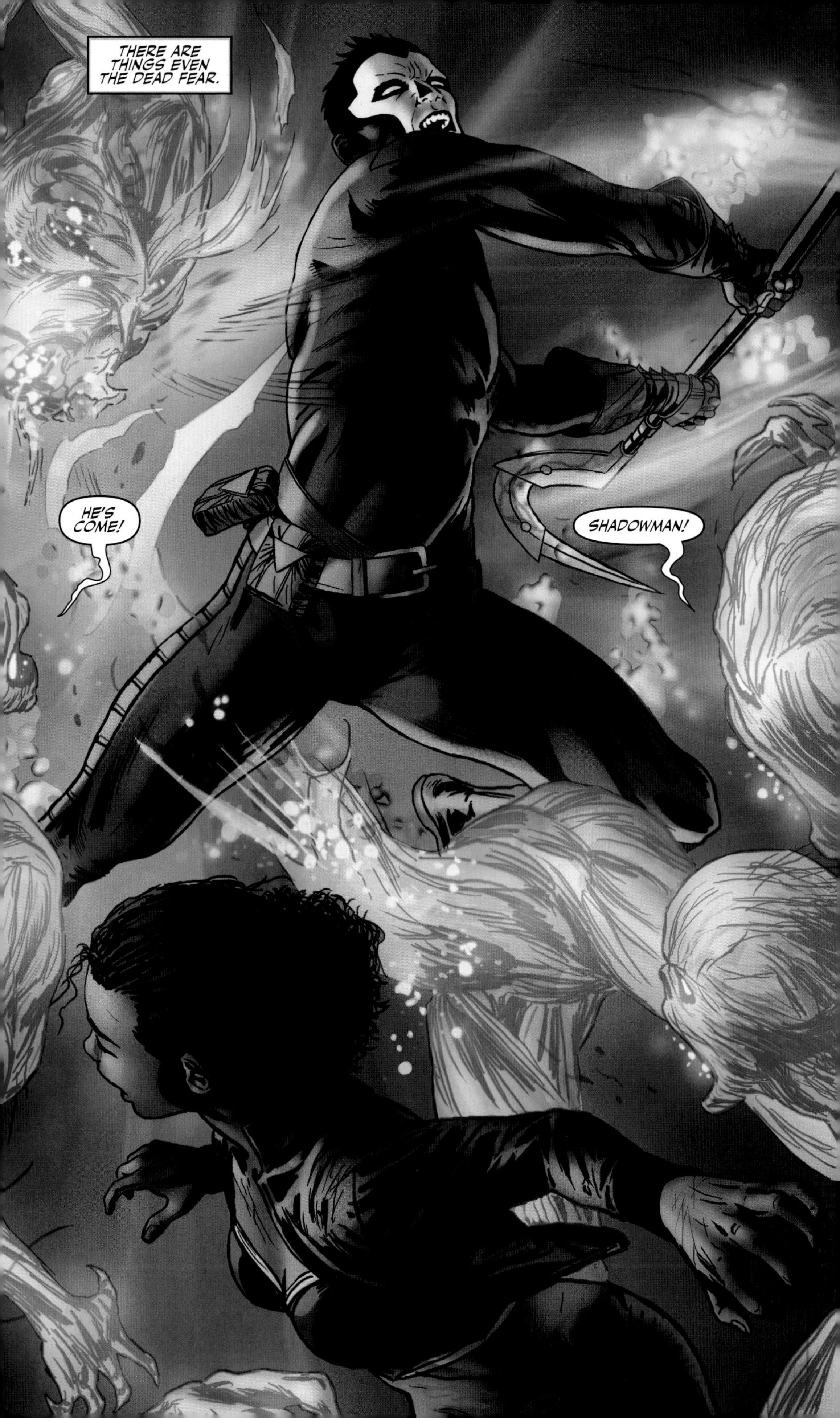
THERE ARE THINGS EVEN THE DEAD FEAR.
HE'S COME!
SHADOWMAN!

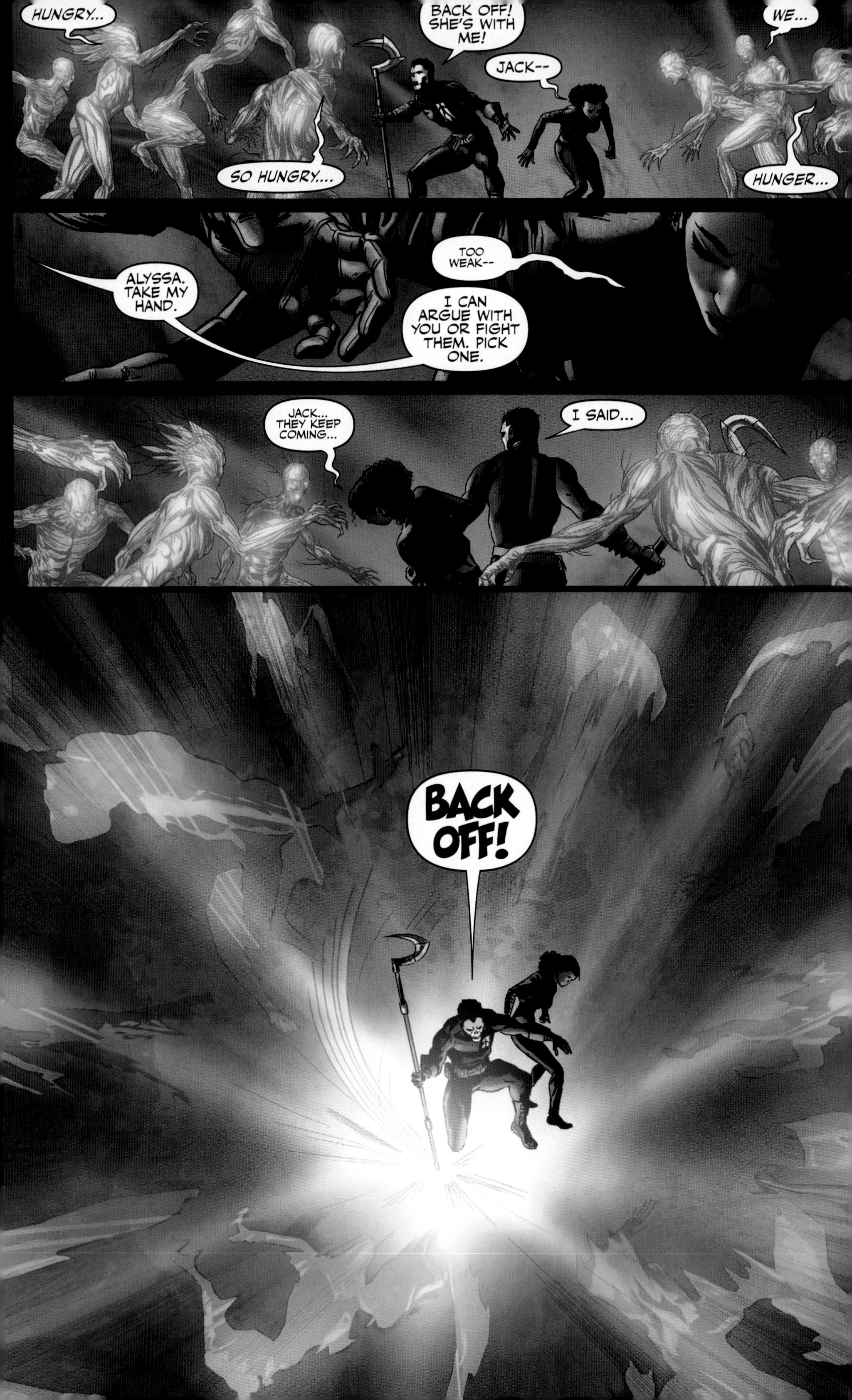
HUNGRY...
BACK OFF! SHE'S WITH ME!
JACK--
WE...
SO HUNGRY....
HUNGER...
TOO WEAK--
ALYSSA. TAKE MY HAND.
I CAN ARGUE WITH YOU OR FIGHT THEM. PICK ONE.
JACK... THEY KEEP COMING...
I SAID...
BACK OFF!

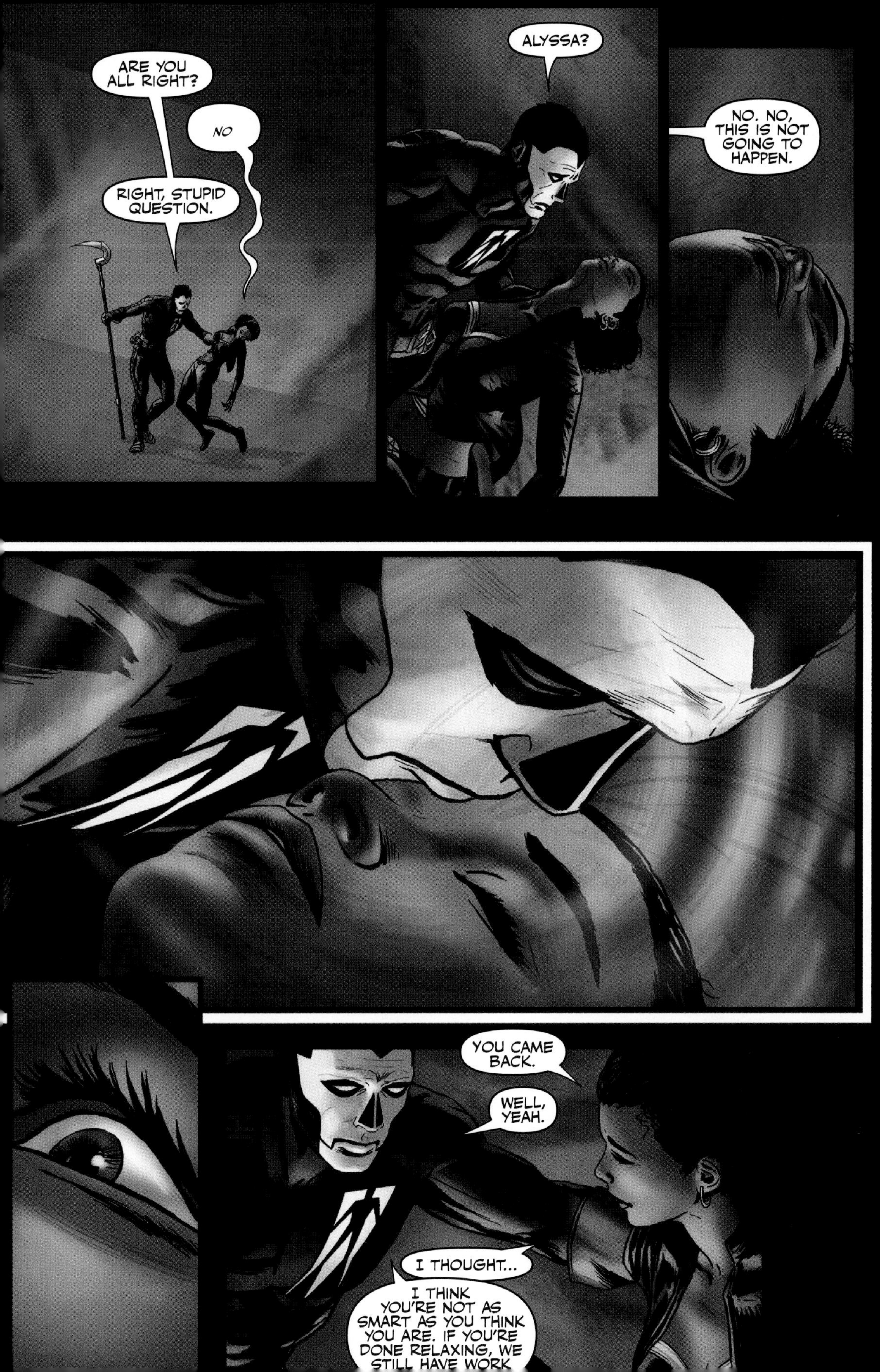

ARE YOU ALL RIGHT?
NO
RIGHT, STUPID QUESTION.
ALYSSA?
NO. NO, THIS IS NOT GOING TO HAPPEN.
YOU CAME BACK.
WELL, YEAH.
I THOUGHT...
I THINK YOU'RE NOT AS SMART AS YOU THINK YOU ARE. IF YOU'RE DONE RELAXING, WE STILL HAVE WORK

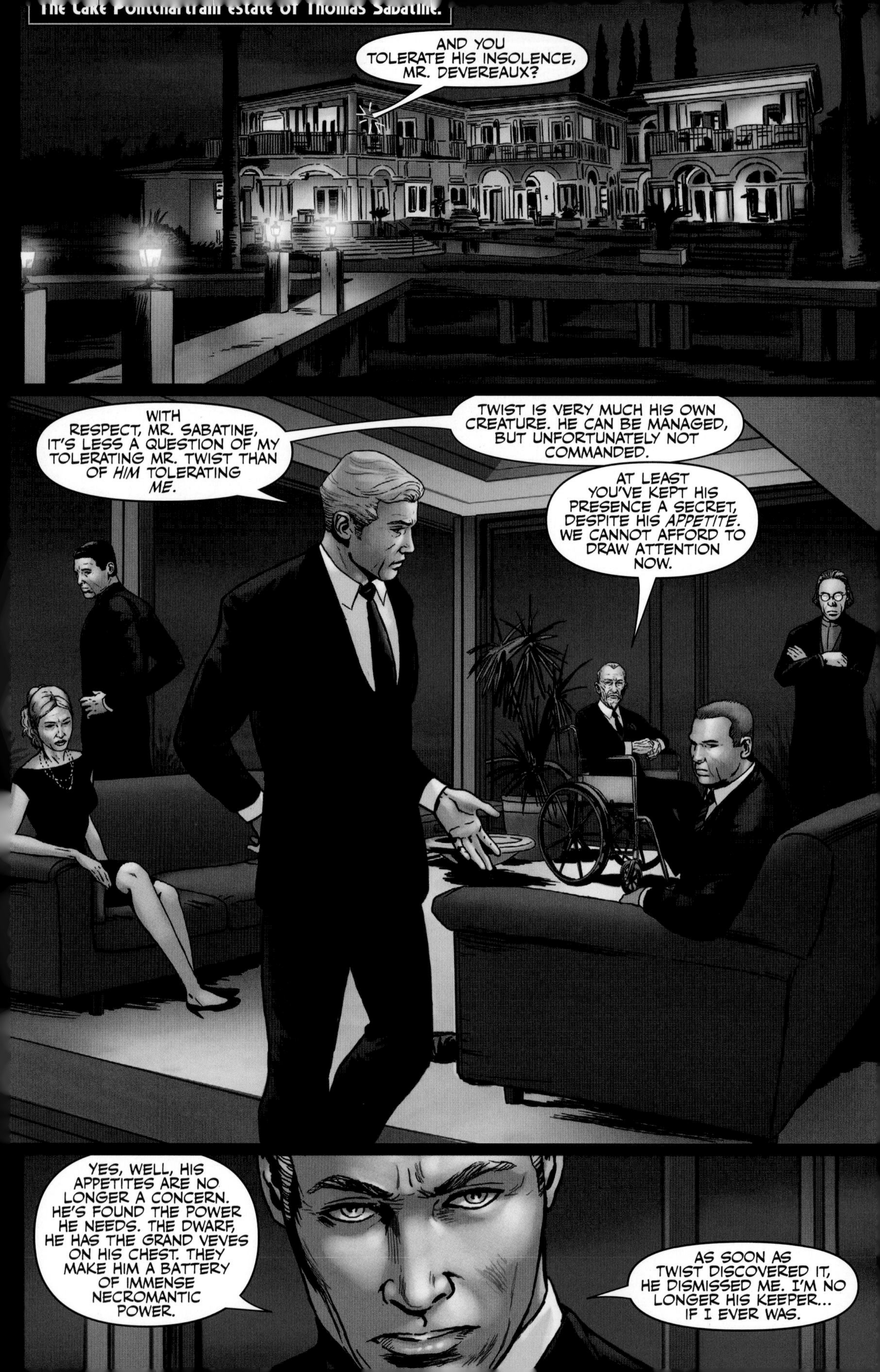
The Lake Pontchartrain estate of Thomas Sabatine.
AND YOU TOLERATE HIS INSOLENCE, MR. DEVEREAUX?
WITH RESPECT, MR. SABATINE, IT'S LESS A QUESTION OF MY TOLERATING MR. TWIST THAN OF *HIM* TOLERATING *ME*.
TWIST IS VERY MUCH HIS OWN CREATURE. HE CAN BE MANAGED, BUT UNFORTUNATELY NOT COMMANDED.
AT LEAST YOU'VE KEPT HIS PRESENCE A SECRET, DESPITE HIS *APPETITE*. WE CANNOT AFFORD TO DRAW ATTENTION NOW.
YES, WELL, HIS APPETITES ARE NO LONGER A CONCERN. HE'S FOUND THE POWER HE NEEDS. THE DWARF, HE HAS THE GRAND VEVES ON HIS CHEST. THEY MAKE HIM A BATTERY OF IMMENSE NECROMANTIC POWER.
AS SOON AS TWIST DISCOVERED IT, HE DISMISSED ME. I'M NO LONGER HIS KEEPER... IF I EVER WAS.

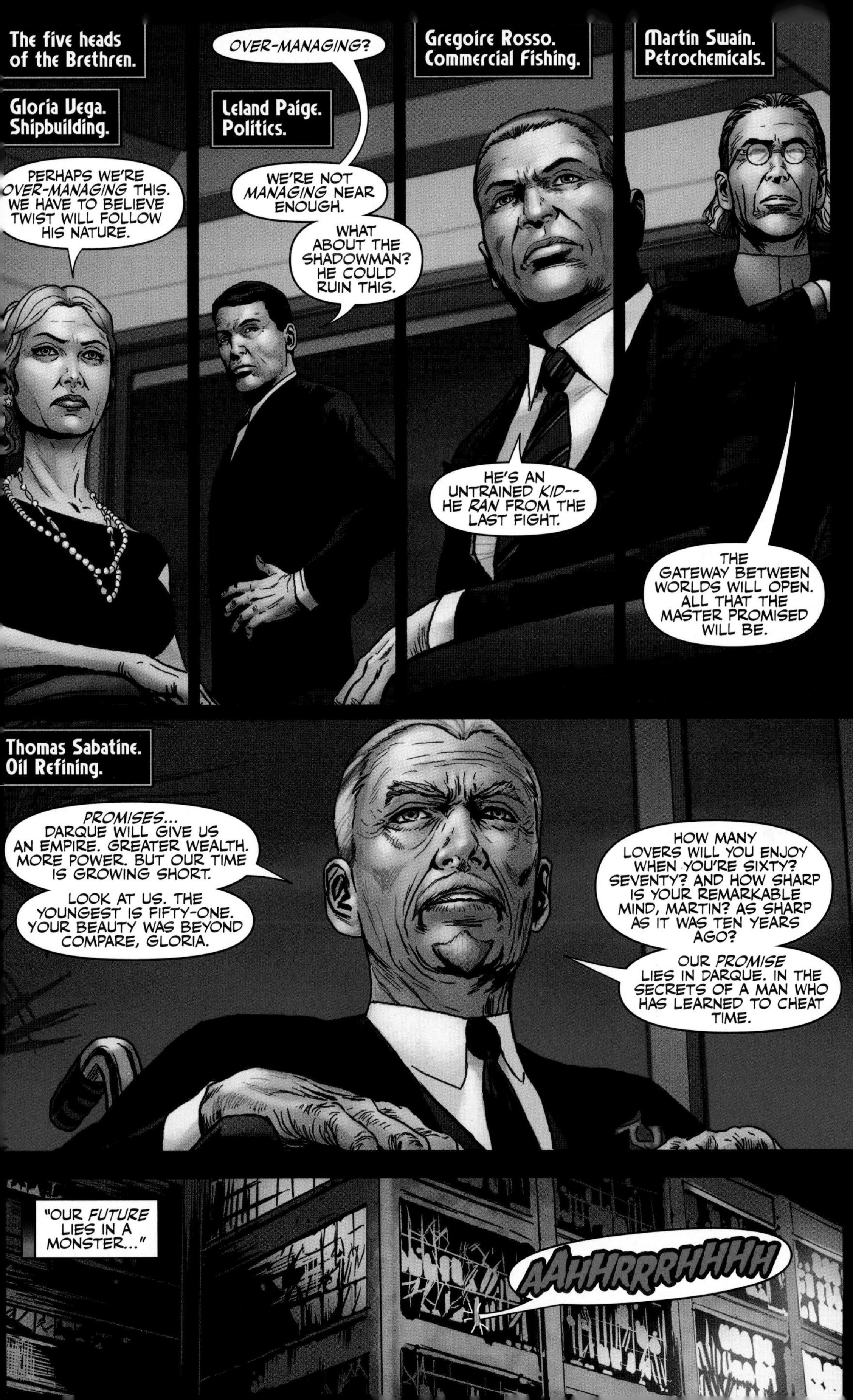
The five heads of the Brethren.
Gloria Vega. Shipbuilding.
PERHAPS WE'RE *OVER-MANAGING* THIS. WE HAVE TO BELIEVE TWIST WILL FOLLOW HIS NATURE.
Leland Paige. Politics.
OVER-MANAGING?
WE'RE NOT *MANAGING* NEAR ENOUGH.
WHAT ABOUT THE SHADOWMAN? HE COULD RUIN THIS.
Gregoire Rosso. Commercial Fishing.
HE'S AN UNTRAINED *KID*-- HE *RAN* FROM THE LAST FIGHT.
Martin Swain. Petrochemicals.
THE GATEWAY BETWEEN WORLDS WILL OPEN. ALL THAT THE MASTER PROMISED WILL BE.
Thomas Sabatine. Oil Refining.
PROMISES... DARQUE WILL GIVE US AN EMPIRE. GREATER WEALTH. MORE POWER. BUT OUR TIME IS GROWING SHORT.
LOOK AT US. THE YOUNGEST IS FIFTY-ONE. YOUR BEAUTY WAS BEYOND COMPARE, GLORIA.
HOW MANY LOVERS WILL YOU ENJOY WHEN YOU'RE SIXTY? SEVENTY? AND HOW SHARP IS YOUR REMARKABLE MIND, MARTIN? AS SHARP AS IT WAS TEN YEARS AGO?
OUR *PROMISE* LIES IN DARQUE. IN THE SECRETS OF A MAN WHO HAS LEARNED TO CHEAT TIME.
"OUR *FUTURE* LIES IN A MONSTER..."
AAHHRRRRHHHH

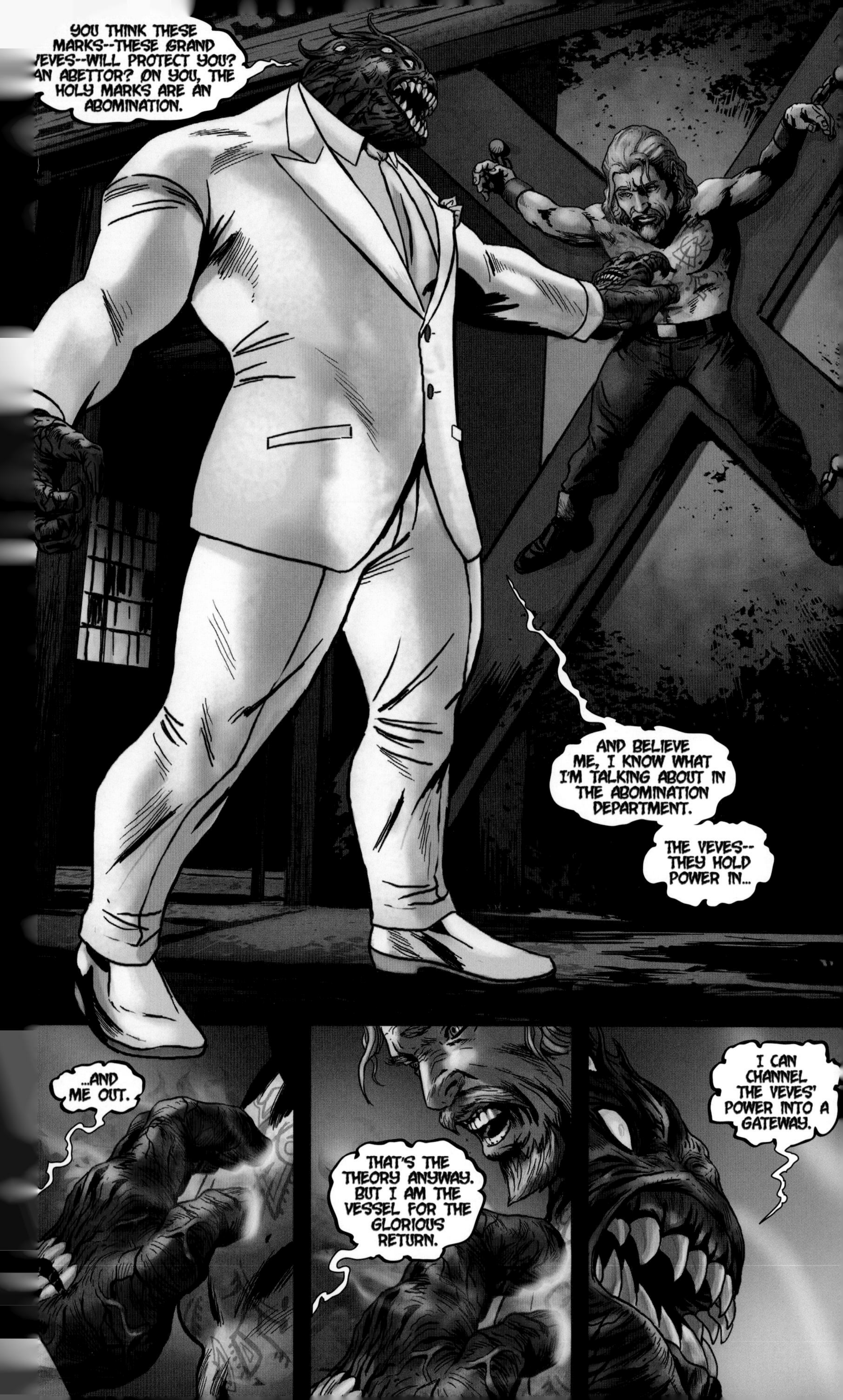
YOU THINK THESE MARKS--THESE GRAND VEVES--WILL PROTECT YOU? AN ABETTOR? ON YOU, THE HOLY MARKS ARE AN ABOMINATION.
AND BELIEVE ME, I KNOW WHAT I'M TALKING ABOUT IN THE ABOMINATION DEPARTMENT.
THE VEVES-- THEY HOLD POWER IN...
...AND ME OUT.
THAT'S THE THEORY ANYWAY. BUT I AM THE VESSEL FOR THE GLORIOUS RETURN.
I CAN CHANNEL THE VEVES' POWER INTO A GATEWAY.

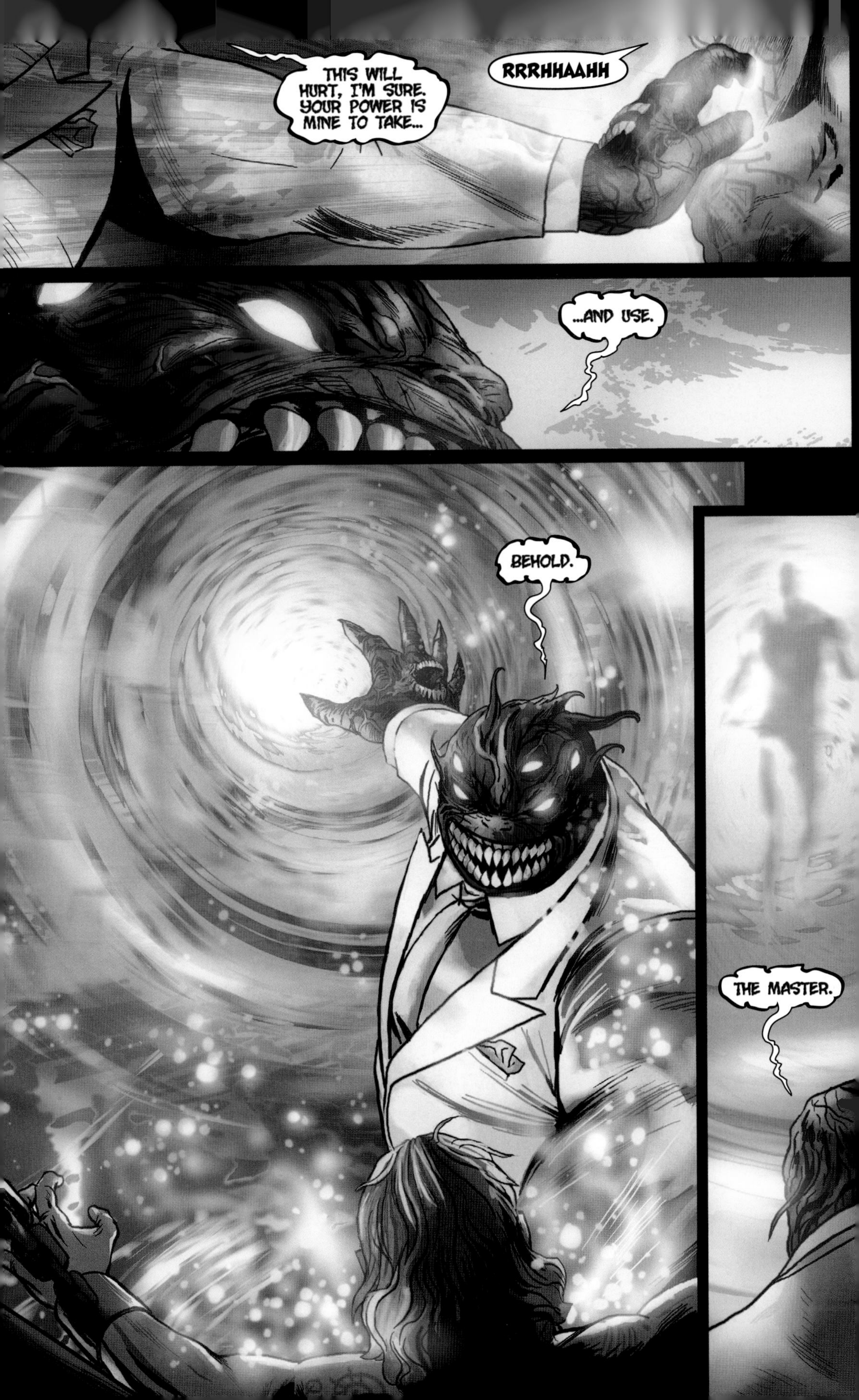
THIS WILL HURT, I'M SURE. YOUR POWER IS MINE TO TAKE...
RRRHHAAHH
...AND USE.
BEHOLD.
THE MASTER.

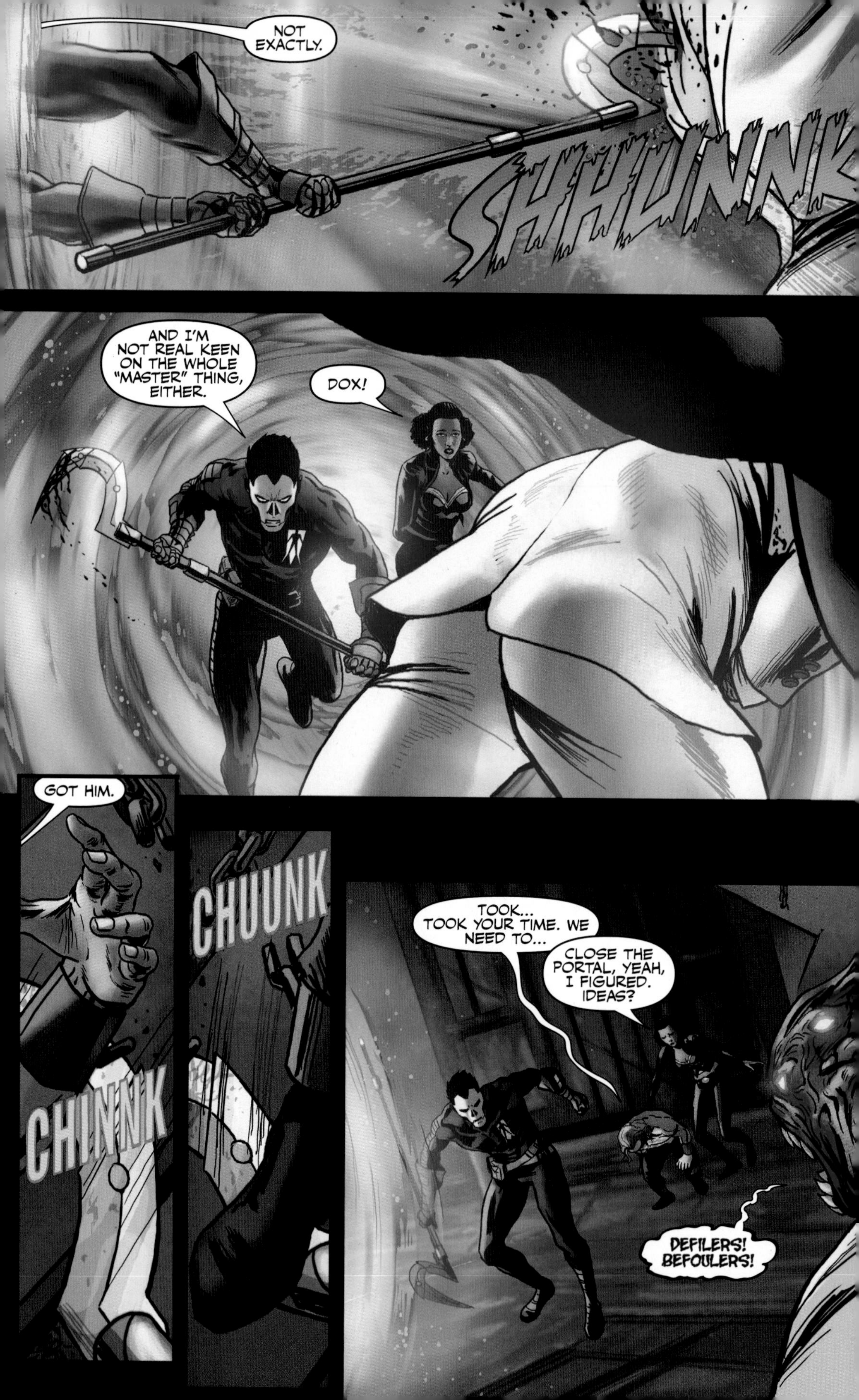
NOT EXACTLY.
SHHUNNK
AND I'M NOT REAL KEEN ON THE WHOLE "MASTER" THING, EITHER.
DOX!
GOT HIM.
CHUUNK
CHINNK
TOOK... TOOK YOUR TIME. WE NEED TO...
CLOSE THE PORTAL, YEAH, I FIGURED. IDEAS?
DEFILERS! BEFOULERS!

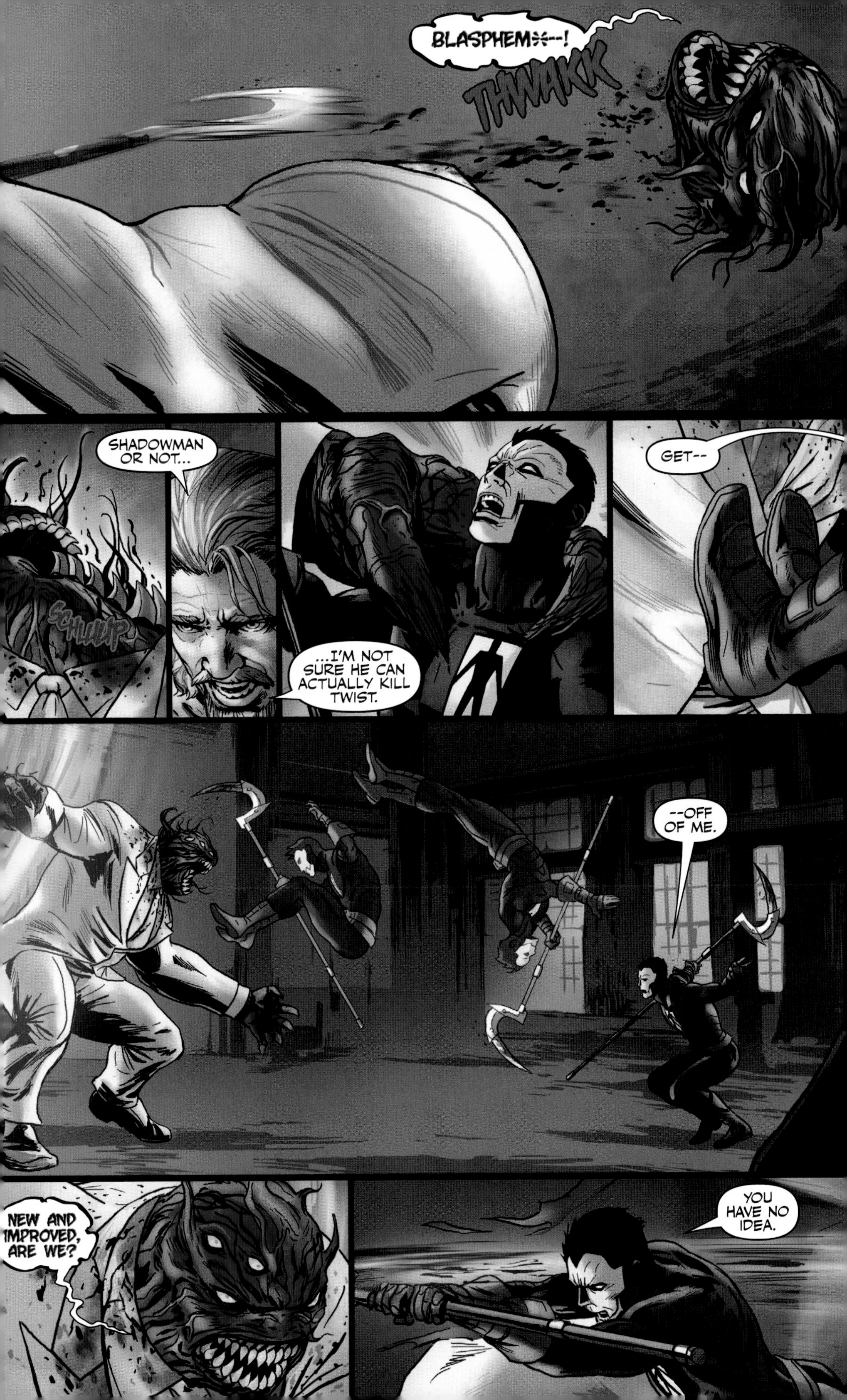
BLASPHEM✱--!
THWAKK
SHADOWMAN OR NOT...
SCHLULP
...I'M NOT SURE HE CAN ACTUALLY KILL TWIST.
GET--
--OFF OF ME.
NEW AND IMPROVED, ARE WE?
YOU HAVE NO IDEA.

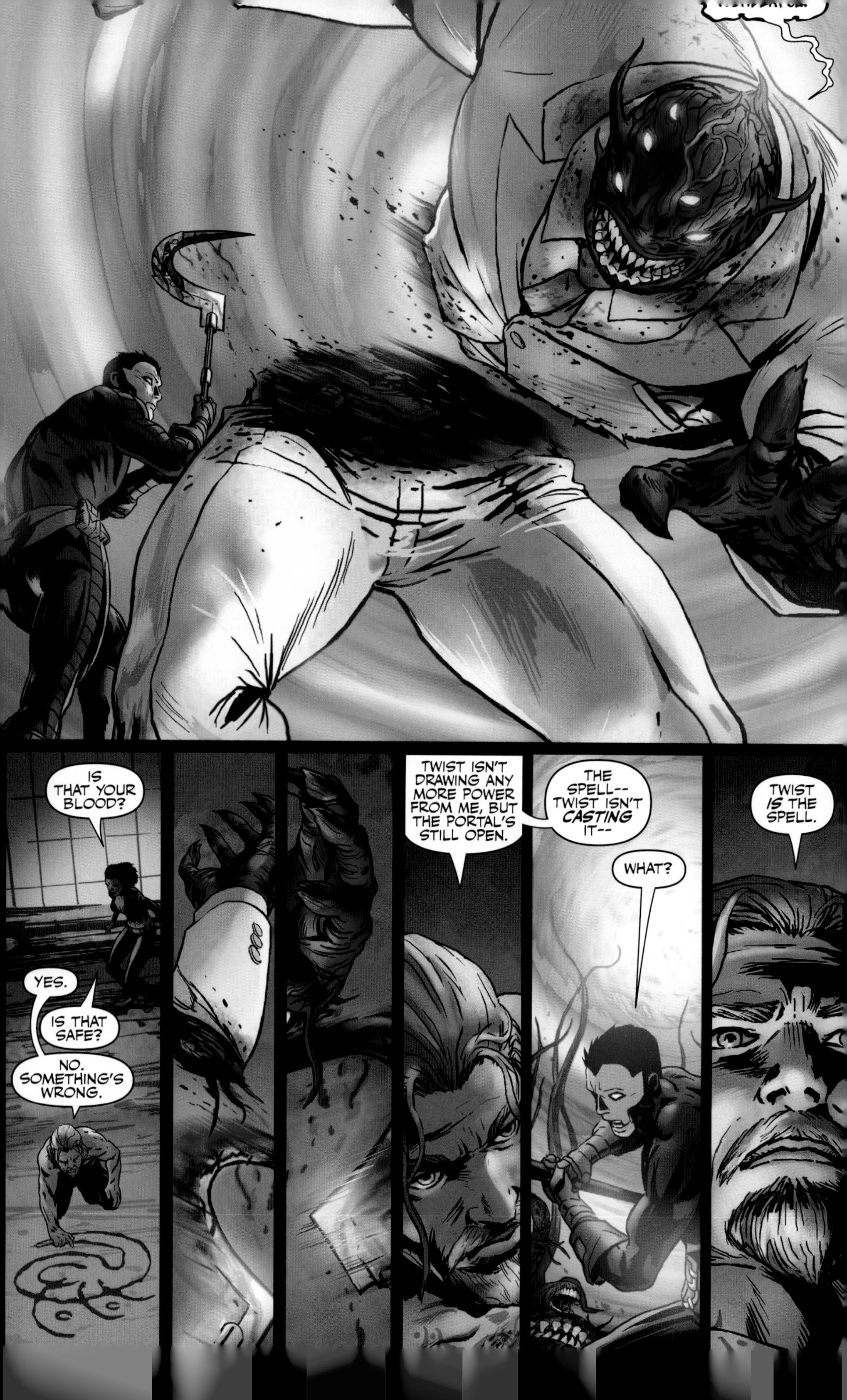
IS THAT YOUR BLOOD?
YES.
IS THAT SAFE?
NO. SOMETHING'S WRONG.
TWIST ISN'T DRAWING ANY MORE POWER FROM ME, BUT THE PORTAL'S STILL OPEN.
THE SPELL-- TWIST ISN'T *CASTING* IT--
WHAT?
TWIST *IS* THE SPELL.

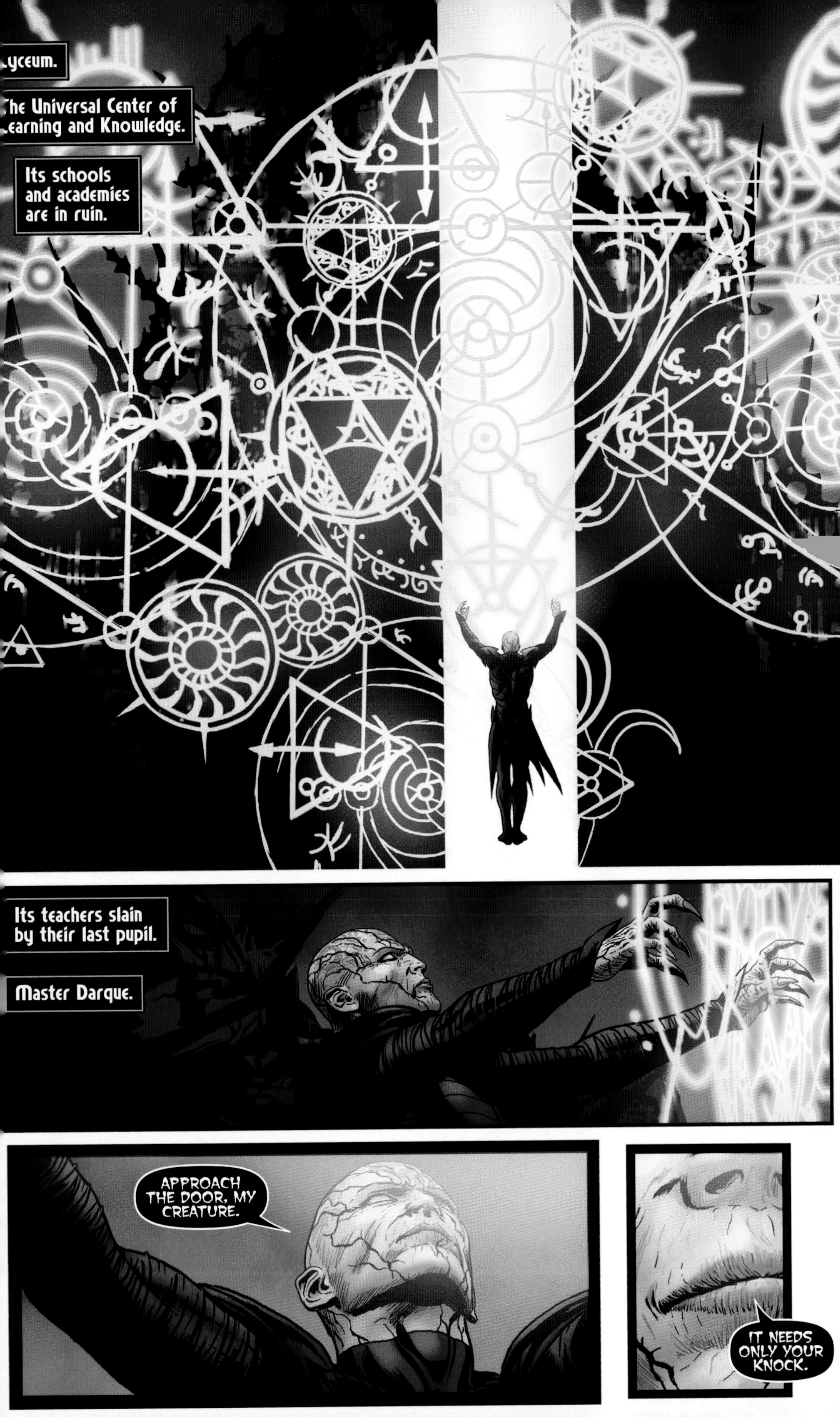
yceum.
he Universal Center of earning and Knowledge.
Its schools and academies are in ruin.
Its teachers slain by their last pupil.
Master Darque.
APPROACH THE DOOR, MY CREATURE.
IT NEEDS ONLY YOUR KNOCK.

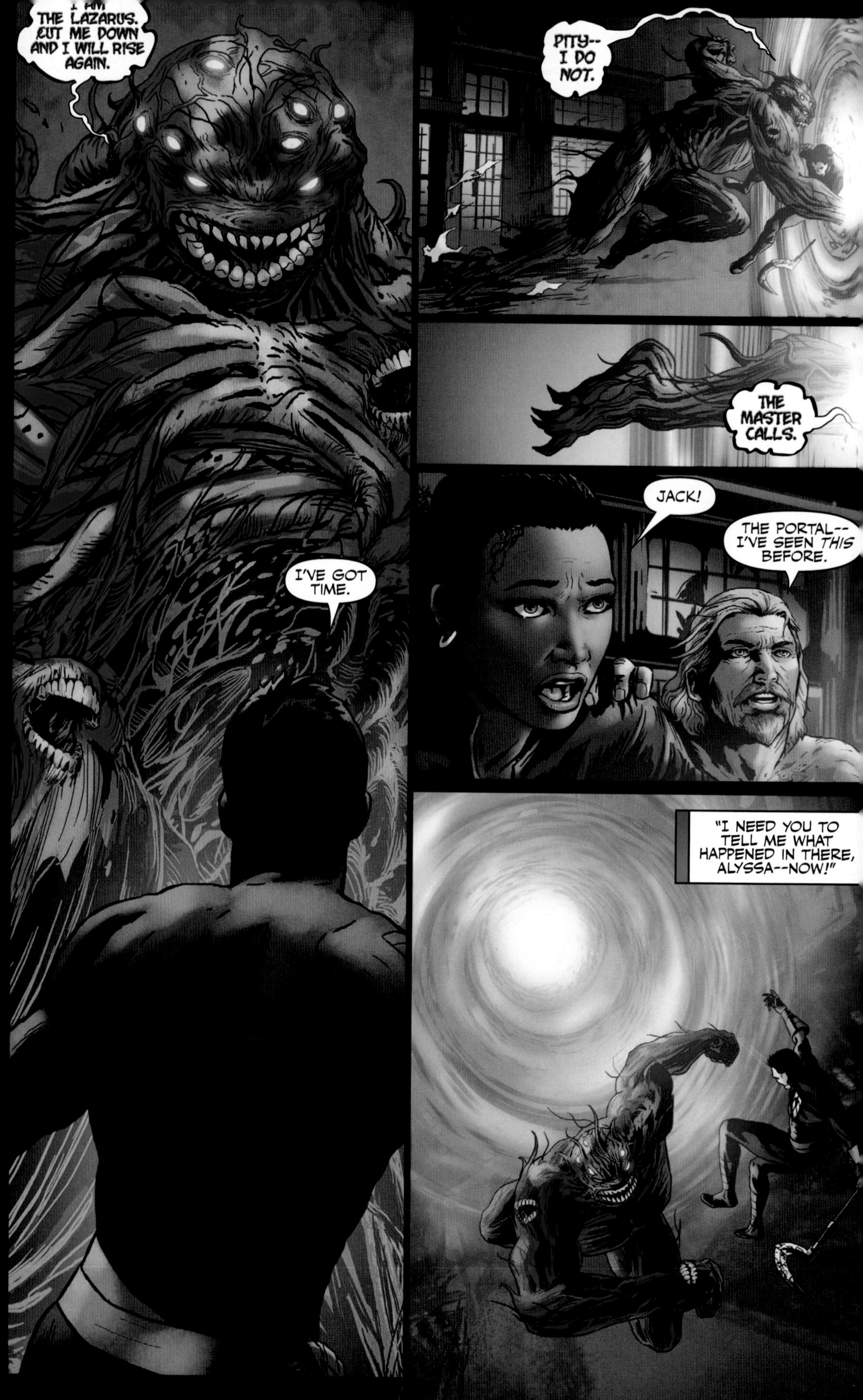
THE LAZARUS. CUT ME DOWN AND I WILL RISE AGAIN.
I'VE GOT TIME.
PITY-- I DO NOT.
THE MASTER CALLS.
JACK!
THE PORTAL-- I'VE SEEN *THIS* BEFORE.
"I NEED YOU TO TELL ME WHAT HAPPENED IN THERE, ALYSSA--NOW!"

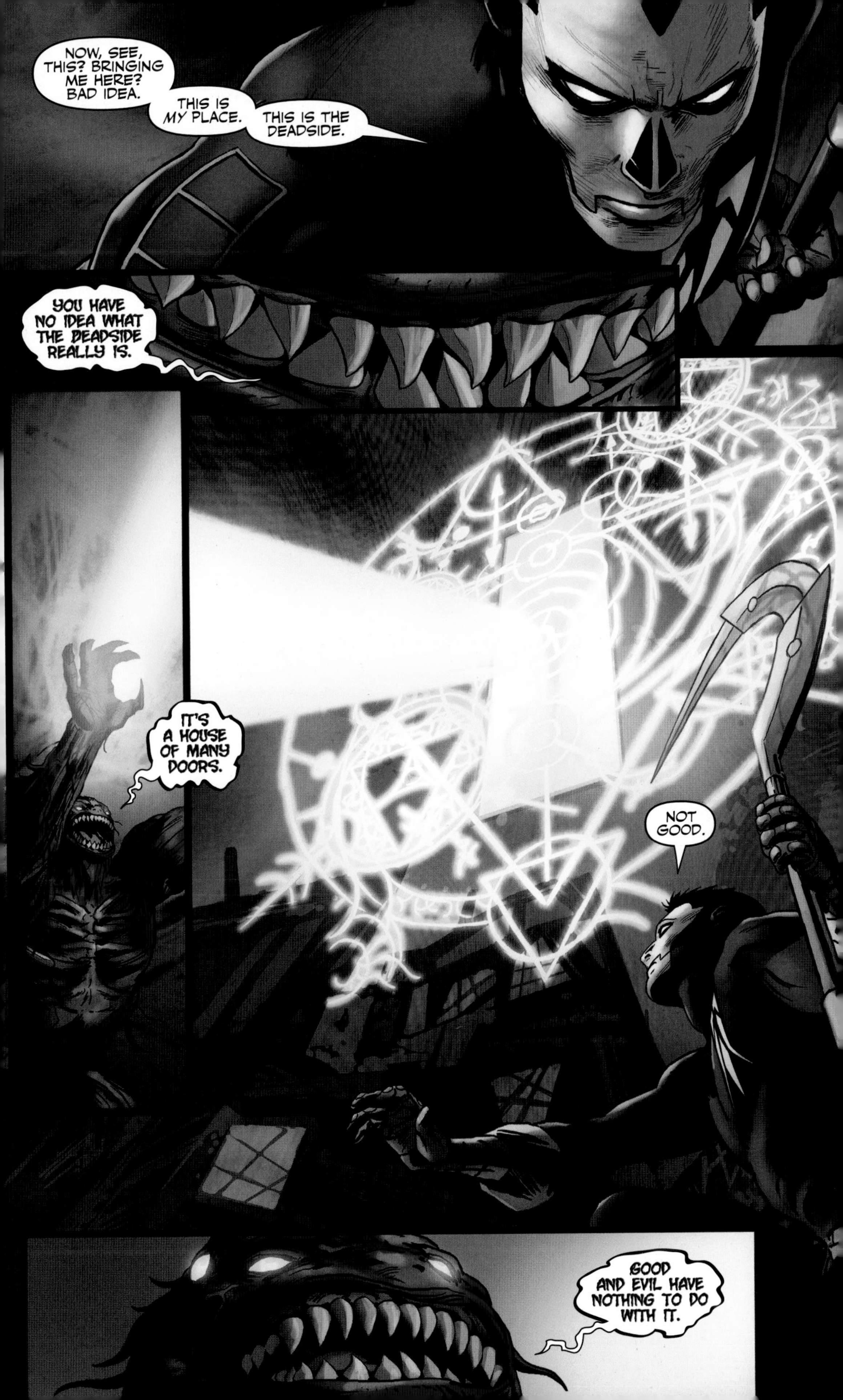
NOW, SEE, THIS? BRINGING ME HERE? BAD IDEA.
THIS IS MY PLACE.
THIS IS THE DEADSIDE.
YOU HAVE NO IDEA WHAT THE DEADSIDE REALLY IS.
IT'S A HOUSE OF MANY DOORS.
NOT GOOD.
GOOD AND EVIL HAVE NOTHING TO DO WITH IT.

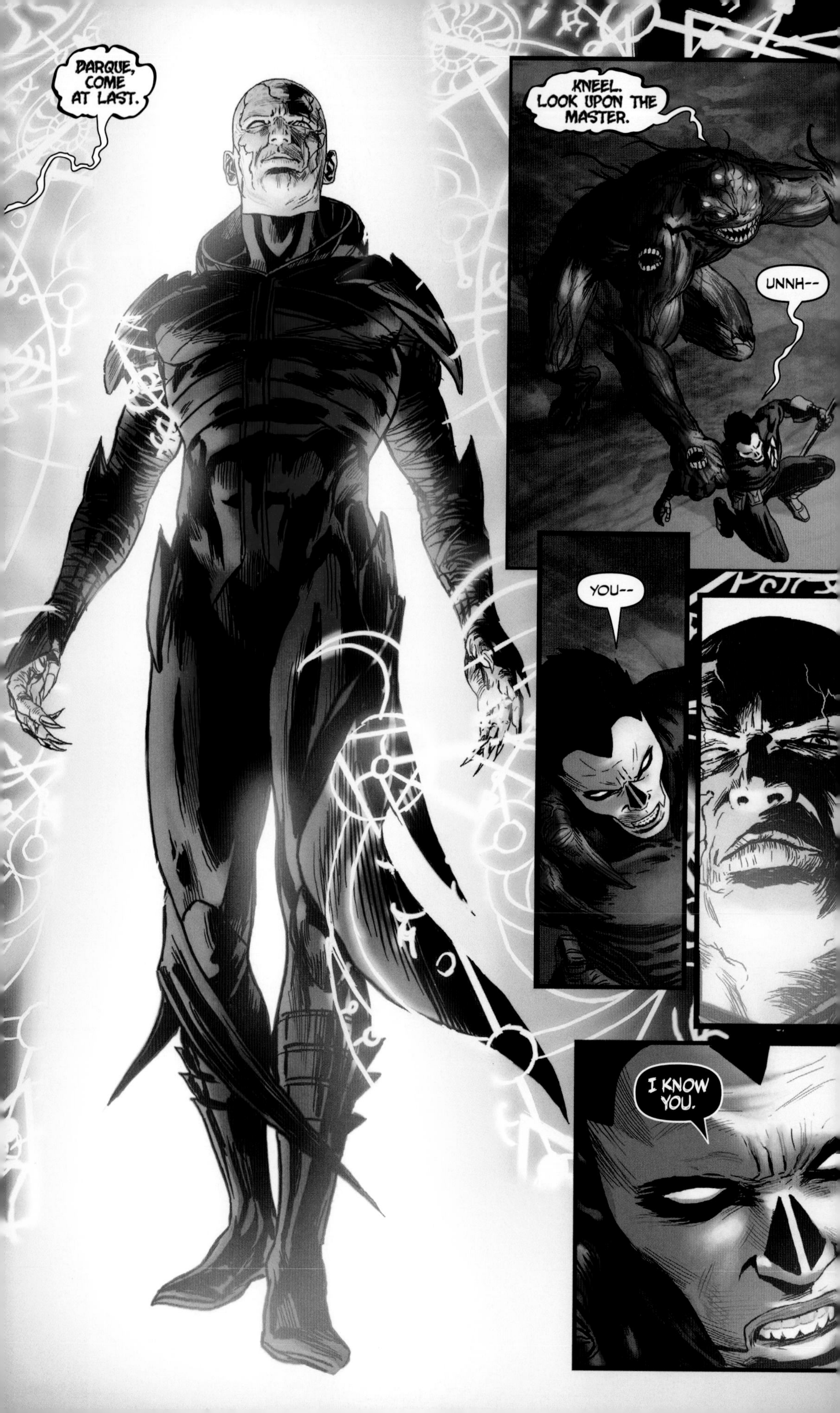
DARQUE, COME AT LAST.
KNEEL. LOOK UPON THE MASTER.
UNNH--
YOU--
I KNOW YOU.

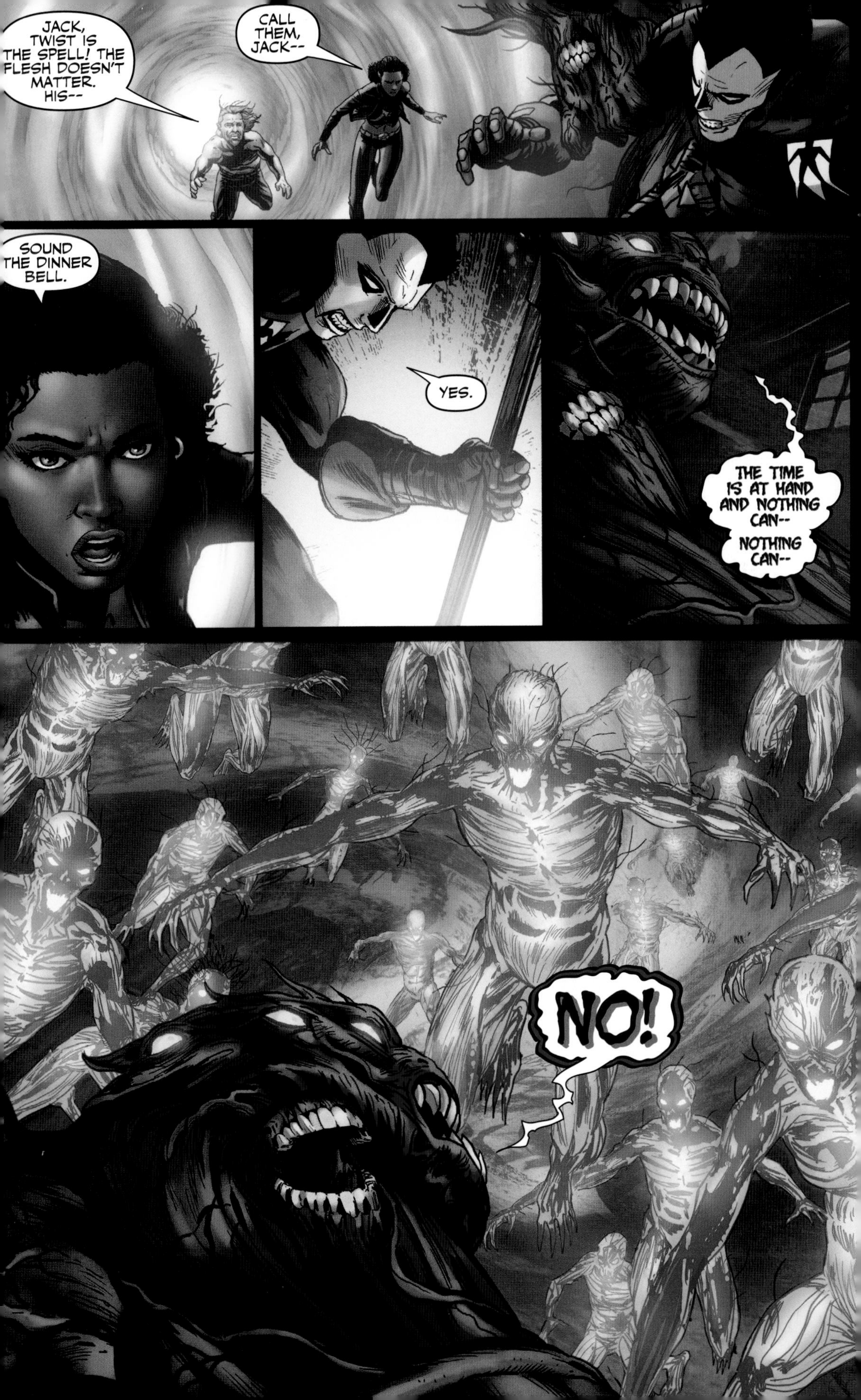
JACK, TWIST IS THE SPELL! THE FLESH DOESN'T MATTER. HIS--
CALL THEM, JACK--
SOUND THE DINNER BELL.
YES.
THE TIME IS AT HAND AND NOTHING CAN--
NOTHING CAN--
NO!

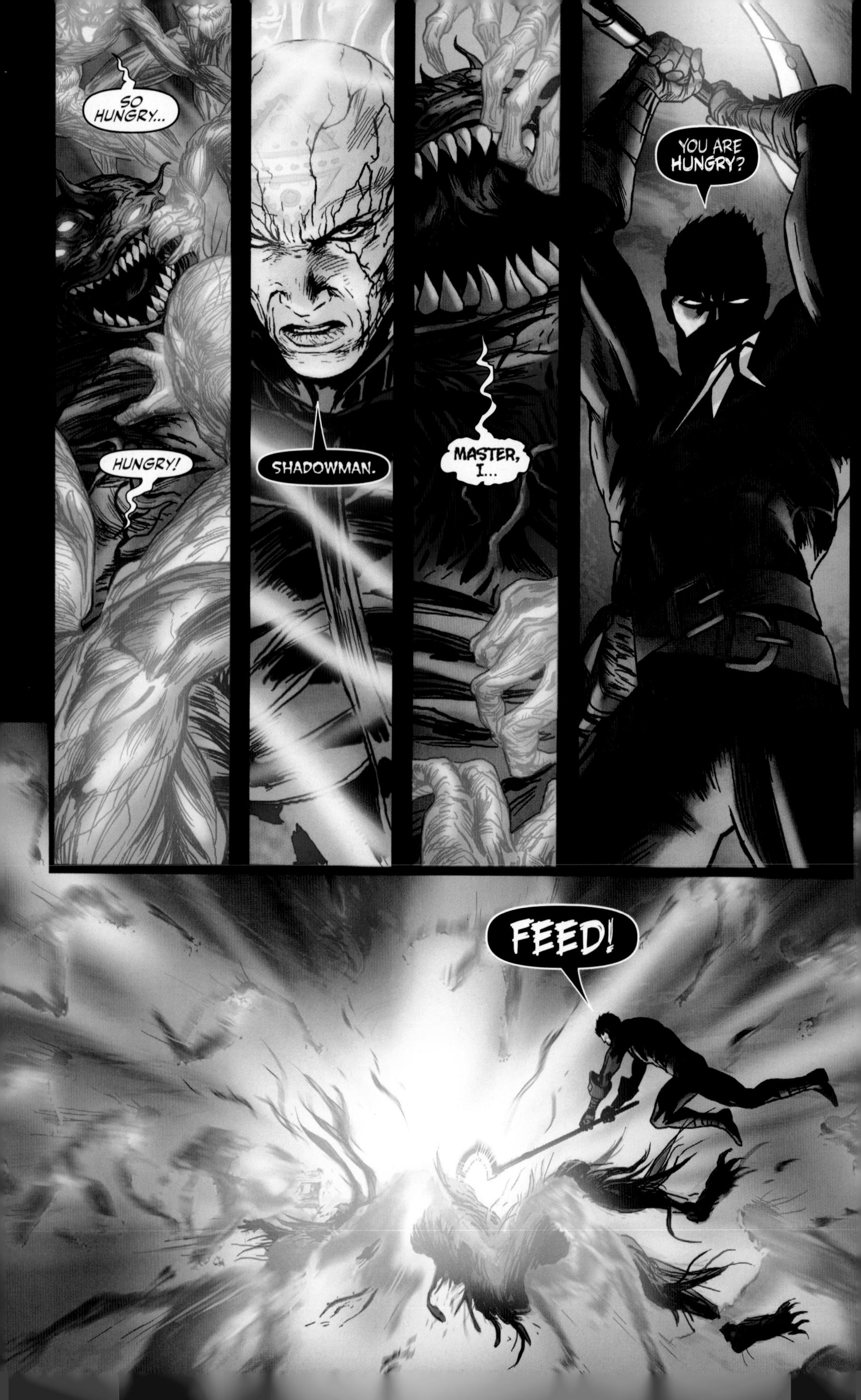
SO HUNGRY...
HUNGRY!
SHADOWMAN.
MASTER, I...
YOU ARE HUNGRY?
FEED!

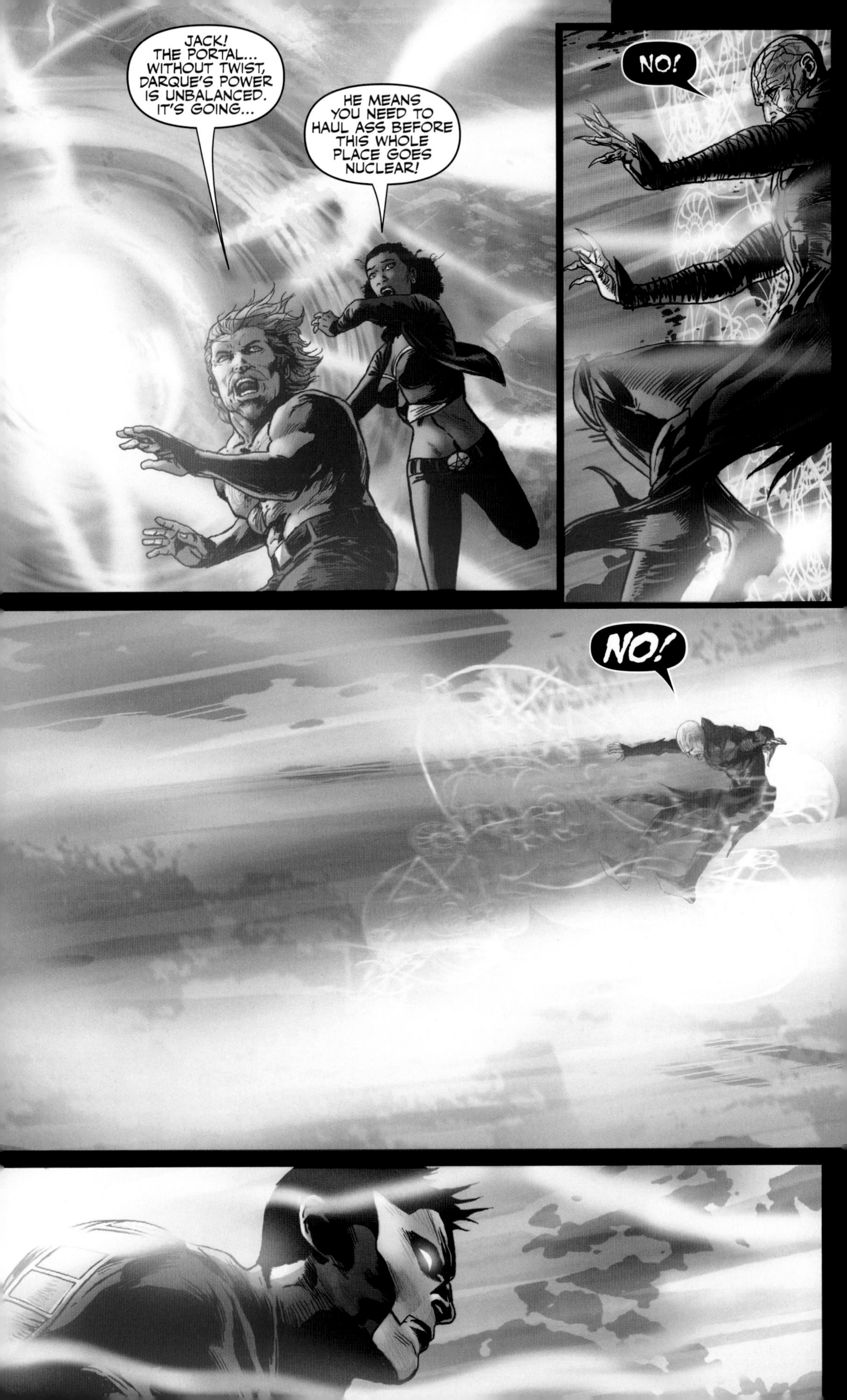
JACK! THE PORTAL... WITHOUT TWIST, DARQUE'S POWER IS UNBALANCED. IT'S GOING...
HE MEANS YOU NEED TO HAUL ASS BEFORE THIS WHOLE PLACE GOES NUCLEAR!
NO!
NO!

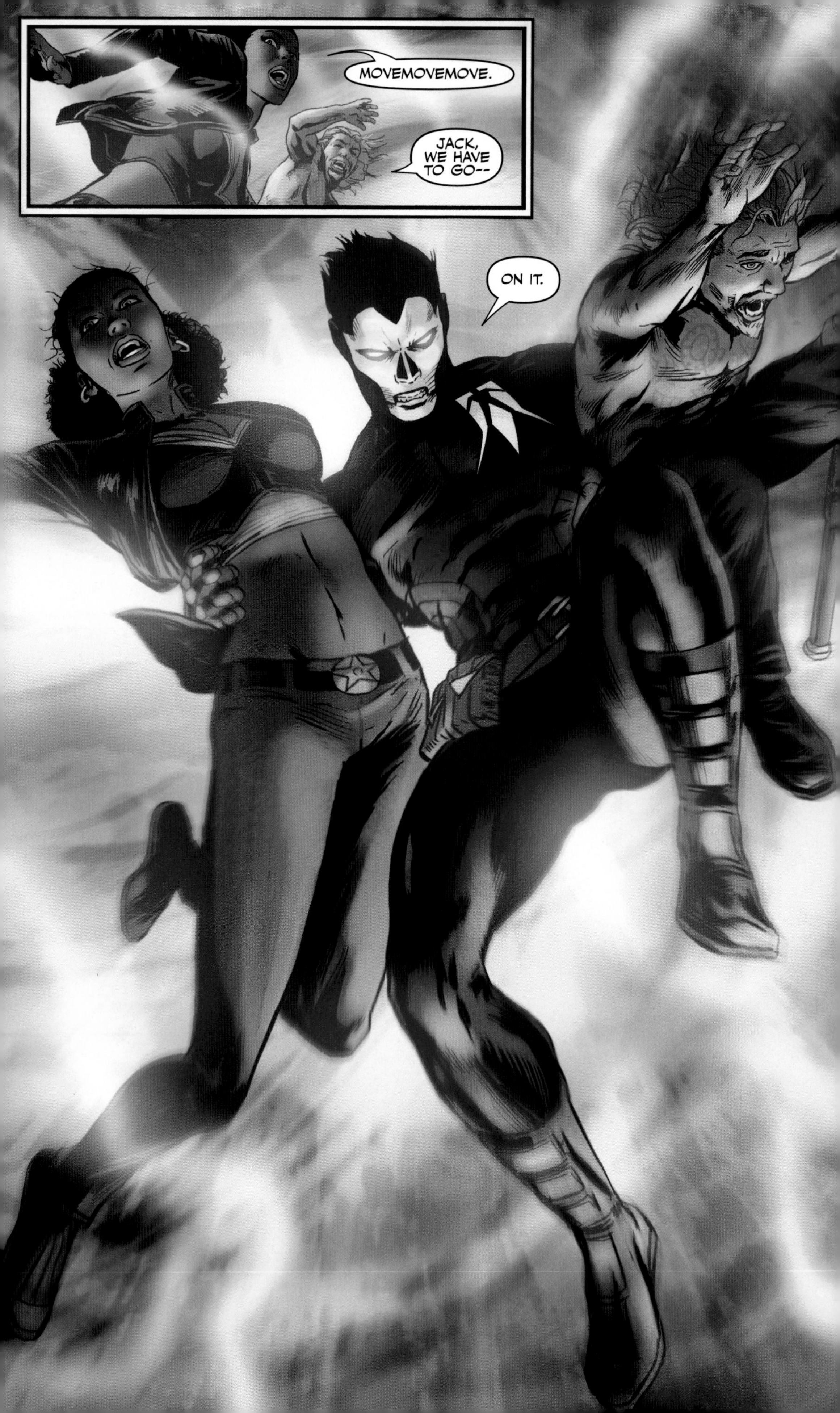
MOVEMOVEMOVE.
JACK, WE HAVE TO GO--
ON IT.

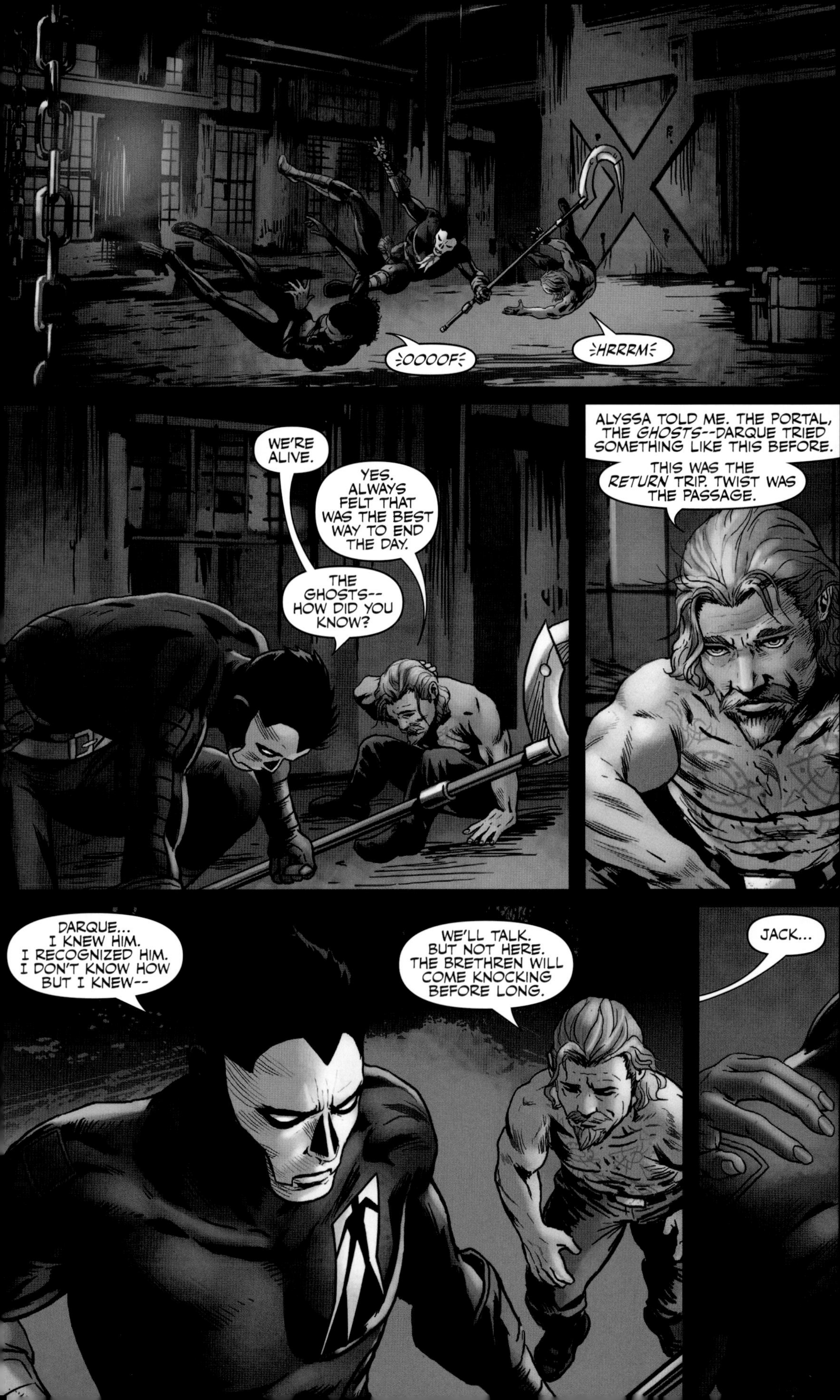

OOOOF
HRRRM
WE'RE ALIVE.
YES. ALWAYS FELT THAT WAS THE BEST WAY TO END THE DAY.
THE GHOSTS-- HOW DID YOU KNOW?
ALYSSA TOLD ME. THE PORTAL, THE *GHOSTS*--DARQUE TRIED SOMETHING LIKE THIS BEFORE.
THIS WAS THE *RETURN* TRIP. TWIST WAS THE PASSAGE.
DARQUE... I KNEW HIM. I RECOGNIZED HIM. I DON'T KNOW HOW BUT I KNEW--
WE'LL TALK. BUT NOT HERE. THE BRETHREN WILL COME KNOCKING BEFORE LONG.
JACK...

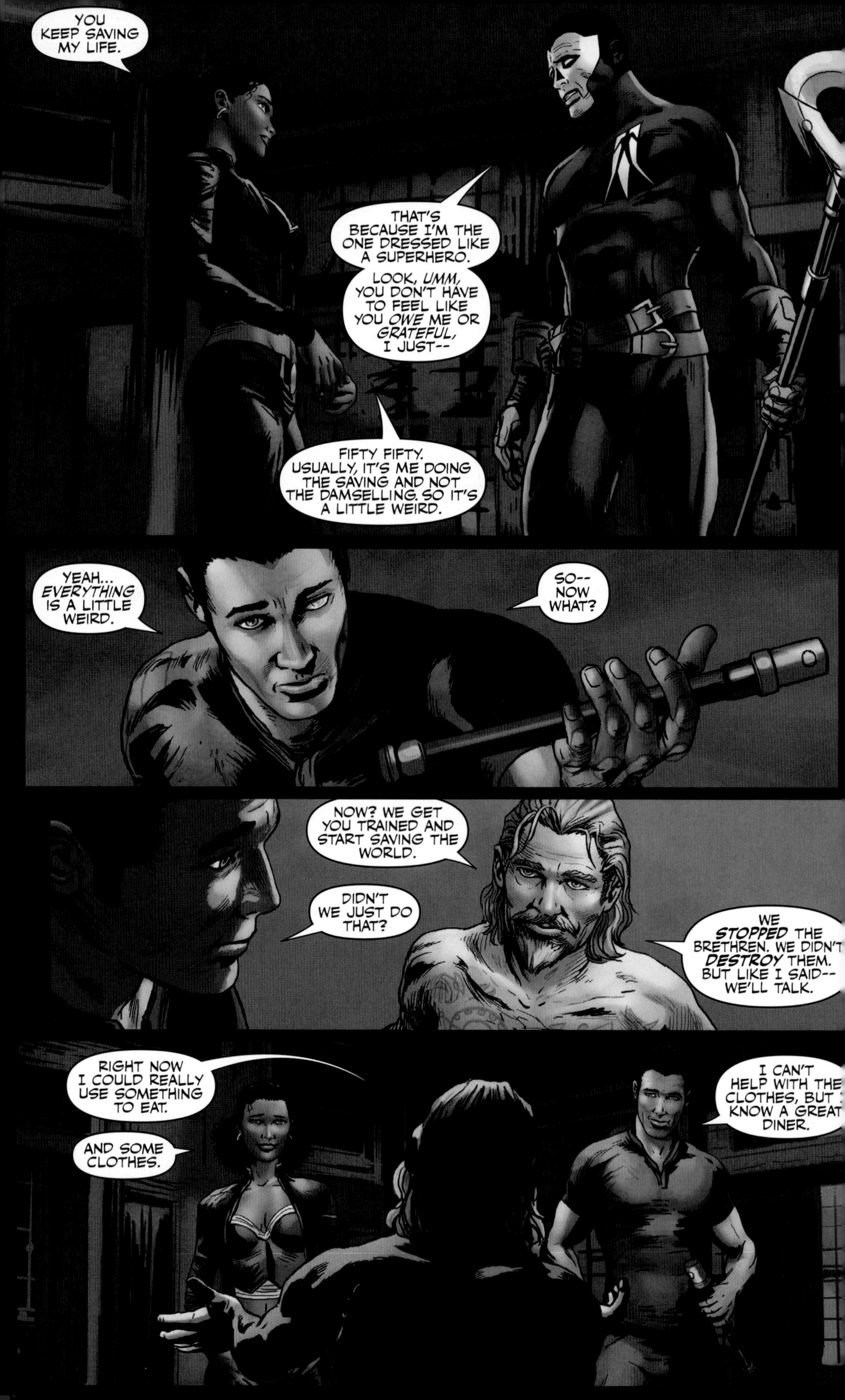
YOU KEEP SAVING MY LIFE.
THAT'S BECAUSE I'M THE ONE DRESSED LIKE A SUPERHERO.
LOOK, UMM, YOU DON'T HAVE TO FEEL LIKE YOU OWE ME OR GRATEFUL, I JUST--
FIFTY FIFTY. USUALLY, IT'S ME DOING THE SAVING AND NOT THE DAMSELLING. SO IT'S A LITTLE WEIRD.
YEAH... EVERYTHING IS A LITTLE WEIRD.
SO-- NOW WHAT?
NOW? WE GET YOU TRAINED AND START SAVING THE WORLD.
DIDN'T WE JUST DO THAT?
WE STOPPED THE BRETHREN. WE DIDN'T DESTROY THEM. BUT LIKE I SAID-- WE'LL TALK.
RIGHT NOW I COULD REALLY USE SOMETHING TO EAT.
AND SOME CLOTHES.
I CAN'T HELP WITH THE CLOTHES, BUT KNOW A GREAT DINER.

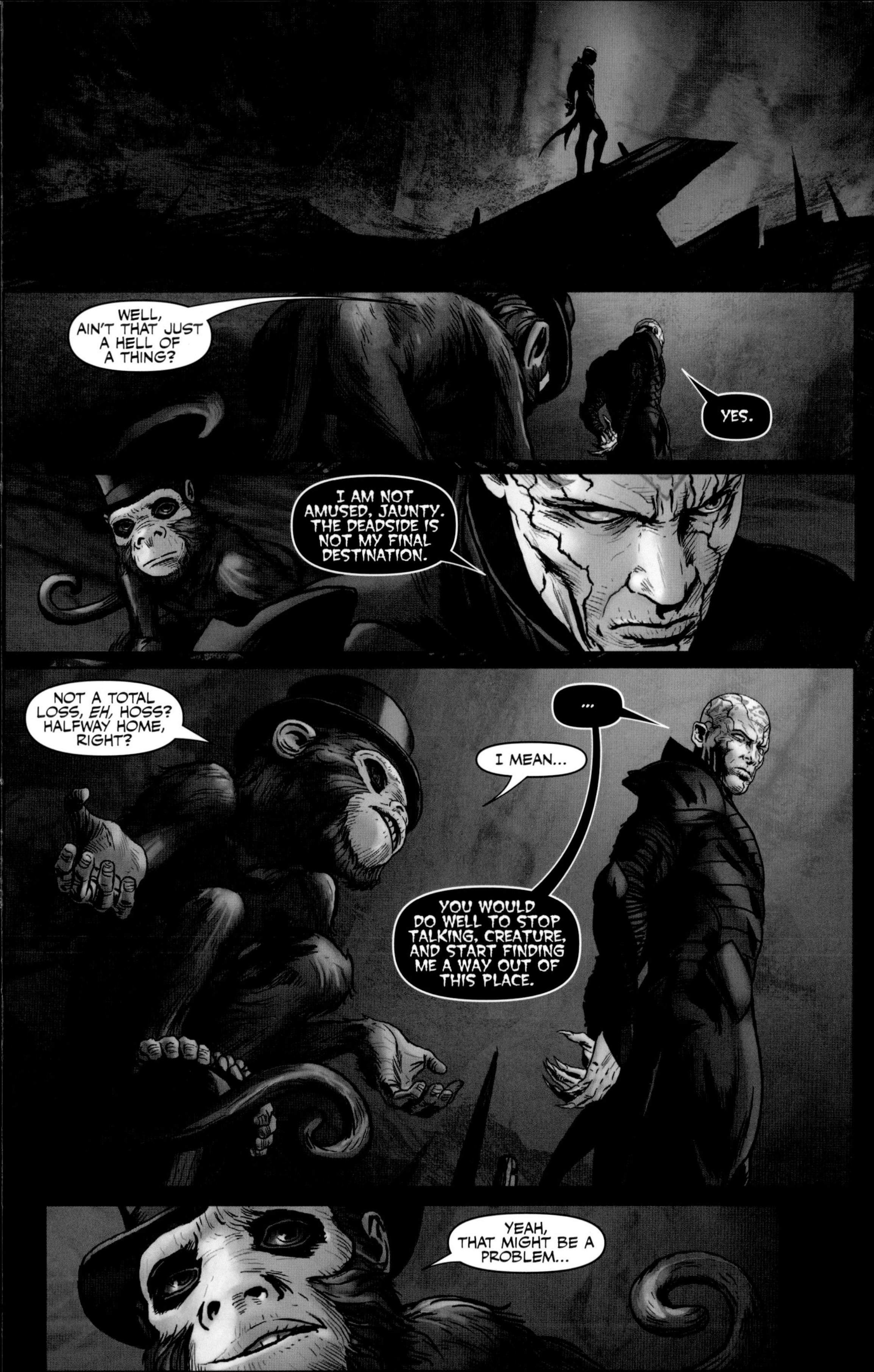
WELL, AIN'T THAT JUST A HELL OF A THING?
YES.
I AM NOT AMUSED, JAUNTY. THE DEADSIDE IS NOT MY FINAL DESTINATION.
NOT A TOTAL LOSS, *EH,* HOSS? HALFWAY HOME, RIGHT?
...
I MEAN...
YOU WOULD DO WELL TO STOP TALKING, CREATURE, AND START FINDING ME A WAY OUT OF THIS PLACE.
YEAH, THAT MIGHT BE A PROBLEM...

Next: DARQUE RECKONING

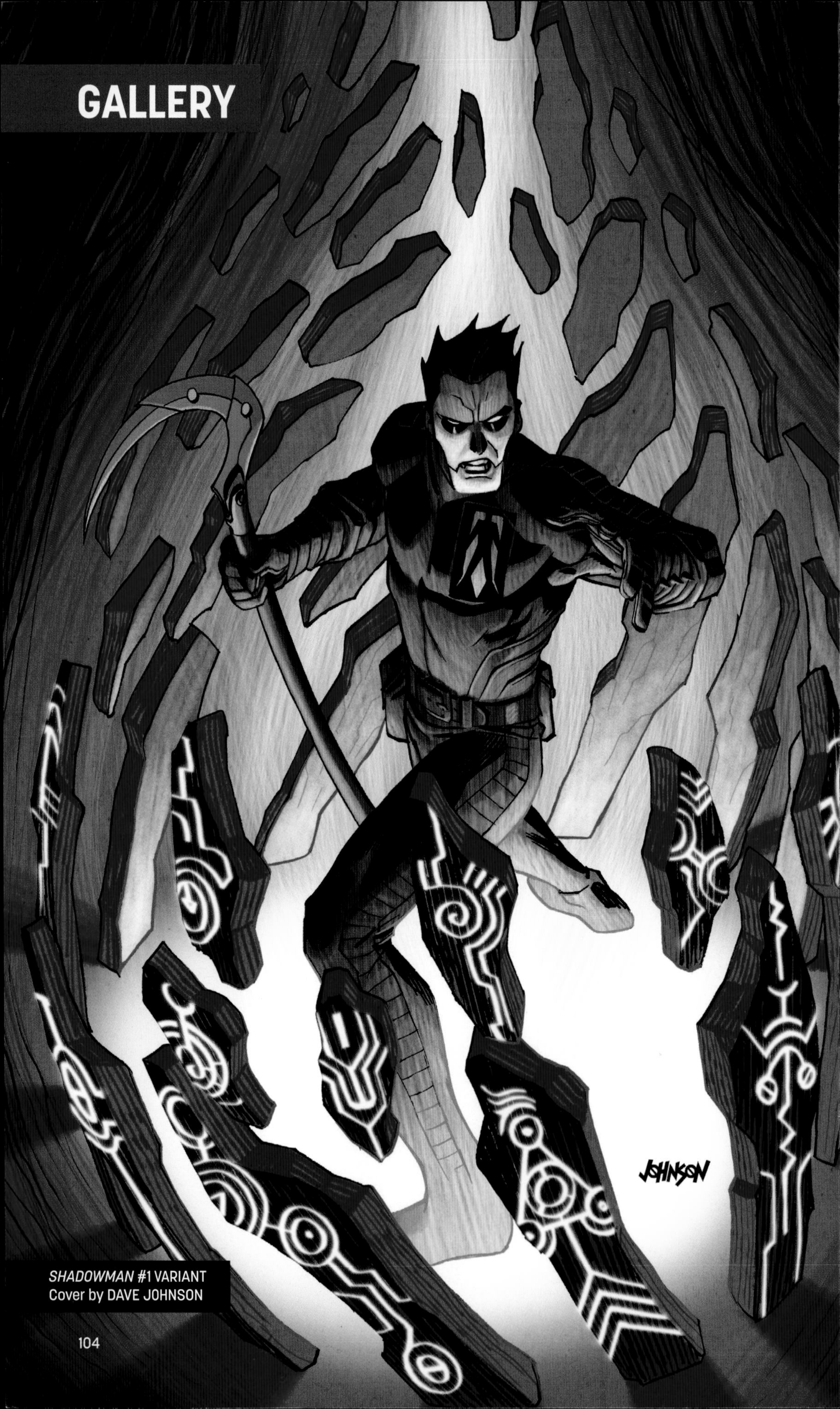
JOHNSON

SHADOWMAN #1 VARIANT
Cover by DAVE JOHNSON

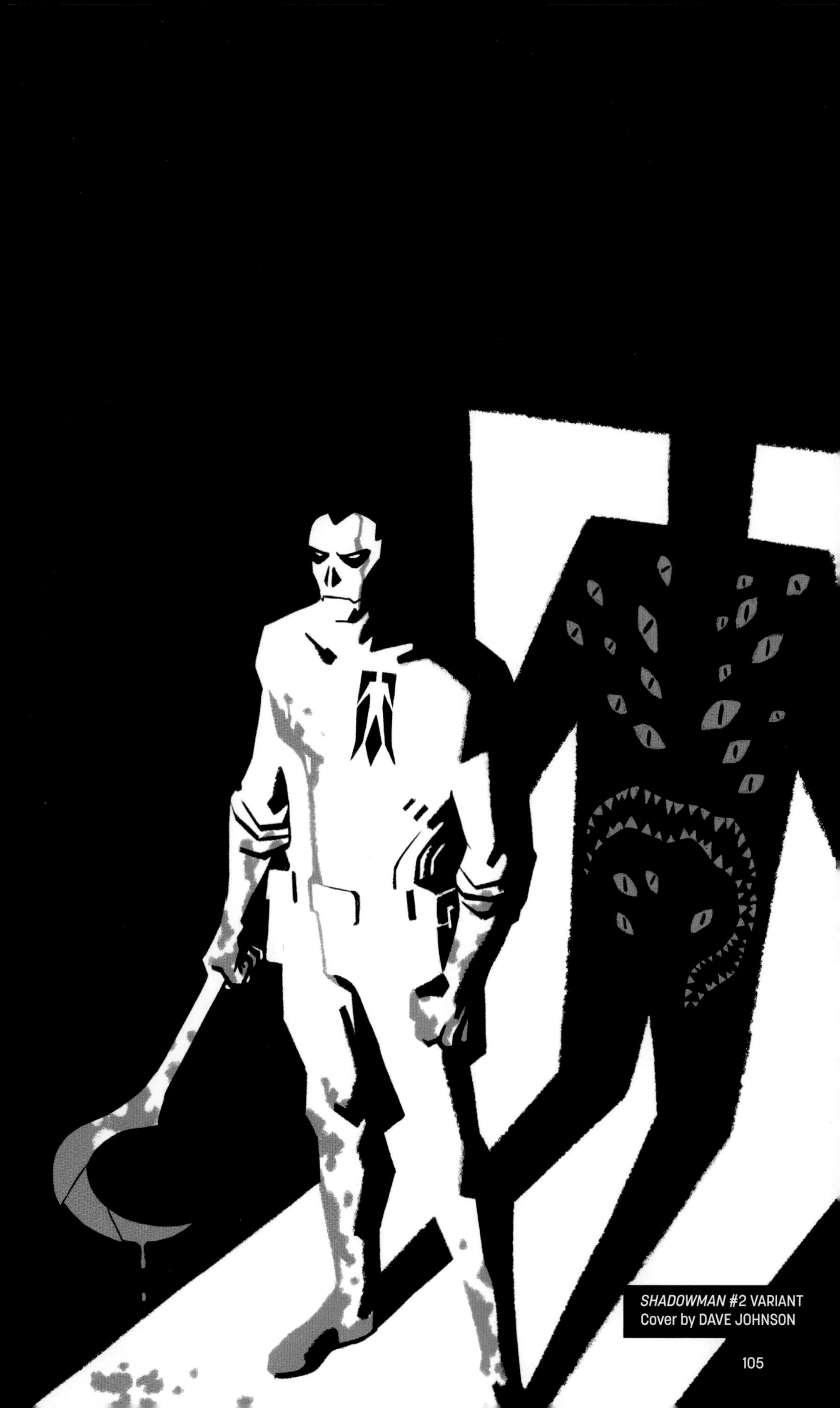

SHADOWMAN #2 VARIANT
Cover by DAVE JOHNSON

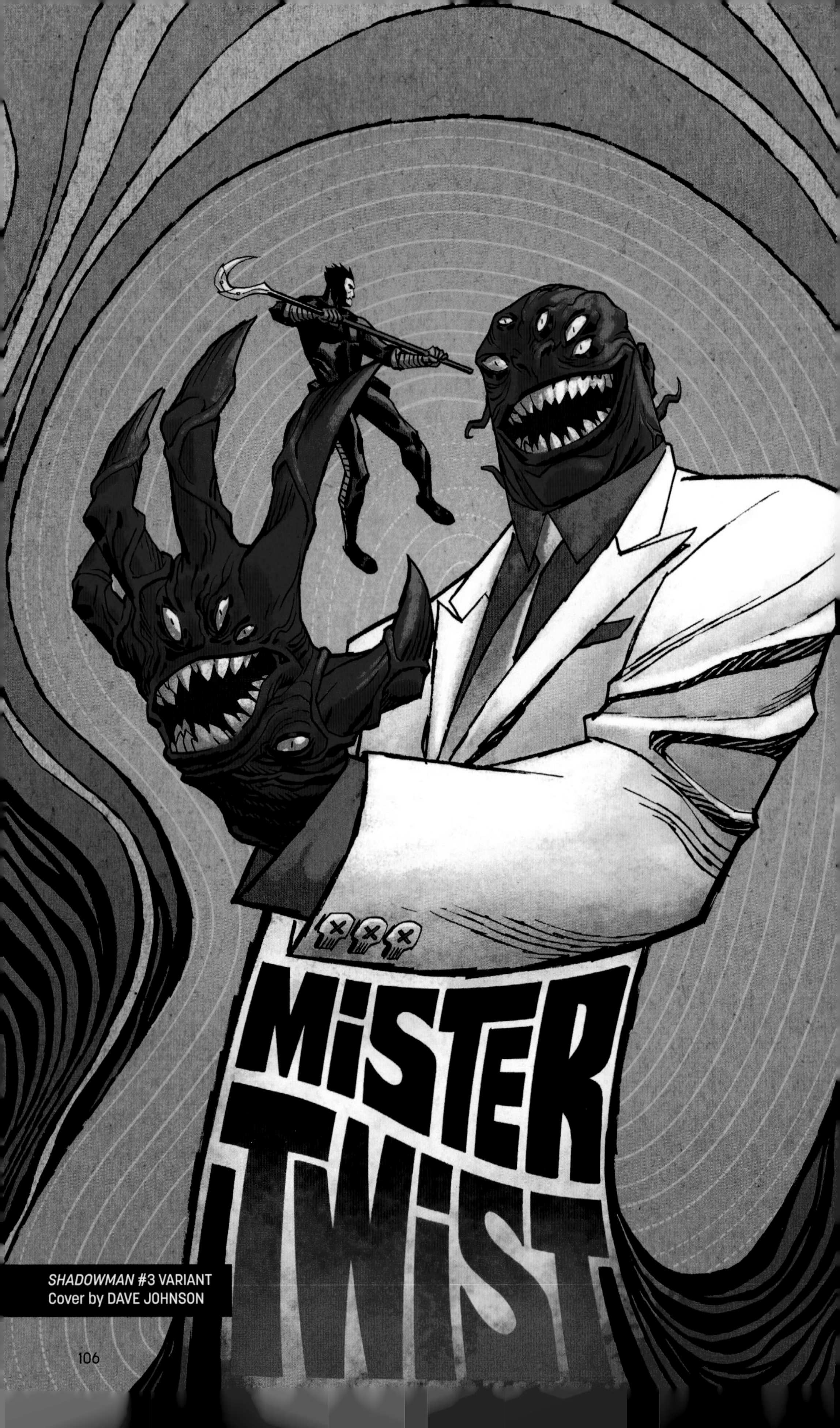
MiSTER
TWiST

SHADOWMAN #3 VARIANT
Cover by DAVE JOHNSON

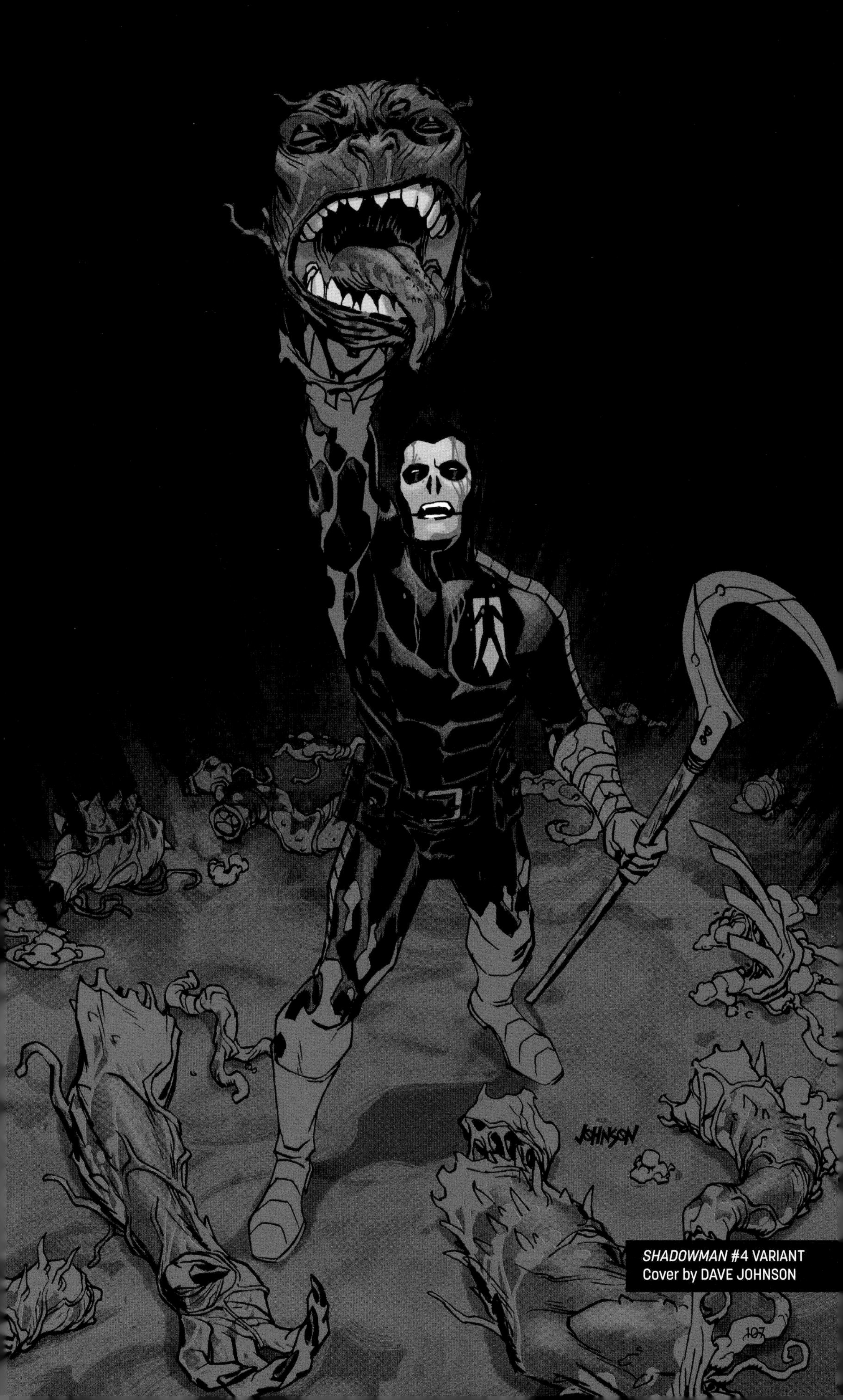
JOHNSON

SHADOWMAN #4 VARIANT
Cover by DAVE JOHNSON

Shadowman #2, page 9
Art by PATRICK ZIRCHER

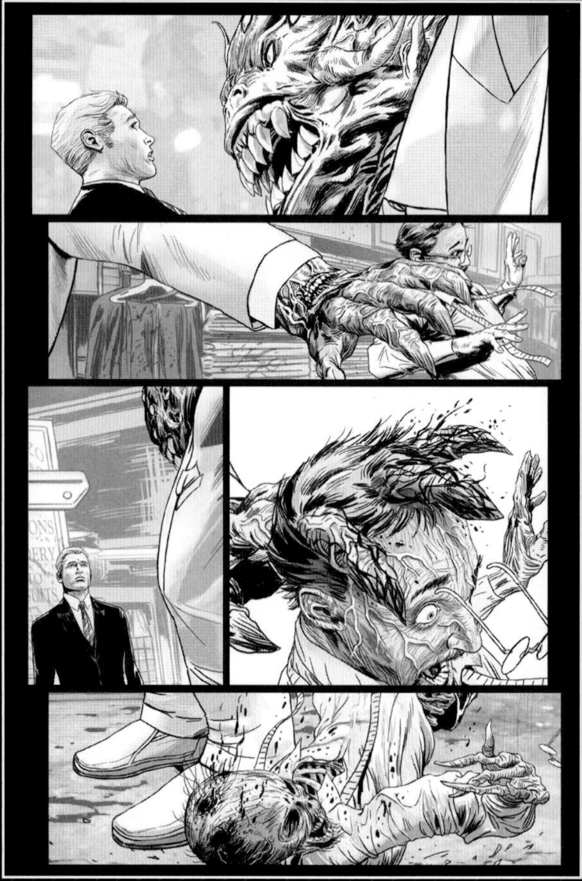

Shadowman #3, page 22
Art by PATRICK ZIRCHER

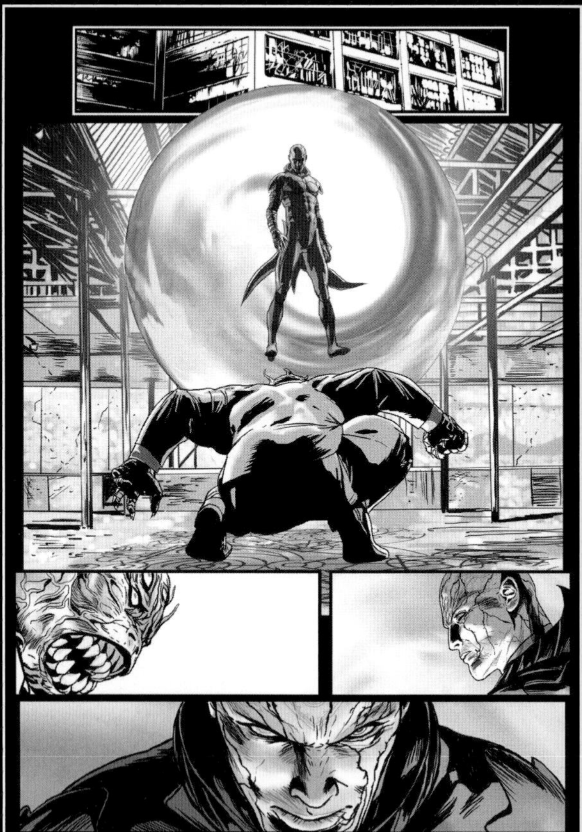

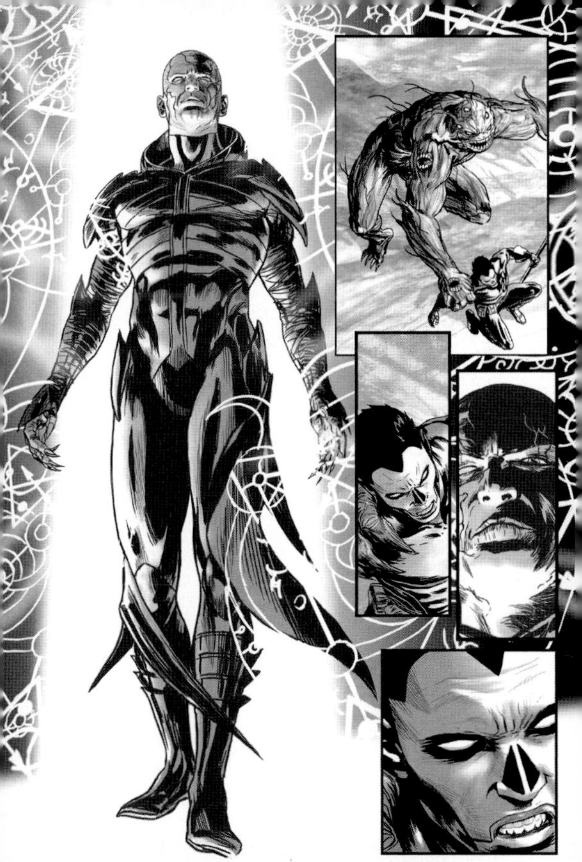

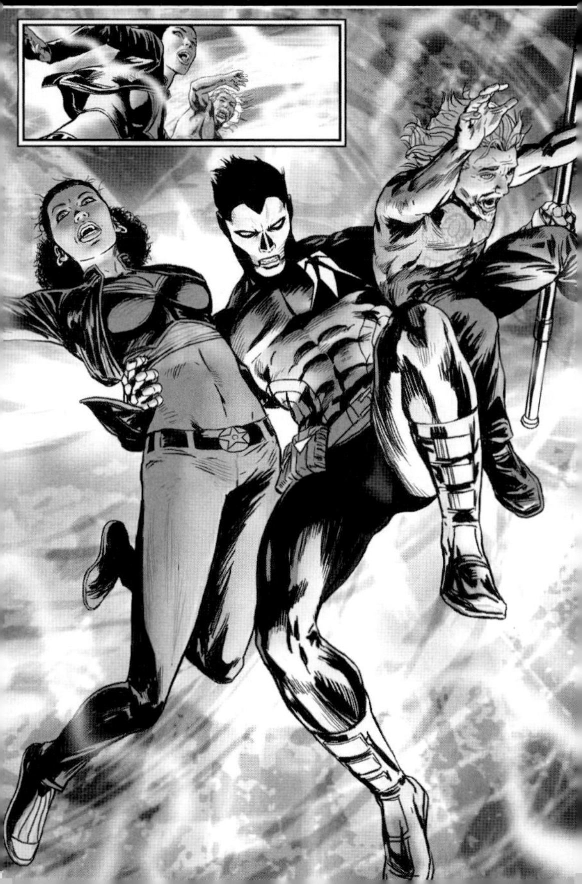

...NG THE ORIGINAL ADVENTURES OF VALIANT'S GREATEST HEROES FOR ...C WORK BY SOME OF COMICS' MOST ACCLAIMED TALENTS.

...LIANT MASTERS: BLOODSHOT VOL. 1: ...OOD OF THE MACHINE

...itten by KEVIN VANHOOK
...t by DON PERLIN
...ver by BARRY WINDSOR-SMITH

- Collecting **BLOODSHOT #1-8 (1993)** and an all-new, in-continuity story from the original **BLOODSHOT** creative team of **Kevin VanHook, Don Perlin,** and **Bob Wiacek** available only in this volume

- Featuring Bloodshot's first solo mission in the Valiant Universe and appearances by **Ninjak,** the **Eternal Warrior** and **Rai**

...RDCOVER
...3N: 978-0-9796409-3-3

...LIANT MASTERS: NINJAK VOL. 1: ...ACK WATER

...itten by MARK MORETTI
...t by JOE QUESADA & MARK MORETTI
...ver by JOE QUESADA

- Collecting **NINJAK #1-6 and #0-00 (1994)** with covers, interiors, and rarely seen process art by best-selling artist and creator **Joe Quesada**

- Featuring the complete origin of Valiant's original stealth operative and appearances by **X-O Manowar** and **Bloodshot**

...RDCOVER
...3N: 978-0-9796409-7-1

...LIANT MASTERS: SHADOWMAN VOL. 1: ...IRITS WITHIN

...itten by STEVE ENGLEHART, BOB HALL, BOB LAYTON, ...M SHOOTER and MORE
...t by STEVE DITKO, BOB HALL, DAVID LAPHAM, ...ON PERLIN and MORE
...ver by DAVID LAPHAM

- Collecting **SHADOWMAN #0-7 (1992)** and material from **DARQUE PASSAGES #1 (1994)** with an all-new new introduction by visionary Shadowman writer/artist **Bob Hall**

- The first-ever deluxe hardcover collection to feature the origin and debut solo adventures of Shadowman in the original

EXPLORE THE VALIANT UNIVERSE

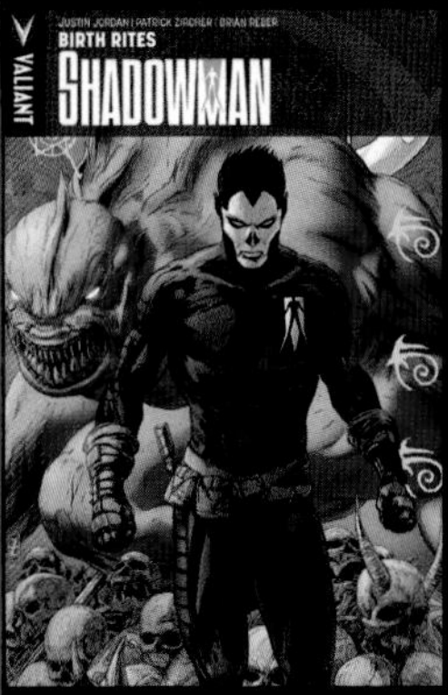
BIRTH RITES
SHADOWMAN

SHADOWMAN VOL. 1: BIRTH RITES
Written by JUSTIN JORDAN & PATRICK ZIRCHER
Art by PATRICK ZIRCHER
Collecting SHADOWMAN #1-4
TRADE PAPERBACK
ISBN: 978-1-939346-00-1

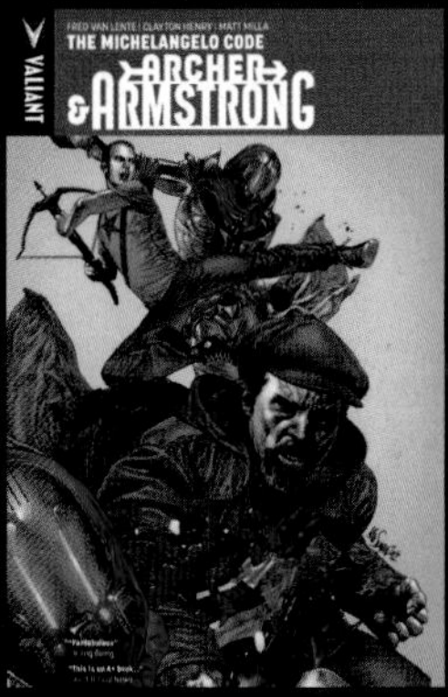
THE MICHELANGELO CODE
ARCHER & ARMSTRONG

ARCHER & ARMSTRONG VOL. 1: THE MICHELANGELO CODE
Written by FRED VAN LENTE
Art by CLAYTON HENRY
Collecting ARCHER & ARMSTRONG #1-4
TRADE PAPERBACK
ISBN: 978-0-9796409-8-8

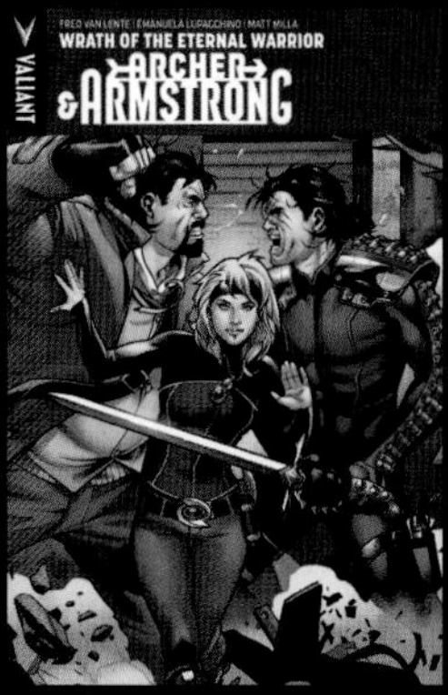
WRATH OF THE ETERNAL WARRIOR
ARCHER & ARMSTRONG

ARCHER & ARMSTRONG VOL. 2: WRATH OF THE ETERNAL WARRIOR
Written by FRED VAN LENTE
Art by EMANUELA LUPACCHINO
Collecting ARCHER & ARMSTRONG #5-9
TRADE PAPERBACK
ISBN: 978-1-939346-04-9

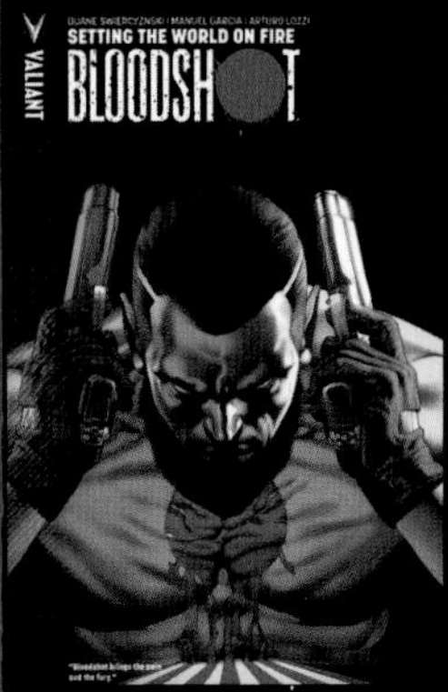
SETTING THE WORLD ON FIRE
BLOODSHOT

BLOODSHOT VOL. 1: SETTING THE WORLD ON FIRE
Written by DUANE SWIERCZYNSKI
Art by MANUEL GARCIA & ARTURO LOZZI
Collecting BLOODSHOT #1-4
TRADE PAPERBACK
ISBN: 978-0-9796409-6-4

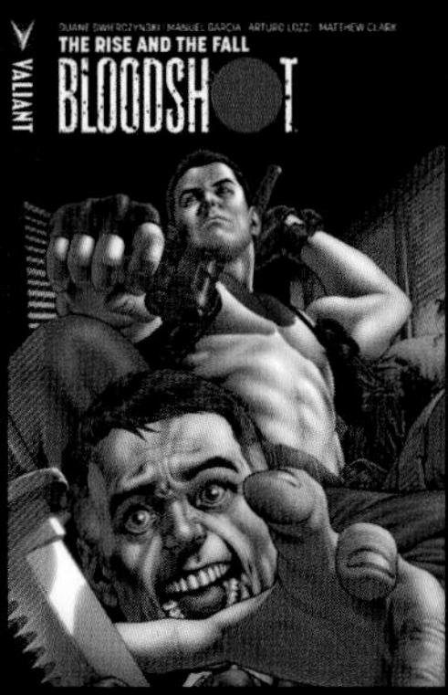
THE RISE AND THE FALL
BLOODSHOT

BLOODSHOT VOL. 2: THE RISE & THE FALL
Written by DUANE SWIERCZYNSKI
Art by MANUEL GARCIA & ARTURO LOZZI
Collecting BLOODSHOT #5-9
TRADE PAPERBACK
ISBN: 978-1-939346-03-2

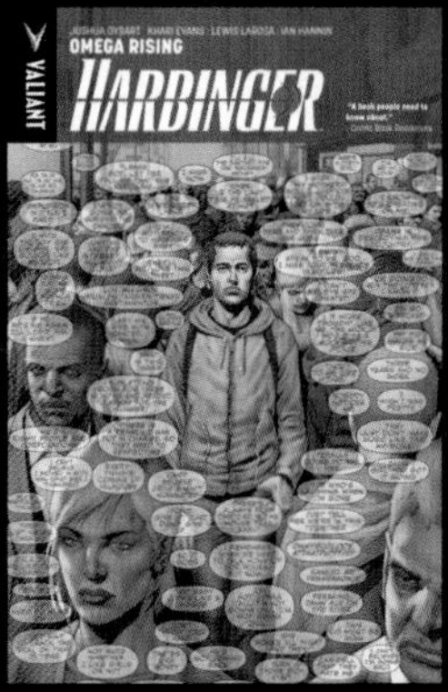
OMEGA RISING
HARBINGER

HARBINGER VOL. 1: OMEGA RISING
Written by JOSHUA DYSART
Art by KHARI EVANS & LEWIS LAROSA
Collecting HARBINGER #1-5
TRADE PAPERBACK
ISBN: 978-0-979-6409-5-7

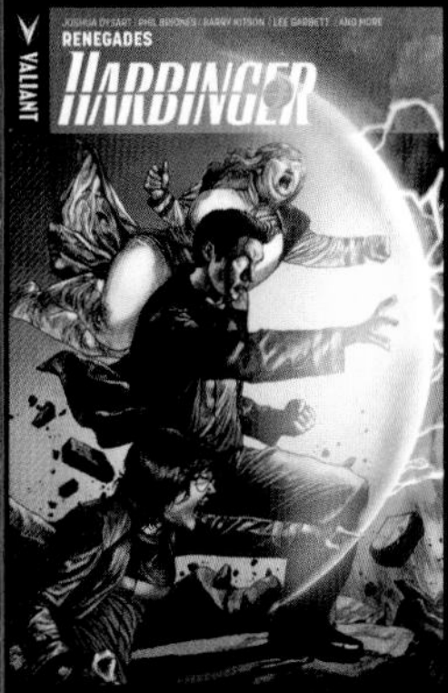
RENEGADES
HARBINGER

HARBINGER VOL. 2: RENEGADES
Written by JOSHUA DYSART
Art by PHIL BRIONES, MATTHEW CLARK, KHARI EVANS, LEE GARBETT, BARRY KITSON and PERE PEREZ
Collecting HARBINGER #6-10
TRADE PAPERBACK
ISBN: 978-1-939346-02-5

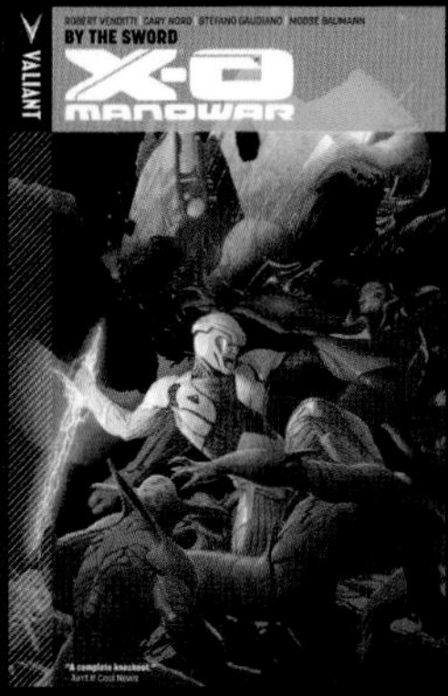
BY THE SWORD
X-O MANOWAR

X-O MANOWAR VOL. 1: BY THE SWORD
Written by ROBERT VENDITTI
Art by CARY NORD
Collecting X-O MANOWAR #1-4
TRADE PAPERBACK
ISBN: 978-0-9796409-4-0

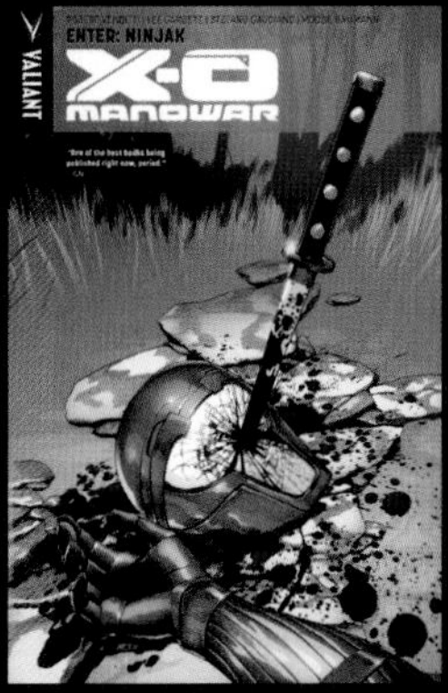
ENTER: NINJAK
X-O MANOWAR

X-O MANOWAR VOL. 2: ENTER NINJAK
Written by ROBERT VENDITTI
Art by LEE GARBETT
Collecting X-O MANOWAR #5-8
TRADE PAPERBACK
ISBN: 978-1-9393460-0-1

VALIANT

SHADOWMAN

VOLUME TWO: DARQUE RECKONING

THE TRUE PRICE OF BECOMING THE SHADOWMAN IS ALWAYS PAID IN BLOOD - AND MASTER DARQUE INTENDS TO COLLECT...

Jack Boniface has just been to Hell and back. After surviving the horrors of the Deadside, Jack is taking his new abilities to the limit and discovering more about the legacy of the Shadowman with each passing night. But what if he wasn't the only thing that managed to escape back to Earth? Something dark has arrived in New Orleans, leaving death and madness in its black wake. What's more, the city's deadliest cartel assassin is after Jack, and he refuses to die - literally...

Collecting **SHADOWMAN #5-9** by acclaimed creators Justin Jordan (*The Strange Talent of Luther Strode*) and Patrick Zircher (*Captain America*) with Neil Edwards (*Dark Avengers*), Lee Garbett (*X-O Manowar*), and Roberto De La Torre (*Daredevil*), start reading here to follow Jack Boniface headlong into the dark side of the Valiant Universe – and find out why *Shadowman* is the thrilling series that MTV Geek calls "everything a gripping horror comic should be."

VALIANT
JUSTIN JORDAN | PATRICK ZIRCHER | LEE GARBETT | ROBERTO DE LA TORRE
DARQUE RECKONING
SHADOWMAN

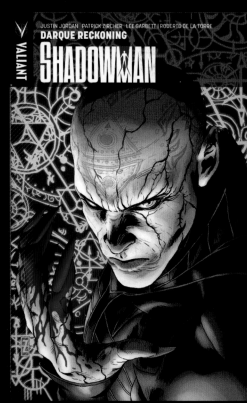

TRADE PAPERBACK
ISBN: 978-1-939346-05-6